MW01254209

Advancing Democracy Through Education?

U.S. Influence Abroad and Domestic Practices

A volume in
Education Policy in Practice: Critical Cultural Studies

Series Editors:
Bradley A. U. Levinson and Margaret Sutton, *Indiana University*

Education Policy in Practice:
Critical Cultural Studies
Bradley A. U. Levinson and Margaret Sutton, Series Editors

Advancing Democracy Through Education?

U.S. Influence Abroad and Domestic Practices

edited by

E. Doyle Stevick
University of South Carolina

and

Bradley A. U. Levinson
Indiana University

Information Age Publishing, Inc.
Charlotte, North Carolina • www.infoagepub.com

Library of Congress Cataloging-in-Publication Data

Advancing democracy through education? : U.S. influence abroad and domestic practices /
edited by Doyle Stevick and Bradley Levinson.
    p. cm. -- (Education policy in practice)
  Includes bibliographical references and index.
  ISBN 978-1-59311-654-5 (pbk.) -- ISBN 978-1-59311-655-2 (hardcover) 1. Democracy--
Study and teaching. 2. Civics--Study and teaching. 3. Democracy assistance--United States--
Case studies. 4. Democracy and education. I. Stevick, Doyle, 1969- II. Levinson, Bradley A.,
1963-
  LC1091.A34 2008
  370.11'5--dc22

                                                  2008013252

ISBN 13: 978-1-59311-654-5 (pbk.)
         978-1-59311-655-2 (hardcover)

Printed in the United States of America

For Kara, eriti tubli abikaasa

For Lilian Alvarez and Maria Eugenia Luna, pioneers of education for democracy in Mexico

CONTENTS

PREFACE

Bradley A. U. Levinson

Democracy is king.

It has become apparent that, over the last 30 years or so, the discourse of democracy has grown ascendant. Globally, societies that existed for long periods under authoritarian regimes struggle in their "transition" to democracy, while consolidated democracies suffer from citizen apathy and a "democracy deficit." At national, regional, and local levels, in government and throughout civil society, democracy is now the watchword. Despite its varied and contested meanings, few would dispute that some version of democracy is the normative rule by which political practice is constantly measured and assessed.

If democracy is king, then education for democracy is its burgeoning stepchild. Of course, the relationship between education and democracy has a long and illustrious history, filling many volumes of political philosophy and pedagogical thought. Yet now more than ever, when a virtual global consensus has been reached on democracy as the most desirable form of government, citizens and politicians alike have turned to education as a means to achieve and consolidate and deepen democracy. Democracy, it turns out, needs tending. Procedures and structures can quicken the arrival of democratic governance, but only education can shape the values and cultures that turn governance into a more far-reaching and deeply rooted form of life.

By exploring democratic citizenship education, this book makes a particular contribution to the discourse on education for democracy, as well as to the critical study of education policy. Since its very origins, the United States has often fancied itself a beacon of democracy for the world. It has also given birth to numerous experiments and programs for democratic education. With its arrival as a global superpower, the United States has sought to use its influence to "promote democracy," and education has been one of the key domains for exercising such influence. Moreover, instruments of **policy** figure prominently in the democracy promotion endeavor. To shape policy, it is typically thought, is to have an irrevocable influence on orders of being and practice down the chain of command.

Yet we now know enough about how policy works to question these assumptions. As we have discussed elsewhere (Levinson & Sutton, 2001), policy is a complex, ongoing social practice of normative cultural production constituted by diverse actors across diverse contexts. On the one hand, the most immediate product of the policy process should be understood as a *normative cultural discourse* with positive and negative sanctions, that is, a set of statements about how things should or must be done, with corresponding inducements or punishments. Such a discourse also crucially presupposes an implicit view of how things "are"—a model of the world, an operative cosmology, as it were. Policy as normative discourse may be what we call officially "authorized," that is, backed by enforcement mechanisms of government or corporate charter. On the other hand, policy may also develop in more spontaneous and informal fashion, outside the agencies or offices that are constitutionally charged with making policy. In either case, policy may be documented and codified, or it may exist in "unwritten" form, through ongoing institutional memory and practice.

Most policy analysis considers only "authorized" policy and its implementation. Yet we prefer to focus policy analysis on the **appropriation** of authorized policy by the actors charged with its implementation. And this is where the volume before you has a lot to teach us: it explores the dynamics of education policy formation and appropriation in the specific domain of civic education for democracy. The studies in the first section of the book, especially, explore the varying dimensions of citizenship and citizenship education in the United States. Together, they excavate and articulate the cultural and institutional bases for the formation of U.S. policy in citizenship education. Historical studies like those of Ben Justice, and ethnographic community studies, like that of Patti Buck, suggest the broad cultural themes and tensions that have informed education policy for citizenship education in the United States. And just as they suggest how such themes make their way into authorized policy, they also show the contingencies of policy appropriation at the local level. Add to theirs the detailed study by

Kathleen Staudt of how a U.S. university undertakes to promote "civic engagement" among its students, and we have a nuanced picture of how education policy for democratic citizenship gets variously interpreted in different American contexts.

But what happens when programs and policies first developed in the United States get recontextualized in other times and places? The latter part of the book suggests the many ways that U.S.-based policies for citizenship education have been appropriated outside the United States. Sometimes the story is less than sanguine. Policies may be attached to ideological and monetary strings, with their implementation strongly channeled or curtailed. Such is the case with the USAID-funded "Tamkeen" project that Ayman al-Sayed describes in Palestine. The conditionalities placed on this project by its donor inevitably lead to a distortion of the very "democratic" goals it espouses. Similarly, Doyle Stevick documents the effects of U.S. aid for civic education in Estonia. The often desperate search for financial security among Estonian civil society actors leads to a kind of amoral pragmatism, in which grants are written and projects accepted regardless of their alignment with the beliefs and ideologies of the donors. Yet donors fail to understand such dynamics, just as they fail to account for the language barrier between themselves and the Estonians. What results is a kind of "skeletal" appropriation of U.S. policies and programs for democratic education, with little regard for democratic substance.

But there are positive stories to be told, too. Working in different parts of Africa, Patty Kubow, and Ron Atkinson and Judy Wyatt, model new forms of dialogue and partnership for contextualizing U.S.-based policies for democratic citizenship education. Showing a humility and openness all too rare in the world of "democracy promotion," and wielding methods of "democratic concept development" or "needs assessment," these authors enable local appropriations of U.S. policies that make sense in the local setting. Similarly, David Landis and Sapargul Mirseitova tell the story of their collaboration in Kazakhstan's Reading and Writing for Critical Thinking project. Through open dialogue, they identify and negotiate points of difference in the assumptions between the U.S.-based creators of Reading and Writing for Critical Thinking and its Kazakh interpreters. Importantly, the project provides enough sustained resources to enable the deep and effective training of local teachers in their own language. Such a commitment makes all the difference for how U.S.-originated policies get locally appropriated.

In Dr. Seuss' *Yertle the Turtle*, Yertle's overweening ambition to rule over all that he sees eventually leads to his own downfall. If democracy is to remain king, it must rely less on the traditional perquisites of an expanding throne and more on the humble outreach born of excitement over a good idea. The volume in your hands provides a great deal of insight into how this should and shouldn't be done.

REFERENCE

Levinson, B. A. U., & Sutton, M. (Eds.). (2001). *Policy as practice: Toward a comparative sociocultural analysis of educational policy.* Westport, CT: Ablex.

INTRODUCTION

Education Policy, National Interests, and Advancing Democracy

E. Doyle Stevick

American influence on education for democracy around the world is complex, diverse, and conflicted.[1] It encompasses U.S. government policy, government-funded programs that operate through recipient organizations, the independent work of foundations, nonprofits and individuals, and the broader influence of American culture and media around the world. It can be found in countries across the globe and throughout the diverse cultures of the United States itself. Aspects of American aid and policy are coercive, manifesting elements of imperialism and colonialism, with counterproductive and deleterious effects. Other efforts thoroughly manifest democratic values, and carry out projects driven by local priorities and needs in cross-national partnerships that come as close to equality as can be hoped under circumstances of great resource and power imbalances. Some influence is inadvertent—little more than the impressions about justice and law left behind by American courtroom dramas. This book explores the diversity of American roles in such cross-cultural engagement in education for democracy, both within the United States and around the world.

Cross-cultural engagement in education for democracy inevitably bears the impressions of each culture involved and the dynamics among them.

Even high-priority, well-funded U.S. government programs are neither monolithic nor deterministic in their own right, but are rather reshaped, adapted to their contexts, and appropriated by their partners. These partners are sometimes called recipients, although that label is problematic. "Recipient" both gives a misleading impression that partners are relatively passive in the overall process, and its use is a reflection of some outside donors' or experts' stance that they are delivering goods or expertise. The authors of these chapters pay close attention to the cultures, contexts, structures, people, and processes involved in education for democracy. Woven throughout this volume's qualitative studies are the notions that contacts between powers and cultures are complex and situated, that agency matters, that local meanings play a critical role in the dynamic exchange of peoples and ideas. The authors span an array of fields that concern themselves with understanding languages, cultures, institutions, the close view of daily life, and the broad horizon of the past that shapes the present: history, anthropology, literacy studies, policy analysis, political science, and journalism.

The contributors have all observed the risks involved when cultural contacts take place amidst extreme imbalances of power, or when some are oblivious or insensitive to the concerns and needs of another. Several (Buck, Staudt, Kubow, Landis & Mirseitova, Shah, and Atkinson & Wyatt) have direct experience teaching in or leading such exchanges and partnerships, and they attempted to manifest their understandings of democracy and cultural sensitivity within the constraints imposed by institutional structures or funders' interests. Others (Alsayed, Stevick, and Levinson & Sutton) have observed the dynamics of appropriation, the impact of poor policy, or the amorphous "influence" that occurs under the label of cultural globalization, from the vantage point of an external but engaged researcher.

It is perhaps too easily forgotten that international and intercultural dynamics have characterized "American" education, at home and abroad, since the establishment of the first colonies in the "New World." Whether we consider Horace Mann's visits to Prussia, the U.S. import of Froebel's kindergarten and Italy's Montessori schools, or the German research university model that inspired the creation of Johns Hopkins University; whether we include John Dewey's early visit to the Soviet Union, or the waves of voluntary immigrants from ever broader swaths of Europe and Asia, the forced journey of countless Africans, and the alternating assimilation and annihilation policies for its Native Peoples, "American" education has inexorably taken shape amidst the melting pot (or tossed salad, mosaic, pizza—choose your metaphor) that is and has been the United States. From this unique assemblage, educators have tried to forge both a citizenry to sustain the American experiment in government by, for, and of the people, as well as a single nation with a common identity to be shared by all.

Benjamin Justice's first chapter enhances our historical perspective and stretches it back to the years straddling the colonies' quest for independence. He identifies and challenges the notion that the history of American education should be viewed through the lens of nationalism, with its presumption of uniqueness or American exceptionalism. The so-called Founding Fathers may well have hoped to shape a new national consciousness, but in fact their own educational plans drew heavily upon ideas that reflected British imperial traditions and, more generally, the European Enlightenment. The education that was to form the foundation of American nation-building was itself quite international, even as education would be used for nation building, at home and abroad, over the coming centuries. Indeed, with such uncertain and ephemeral plans for a single government to rule the 13 colonies and territories that had been captured during the Revolution, leading American educational writers envisioned educational reforms built on what they deemed to be universal, and not uniquely American, truths. The ideals would be enacted within the United States, but not limited to them. The United States became a means to manifest these universal truths, and set the stage for these truths to be exported in turn, fulfilling their universalist mandate. By comparing the writings of two important "Smiths" who helped forge educational thought in the early American Republic, Justice argues that in the decades preceding and following the revolution, the relation of educational thought in the early United States to its European origins showed far more continuity than change. The success of nineteenth century American educators in constructing a national identity in the United States should not cloud the vision of modern scholars looking back to its origins.

Justice cites an extraordinary passage from Noah Webster that reveals how tenuous the new political experiment that was the United States seemed at the end of the late eighteenth century, and shows that Webster was prepared for his nation-building project—to forge an American people, largely through the imposition of a standardized language—to occur among an American people dispersed among a large number of independent political regimes:

> Within a century and a half, North America will be peopled with a hundred millions of men.... Even supposing that a number of republics, kingdoms or empires, should within a century arise and divide this vast territory; still, the subjects of all will speak the same language, and the consequence of this uniformity will be an intimacy of social intercourse hitherto unknown, and a boundless diffusion of knowledge. (quoted in full in Justice, this volume, p. 4)

Webster's passage points to the interrelated but separable projects of state-building and nation-building, each of which has a long history in the United States.

The crucial terms of "state," "nation" and "nation-state" are used loosely in colloquial American English, yet their precise definitions are important for understanding the colonial legacy of Europeans in the world. The distinction is also critical because "so many of the world's problems involve the lack of correspondence between the two" (Maybury-Lewis, 1997 p. 131). The "state" signifies a country's government and the institutions controlled by the government that are responsible for administering its internal affairs and foreign relations. State-building refers to the process of constructing the institutions of governance and control within a territory. Education for state-building thus entails knowledge of governmental institutions and how they function, the duties of citizenship, and the like. Webster, keenly aware of the uncertainty facing the country, the United States, invested his energies instead in the construction of a people and a language that would transcend whatever political forms the future might hold. He was concerned with the American nation.

"Nation" derives from the Latin word for birth and refers specifically to a people. The people of a nation are often defined by their shared characteristics, such as ethnicity, culture, religion or language. So, for example, the United States has several quasi-autonomous nations within it—the Navajo nation, the Spokane nation, and so forth. If the people of Europe once identified themselves primarily as Christians under the rule of the Pope in Rome, they would later be clustered into multicultural (or properly, multinational) empires, such as the Austro-Hungarian empire, which included Germans, Czechs, Slovaks, Hungarians, Serbs, and so forth (Agar, 1994, p. 213). Education for nation-building clearly involves identity-development, patriotism, loyalty, and so forth. Webster's nationalism and emphasis on language go hand-in-hand with his nation-building efforts in education.

The expansion of the ideology of nationalism in Europe in the nineteenth century was a major contributing factor to the development of a new political formation, the "nation-state." While the term "nation-state" is sometimes used mistakenly as a synonym for "country," in fact it designates an attempt to make a specific group of people (the nation) and a country's political boundaries and institutions (the state) coextensive. France for the French, for example. As Brecher (1995) has explained, "nationalist movements ... sought to align states as power centers with nations as communities of people who asserted common linguistic, ethnic or historical bonds" (p. 346). Very few countries approach the homogeneity presupposed by this overlap between a people and the borders of a state. Nevertheless, the recent notion that countries do and/ or should have a single common language, for example, is today often taken for granted as almost a natural condition. This prevailing ideology of the nation-state, emerging out of Europe and imposed around the world, with its exclusionary or assimilationist pressures, has profound consequences for minority populations around the world.

Yet nations and nation-states are anything but naturally-occurring entities. As Maybury-Lewis (1997) points out, nations "are created by feelings of nationalism. People have to come to feel that, for whatever reason, they are members of a nation for that nation to exist" (p. 128). In other words, nations must be created, very often through deliberate and calculated means, and very often by targeting children. Hence, schools are "the primary site for integrating social and cultural differences into a predefined national whole" (Baumann, 2004, p. 1).

The projects of nation-building and state-building are often brought together within the realm of formal public schooling for children under the rubric of civic education. Civic education itself varies dramatically around the world, and implicates issues of national identity, citizenship, rights, duties, laws, institutions, and so forth (see, e.g., Stevick & Levinson, 2007). In countries where the nation-state is the prevailing ideological and political form, the distinction between the political institutions and the leading ethnic/national group of a country can be elided. One's ethnicity, religion, or language can become a virtual or real criterion for political membership and rights. People are not identified first as citizens, but as members of particular groups. Political membership may be premised upon admission to the nation through such proxy criteria as language ability or ancestry. Yet just as nations are not naturally-occurring, they are also in flux: reproducing "national identifications, civil structures and civic credibility requires continuous labours of adjustment, re-definition, and reformulation of what 'the nation' is thought to stand for" (Baumann, 2004, p. 1).

A nation's self-understanding evolves in symbiotic relation to the changing role and status of its home country in the world. As the United States expanded across the continent and from 13 to 50 states, and increased its holdings around the world, it pursued its ends and exercised its influence in no small part through education. In doing so, it inevitably advanced its own values and interests—often in destructive ways—even when it had explicit benevolent intentions towards other societies.

Julian Go's and Ann Foster's excellent 2003 book, *The American Colonial State in the Philippines*, shows that by the end of the nineteenth century, the United States was already involved in political education for democracy in Puerto Rico and the Philippines by providing the inhabitants with their first experience in managing their own affairs in municipal governments—with American oversight. Go and Foster argue that "U.S. colonial rule was not exploitative or tyrannical," but aimed, in the words of Daniel Williams, Secretary of the Philippine Commission, at something that he doubted "if in the world's history anything similar has been attempted; that is, the transplanting so rapidly of the ideas and improvements of one civilization upon another" (Go, 2003a, p. 1). The notion that such "improvements" were culturally and historically specific, and not simply portable goods that could be directly transferred into any given context, was not yet on the horizon. Here we feel acutely the universalism identified by Justice, and the almost missionary enthusiasm for the "boundless diffusion of knowledge" endorsed by Noah Webster.

The reality of these attempts to transfer advances and diffuse knowledge differ significantly from the hopes expressed by these early proponents of disseminating things American. The experience of the overseers in Puerto Rico and the Philippines—once brought into comparative perspective—demonstrated that cultural and contextual differences mattered a great deal. Although the U.S. adopted nearly identical developmental programs in each case, faced both resistance from below and corruption, and manifested logical contradictions and competing priorities, it was only once "those factors internal to the colonies converged with the different stances taken by Congress" that political education in the Philippines and Puerto Rico parted paths dramatically (Go, 2003b, p. 207). The U.S. tightened control over Puerto Rico after Congress propped up foreign investment, thus exacerbating the problem of corruption, while their failure to do the same in the Philippines led to loose oversight and a blind eye towards corruption (pp. 207–208).

The continuing expansion of the United States westward, and its expanding dominion over places like the Philippines, raised new questions about what the United States and the American people were. A Shining City on a Hill? A Beacon for Freedom and Democracy? More specifically, was the United States, by 1900, an empire? Go (2003a) argues that the particular approach of the United States to colonial rule constituted a "benign, civilizing mission" rather than one of "conquest," the type that characterized previous imperialism (p. 2). Indeed, important distinctions between "settler" and "administrative" colonialism, and "formal" and "informal" imperialism, are needed to understand the United States' evolving role in the world (p. 4). Unlike the original 13 colonies, or the approach taken with the Louisiana Purchase and the American West, where settlers were planted permanently, administrative colonialism involved extended political control over a region, but without a permanent population transfer (p. 6). The new territories and new peoples would not be incorporated into the United

States or the American nation (pp. 8–9). They were, however, through their direct control, an example of "formal" empire, as opposed to the collection of strategies for meddling in domestic affairs—economic, political and military interventions—that are techniques of "informal" imperialism, and characterized U.S. involvement in Latin America. Accordingly, the educational tasks in the Philippines and Puerto Rico were specifically political—state-building rather than nation-building.

The emergence of the U.S. as a superpower and the growing chill of the Cold War followed in the wake of perhaps the U.S.'s least controversial occupations, those of Germany and Japan following the Second World War. (For an alternative perspective, see Giles MacDonogh's *After the Reich: The Brutal History of the Allied Occupation*, 2007). Study of the role of the United States in the reconstruction of Germany's education system has received an important recent boost from Brian Puaca, whose dissertation "Learning Democracy Education Reform in Postwar West Germany, 1949–1965," won the 2006 Eggertsen Dissertation Prize from the History of Education Society. Although historians tended to regard the occupation as a period of failed reform, Puaca argues that classroom experiences played a great role in changing how German children conceived of their identities and their responsibilities as citizens. Through an examination of civics instruction, history textbooks, exchange programs, student government, school newspapers, and teacher training, Puaca was able to document the subtle, local and regional-level reforms that transpired through the occupation and into the 1960s, connecting these changes to the steady development of democracy in the Federal Republic. While recently developed approaches such as multisited ethnography have been coming to grips with the complex dynamics between the global, national, local, and classroom levels in contemporary school reform, it is particularly rewarding to discover such fine-grained analysis in historical explorations of international and domestic influences in educational transformation. The reconstruction of the German education system unfolded as the world came to grips with the horrors of the Holocaust, and it involved highly regarded figures in American education, including Indiana University's visionary president, Herman B. Wells.

The major wave of education reform that occurred in Japan during the postwar U.S. occupation involved the promotion of peace and democracy through education for the reconstruction of Japanese society (Motani, 2007, p. 277). Many of these reforms are still controversial with conservatives and nationalists in Japan. Germany does not seem to be beset with the same concerns, and the divergence of Japan and Germany seems to echo the differences Go revealed in Puerto Rico and the Philippines. Beate Rosenzweig (1998) compared educational reforms in postwar Japan and Germany, finding that although changes in the structure of the school system as a result of the American occupation were much more evident in Japan than in Germany, the more meaningful curricular and pedagogical changes, which are less visible, took place in the German schools. Structural change should therefore not be conflated with "success" in democratization of the education system, although it was a leading criterion for officials of the American occupation. Although both Germany and Japan evolved in the half-century after the war into relatively peaceful and prosperous societies, the extent to which U.S. involvement in reforming their education systems should be credited is extremely difficult to assess. In fact, the victors' goals could often be ethnocentric and inappropriate to the context. For example, presiding general Douglas "MacArthur's greatest disappointment may have been his failure to convert the Japanese masses to Christianity, despite his conviction that 'true democracy can exist only on a spiritual foundation,' and will 'endure when it rests firmly on the Christian conception of the individual and society' " ("MacArthur and the Japanese Occupation," n.d., para. 3). American ventures in educational reform around the world were, and continue to be, fraught with cultural baggage and assumptions, some explicit, many not, others embedded in larger policies and practices.

If the general feeling within the United States that the country had a positive influence around the world, at a peak following the transformations of Germany and Japan, waned during the Korean and Vietnam conflicts, it was certainly reinvigorated with the collapse of the Soviet Union and apartheid South Africa and the military engagements of the First Gulf War and the toppling of the Taliban in Afghanistan. Skepticism about the use of American power and the agendas driving it vary around the world and shift over time, but reached a summit with the ongoing conflict in Iraq. The sense that the U.S. might be advancing hidden agendas through its policies, particularly the promotion of Christianity, emerged again as rhetoric of a "Crusade" presaged the invasions of Afghanistan and Iraq. Despite perceptions that the U.S. feels a sense of entitlement to remake the world through violence, without regard to or understanding of foreign cultures or countries, or that economic agendas of expanding markets trump true support for democracy, many who operate within the U.S.'s broader involvement in promoting democracy adamantly oppose their contemporary administration's foreign policy and simultaneously advocate different values, even as they are caught up within larger geopolitical agendas. This seemingly bifurcated view is not new, however; President Dwight Eisenhower, who warned the country of the growing "military-industrial complex," also provided the country with the notion that it was in a global struggle to "win hearts and minds." Indeed, whether seeking to stem the tide of spreading communism or militant Islam, American engagement with and influence in the world has been an oscillating formula of military and diplomatic means, wedding coercion with persuasion in different ratios

Where its military ventures proved unsuccessful, the U.S. had no opportunity to attempt to repeat the system reconstruction pursued in Japan and Germany. Divided Korea manifests the problem that Noah Webster feared for the United States: both North and South Korea embrace a rhetoric of one Korean nation, divided into two political units, as Ford, Wilson, and Jones (2005) have shown. They thus identify what they call two strains of nationalism in the history curricula of North and South Korea: " 'civic nationalism' that emphasizes the rights and duties of citizenship and identification with the [particular] political state ... [and] 'ethno-cultural nationalism' that highlights the inherent unity of the Korean 'national people' (*minjok*)" (Wilson, Ford, & Jones, 2005, p. 228). Had the U.S. been able to fully implement an educational component in the reconstruction of Iraq, it is likely that state-building would have had to take a secondary role to nation-building. Although foreigners may refer primarily to its citizens as Iraqis, the extent to which the peoples of Iraq feel themselves to be above all Iraqi, or Muslim, or Kurdish, or Sunni, or Shiite, is of critical importance to the prospects for crafting a united Iraqi nation and identity, lest the centrifugal forces of separatist identities lead ultimately to partition, ethnic cleansing or genocide. Iraq, after all, did not evolve "naturally" as a "nation-state" in the European mold, but rather was the outcome of foreign interventions and conquests that shoe-horned distinct and often rival groups into a common territory.

The situation of Iraq through 2007, which underscores the importance of understanding different cultures and societies and their histories, is all the more complex now that failed states are perceived to be a direct threat to the national security of the United States. The fear that failed states in the Islamic world like Afghanistan and Somalia are potential havens for anti-American militants has renewed American interest in the recently discredited projects of nation-building and state-building. Such projects were called into question after the events in Somalia, when a U.S. humanitarian intervention escalated into state-building and led to direct military confrontation with a Somali warlord. Failed states, of course, are not simply a potential threat to distant enemies, but take a terrible toll on the people living there. The collapse of Somalia led to a flood of refugees, which can in turn contribute to instability in neighboring countries. But the instability in Somalia did not arise without foreign involvement. Somalia had been a pawn in the Cold War struggle between the Soviet Union and the United States, shifting allegiance from one to the other as the perceived benefits shifted.

When the refugees of a place like Somalia, destabilized in part through a deluge of arms sent in during the Cold War, are then admitted into the United States itself, what happens to the self-understanding of those that receive them? Will integration mean the "incorporat[ion of] an originally autonomous entity into the fabric of another pre-existing and pre-defined whole" (Baumann, 2004, p. 1)? Must the newcomers adapt themselves totally to their new context? Or, as Patricia Buck asks in the second chapter of this book, is there a moral obligation on the part of the citizens of the United States to make accommodations for refugees, when their own government bears part of the responsibility for the horrors the refugees have endured? Will the refugees follow the assimilation patterns of previous generations of immigrants, or will their arrival challenge existing regimes of integration?

The situation of the Somali refugees is caught up in complex cycles. A Cold War spot of contention, Somalia collapsed, a major diaspora ensued, and its territory opened to independent armed groups. The events of this century, stoking Americans' fears and generating suspicions of Muslims generally, exacerbate the obstacles to the Somalis' inclusion into American society. Hollywood blockbusters like *Black Hawk Down* shape the image of Somalis in the minds of the American public, further influencing how they are perceived and received within the country. The fears and perceived threats of failed states meanwhile instigate further American military intervention in Somalia through Ethiopian intermediaries, increasing Somali refugees' anxiety about relatives and friends still within the country. Against this evolving backdrop, Buck explores some of the different ideologies that shape the treatment of adult Somali women studying the English language in Maine.

Buck plumbs the dynamics of an adult education center in a small northeastern town that has witnessed a surge of Somali refugee immigrants, and that struggles to cope with the sometimes nativist, occasionally openly racist reaction to their presence.[2] While the director and a senior instructor at the center impose a traditional authoritarian model of schooling that constructs the refugee immigrants as children who need to embrace and conform to American notions of punctuality and hard work or be denied services, Buck embraces a more accommodating posture that makes room for the exigencies of the lives of these Somali women, who are often traumatized, single, and child-rearing in an alien culture. Buck shows how different implicit ideas about immigrants and citizenship underlie the divergent perspectives that clash in the contested space of the adult center. This exploration reveals that the liberal school of thought about immigrants, a philosophy that guides the director and senior instructor, is framed in opposition to nativist or racist discourses, and therefore fails to see beyond the imagined other to the historical realities of their lives, or to the wider responsibilities Americans carry for their welfare in light of the suffering incurred by Somalia's role as a U.S. proxy warrior during the Cold War. Through direct engagement, Buck hopes to break down the ongoing dominance of mainstream culture in favor of multiplicity and cultural citizenship rights.

Buck's struggles to humanize and accommodate the Somali women take place within the structure of the institution that allows her to work with the women in the first place, even as that institution strives to provide a route to inclusion and opportunity against a resistant community. Buck's layered struggle, simultaneously pushing and challenging the boundaries that enable her work, prefigures the work of American political scientist Kathleen Staudt, who feels such constraints keenly even from her leadership role in a large U.S. university.

Staudt's contribution both completes a trio of chapters that are based primarily within the United States and initiates a cluster of essays that involve larger policy structures and their limitations. Staudt, a faculty member and some-time administrator at a U.S. university on the border with Mexico, draws upon her professional experiences to explore the democratic potential of the new "civic engagement" movement in U.S. higher education. Since this movement began to gain steam in the 1990s, as Staudt shows, different meanings of democratic citizenship have been embodied and advanced through different kinds of civic engagement programs. Such programs have ranged from volunteer "service learning" in social service agencies, to technical assistance projects in the community, to more radical advocacy, empowerment, and social justice movements. Staudt suggests that university administrative elites favor the more limited meanings of democratic participation entailed in service learning and technical assistance projects. Yet she also questions the "monolithic" view of the corporate university and its entrepreneurial ethos advanced by recent radical critics, such as Stanley Aronowitz. Drawing on her own participation in a variety of local and national initiatives, Staudt asks how the entrepreneurial ethos can be productively engaged for deeper democratic goals. She wonders how civic engagement advocates with a more radical orientation can craft a message that appeals to university administrators and the economic bottom line, even while advancing social justice goals. Based on her experiences, Staudt has few illusions about the challenges involved; she recounts the dilemmas of educating college students for democratic citizenship through university-community partnerships, when the conditions for such partnerships are so constrained by university structures (such as low faculty incentives for participating), bureaucratic infighting, and the like. Yet even by charting these dilemmas, Staudt points us toward further possibilities.

   Staudt's work is keenly sensitive to the structures that both enable and
constrain our attempts to advance democracy through education. Her
title's citation of budgetary, spatial, and disciplinary borders helps us to
appreciate how substantial the obstacles can be just within the confines of
an American university. These structures can be all the more imposing
when they are augmented by impermeable linguistic boundaries, time
constraints, thousands of miles, religious differences, and the like. The
following two studies build upon her insights into the structures at play in
educational projects, international policy, and institutional design. Ayman
Alsayed's chapter on U.S. involvement in education in Palestine and Doyle
Stevick's chapter on U.S. support for civic education in Estonia reveal
complementary patterns. Alsayed's chapter 4 also marks a transition from
considering American responses within the U.S. to Muslims from a failed
state (chapter 2), to the policy manifestations and implications of American
fear of terrorism within a nation that is still seeking state-hood.
   A Palestinian educator and scholar, Ayman Alsayed presents a critical
account of "discourse versus practice" in efforts by international donors to
help develop democratic civic education in Palestine. In his chapter,
Alsayed fundamentally questions the very meaning and direction of
national "development." He contrasts grassroots Palestinian normative
goals of social justice, and fulfillment of human potential, with the
prevailing developmentalist goals of free markets and macroeconomic
prosperity. He notes that international donors consider democracy and
"good governance" absolutely necessary to development, but then he
wonders why donor-supported civic education programs tend to carry
forth such a narrow vision of democratic education. Taking up the debate
over what really constitutes "democracy" and democratization, Alsayed
contrasts the urban and elite orientation of donor programs for
democratic civic education with the often more radical, and popularly
rooted, education of other nongovernmental organizations (NGOs). He
uses document analysis to focus his attention on these problems in a
particular USAID (United States Agency for International Development)
program for adult civic education in Palestine, called *Tamkeen* (Arabic for
"empowerment"). According to Alsayed, the Tamkeen program
illustrates many of the problems with international donor funding of so-
called democratic civic education. Because of geopolitical exigencies, he
argues, the USAID program enforces narrow definitions of democracy,
restricts participation to government (i.e., Palestinian National Authority)
allies, exemplifies authoritarian rather than democratic means of
governing, and marginalizes popular groups. In the end, the application
of USAID funding rules has the effect of limiting the successes of civic
education to the realm of formal, cognitive knowledge, while dampening

the participation and behavioral transformation that democratic theorists agree are truly the ingredients of successful democratic citizenship.

It is perhaps unsurprising that security considerations for the U.S.'s strong regional ally, Israel, drive American policy towards Palestine. It is more surprising to find an emphasis on Holocaust education as a primary policy-driver for American involvement in Estonian education reform. Yet, as Stevick found (2007), both NATO (North Atlantic Treaty Organization) and the European Union used Estonia's prospective memberships in those organizations as a carrot to advance the creation of a Holocaust education day in that country. While the policy was implemented officially on paper, in practice it was made voluntary and, in effect, never actually encouraged. In Estonian schools, the policy scarcely exists. Basic knowledge of the historical experience of Estonia, however, sheds light on its resistance to Holocaust education. Estonia was initially handed over to the Soviets in the Molotov-Ribbentrop pact, and endured a terrible year under Soviet occupation before the Nazis arrived, forcing out the Soviets and therefore being perceived as liberators, which led many Estonian patriots to enlist with the Germans in the fight against the Soviets. While the Nazi occupation was itself horrible, the reoccupation of Estonia by the Soviets then lasted another half-century, and the collective memory of the Estonian nation is dominated by the murder, deportation or exile of fully 20% of its pre-war population. The Soviet occupation in turn diluted Estonia's nation-state (which had been a relatively homogenous 90% before the war) with settler colonialism, flooding the allegedly autonomous Soviet republic with Russian-speakers and attempting to Russify Estonian society.

An understanding of the historical background of Estonia and the hostility that remains between Estonia's ethnic Estonians and Russians goes a long way toward explaining why this policy has been such a failure, but it is precisely this kind of knowledge that has too often been absent in American involvement in promoting democracy, whether in Palestine or in Central and Eastern Europe after the fall of the Berlin Wall and the collapse of the Soviet Union. Anthropologist Janine Wedel (2001) provides this scathing account from her outstanding book, *Collision and Collusion: The Strange Case of Western Aid to Eastern Europe*:

> Deficient in cultural and historical sensibilities, consultants and aid repre-
> sentatives often made social fools of themselves, failing to realize that their
> chief source of attractiveness was in their own pocketbooks or their per-
> ceived access to others' pockets. (p. 92)

As American educational researcher Doyle Stevick demonstrates in the fifth chapter, in foreign partnerships for civic education in Estonia the problem of deficient sensibilities is most acute with regard to the language barrier. The language barrier is impermeable to outsiders, who therefore lack unmediated access to the local context; the difficult Estonian language undercuts the possibility of accountability to foreign donors and partners even as it provides more freedom to operate for domestic partners who are sufficiently capable in English. Stevick's chapter considers the selection criteria used at three different levels in these partnerships: the American selection of Estonian partners for civic education work within Estonia, the outside presenters selected by the Americans for civic education teacher-conferences within Estonia during the years immediately following the Soviet Union's disintegration, and the selection of participants within the country. The first section demonstrates that, although government funding does create a level of public accountability and a vague mandate to advance the national interest, organizations can circumvent such restrictions by funneling money through a series of nonprofits and thereby advance a more ideological agenda. The foreign speakers who presented at teacher-training sessions in Estonia, for example, shared strong links to conservative American foundations and think-tanks such as the Cato Institute and the Heritage Foundation. Moreover, the desire to advance particular ideas converged with what Stevick calls a "transmission-orientation" on the part of donors and foreign partners.

The Americans, Stevick found, had less success advancing an ideological agenda than in shaping the forms and functions that civil society took on. Yet civil society acted both as means and ends for the Americans: its development was a major goal of American involvement in democracy promotion, but it was not always the most effective channel through which to promote citizenship education reform. While Americans in the administrative colonies of the Philippines and Puerto Rico a century before had advanced political education by providing direct municipal experience to local leaders, the new reigning ideology of civil society impelled American partners to work in just the opposite manner, independent of government institutions. This was a policy decision that limited their own influence and resulted in the exposure of their partners to the insecurity of market forces in the competition for foreign funding. In order to secure their own economic viability, domestic partners who were responsible for generating their own revenue streams had a strong incentive to be—and often were—more concerned with foreign mandates than with domestic issues. Activities undertaken more from economic insecurity than from personal commitment were undertaken in rapid succession and dropped upon completion, resulting in a pattern of inconsistent focus that Stevick dubs "project-hopping." Partners would even sign on to projects to which they were ideologically opposed, which made them ineffective advocates for foreign agendas. To help bring such dynamics to light, Stevick develops a typology of NGOs according to their funding sources and economic security. An analysis of partnerships conducted by an Estonian civic education NGO reveals that projects undertaken with American and Western European partners hewed closely to donor goals, while self-funded activities ventured into subjects seldom touched by foreign projects. The selection of participants for teacher-training sessions was generally left in the hands of national coordinators, and reflected their own priorities, power structures, and networks of trust. The failure of foreign partners to establish and enforce meritocratic criteria for selection subverted their ability to disseminate ideas and to advance either their own agendas—or even the shared goal of advancing citizenship education.

Given the American preference for working with civil society, influence on government could be either indirect, if any (see Levinson & Sutton, this volume, chapter 6), or occur only once civil society, functioning as a bastion for the opposition movements, sweeps to power, which portends a cyclical influence at best (as in Atkinson & Wyatt, this volume). As Levinson and Sutton remind us, influence need not be direct or deliberate, as when Estonian children falsely assume, after watching American movies, that their country's justice system also renders verdicts by a jury of one's peers. Such is the situation with Mexico and Indonesia, where American discourses about civic education circulate as one of a body of global resources available to be appropriated for local ends. Pioneers in the anthropology of education policy and in the theory of policy as practice, anthropologists Bradley Levinson and Margaret Sutton define policy as "a complex social practice, an ongoing process of normative cultural production, constituted by diverse actors across diverse social and institutional contexts" (Levinson & Sutton, 2001, p. 1). This insight, which dovetails with the development of multi-sited ethnography, was an important development in the understanding of educational change under globalization because, as Wedel and Gregory Feldman note, "policies connect disparate actors in complex power and resource relations" (Wedel & Feldman, 2005, p. 1).

Although policy elites who work from a implicit model of "from the top-down" policy may regard deviations from their goals and expectations as "failures of implementation," in fact, individuals throughout these policy networks inevitably appropriate policy in ways that alter it from the initial conception. The top-down policy and coercive diplomacy of informal imperialism are no more likely to be successful than the transmission-orientation discussed in the previous chapter. As we strive to manifest democratic values and processes in the advancement of democratic education in our own societies and others, the needs for openness, for deep engagement, for relating across differences, are highlighted within Levinson's and Sutton's (2001) definition of appropriation itself as,

> an active process of cultural production through borrowing, recontextualizing, remolding, and thereby resignifying cultural form.... [It] emphasizes the agency of local actors in interpreting and adapting [resources] to the situated logic in their contexts of everyday practice. (p. 17)

For their chapter, Levinson and Sutton explore what happens when concepts and models of democratic education that were first developed in the Euro-American context meet the conditions of large, poor, newly democratizing countries. They draw on a historical-institutionalist perspective that takes seriously the possibility that there can be "modernization without Westernization." Thus, they find that globally circulating concepts of democratic citizenship education undergo important modifications in Mexico and Indonesia, where unique circumstances—such as historical experiences with the dominant religions of Roman Catholicism and Islam, or different roles of the military—as well as diverse understandings of democracy, insinuate themselves into policy making and implementation. The chapter begins with an historical overview of important political and structural changes in the two countries, and then moves on to compare their "policy processes and the production of new curriculum for civic education." It closes with a conceptualization of how the "local and the global" intersect in complex ways to give particular shape to civic education programs. Based on this comparative study, Levinson and Sutton conclude that countries that are modernizing and democratizing their political structures can—and indeed, must—recover and elaborate democratic traditions from within and, in the process, define democratic citizenship in terms uniquely inflected by local cultural contexts.

The work of the scholars who follow—Kubow, Landis and Mirseitova, Shah, and Atkinson and Wyatt—join Buck and Staudt in their attempts to manifest democratic values in the means and ends of cross-cultural educational engagement. Reflective scholars of deep commitment, they know the problematic legacy of colonialism and the challenges of cross-cultural work, they are informed and motivated by the latest work in research, theory and philosophy, and they bring the experience and insight produced by extended periods of cultural immersion. They are aware both of their own position within larger structures and systems of power, as well as what they represent for the people with whom they are engaged. Together, they model the best of what is possible in international and cross-cultural partnerships, even as they reveal the diversity of contexts and approaches that such enterprises can embody. In these qualities, they are emblematic of what Heidi Ross (2002) calls "relational theories," and embrace what Patricia Hill Collins characterizes as "the necessity of linking caring, theoretical vision with informed, practical struggle" (cited in Ross, 2002, p. 409).

Ross's (2002) articulation of relational theory resonates with the work of these scholars. She argues that "[k]nowing particular people across spaces of difference requires the moral capacities of response, care, emotional sensitivity—the ability to see the other as a being in her own right" (p. 412). This is not a group of people who arrive in foreign contexts with all the right answers graciously transmitting their truths to others who have not yet seen the light. They do have values, ones they are eager to share, but only through an open dialogic process, and not in one direction only: they are themselves open to transformation through these engagements.

Relational theories call for a certain intellectual and moral posture from the individual, because "understanding is not contained within me, or within you, but in that which we generate together in our form of relatedness" (Schwandt, 1999, p. 457). Building understanding communally between people is a complex, dynamic, imperfect process that neither submits itself to clear, methodological formulae for achieving "truth" nor occurs in a moral vacuum. As Blum puts it, "Never is 'knowledge of individual others a straightforwardly empirical matter requiring no particular moral stance toward the person' " (cited in Ross, 2002, p. 412). Relations with others involve a flickering between the familiar and the alien, a sense of liminality, of simultaneous knowing and not knowing.

> [U]nderstanding requires an openness to experience, a willingness to engage in a dialogue with that challenges our self-understanding ... and [we] simultaneously risk confusion and uncertainty both about ourselves and about the other person we seek to understand ... one does not simply defend one's own beliefs or criticize what the other believes, but rather seeks to become clear about oneself, about one's own knowledge and ignorance ... [only then can we] engage in checking one's own prejudices.... "I both allow some play to my own thinking and, in so doing, expose it to the counterweight of the other's contribution, which may confirm me in it or force me to amend or abandon it." (Schwandt, 1999, p. 458, citing Molander & Dunne)

Understanding is always tentative and open, subject to revision and reinterpretation, not a final state that is achieved. "[T]he space between us—including the relationships between researchers and subjects ... is first and foremost one of partial and negotiated meaning. The space between us is never transparent or completely knowable and is inevitably subject to conflict and misunderstanding" (Ross, 2002, p. 411). In bell hooks's words, this is "transforming selves in relationships" (Ross, 2002, p. 412).

It is in this idea of transformation that important work in education and democratic theory come together. Transformational learning, the theory developed by Jack Mezirow, is broken down into four key components or stages:

1. Critical reflection on assumptions supporting a problematic belief, feeling or value judgment—its source, nature and consequences.
2. Engagement in discourse (dialogue devoted to assessing contested beliefs) to arrive at a tentative best judgment upon which to act until new perspectives, evidence or argument are encountered that are found to be more justified through further discourse. Free full participation in discourse is central to adult learning and education in a democracy.
3. Reflectively and critically taking action on the transformed frame of reference.
4. Developing a disposition for critical reflection on one's own assumptions and those of others. (Marsick & Mezirow, 2002)

The authors of these chapters opened themselves to transformation and, in Mike Rose's sense of education as an "invitation," invited their partners to participate with them in the process of transforming of selves in relationships. Rather than avoid conflict, and in so doing erase difference, relational theories seek to bring differences out into the open and to deal with them directly. Indeed, it is often the discomfort and challenge of difference and conflict that lead us to our more profound learning and transformation. Gutmann and Thompson (1996) encourage people confronting moral disagreements to seek out together points of convergence within larger conflicts and to elevate others' moral concerns within one's own priorities. Not only are conflicts inevitable, argues Stuart Hampshire (2000) in *Justice as Conflict*, they are essential. The issue is in the manner in which we approach and manage those conflicts. Hence, agonistic democracy advocates call for transversal politics, which gets

> around and above the immobilizing contradiction...between a universal sisterhood and a relativist stress on difference that dooms us to division and fragmentation.... [P]erceived unity and homogeneity are replaced by dialogues which give recognition to the specific positioning of those who participate in them. (Ross, 2002, p. 425, as cited in Cockburn)

Habermas's conception of instrumental and communicative learning highlights the distinction between partnerships that are premised on transmission and those that are premised upon transformation.

Transformative learning differentiates between instrumental and communicative learning. Instrumental learning involves control or manipulation of the environment. Communicative learning involves shared meaning through interpersonal interaction. Communicative learning involves critical assessment of assumptions that support contested beliefs and dialogue that results in a dialectically derived, tentative best judgment upon which to act. (Marsick & Mezirow, 2002)

This invitation, if accepted, becomes a means for cultural transformation from within and for civic self-empowerment, which is to say, a foundation for democratic citizenship.

Patricia Kubow's work with South African and Kenyan educators is exciting in part because it eschews the transfer of expertise from developed to developing countries—even south-south transfer—in favor of a dynamic process through which educators from different sub-Saharan African societies coconstruct curriculum within their own similarities and across their differences. Kubow's participation with the participants self-consciously encourages the development of educational materials based on local knowledge and expertise, which is particularly significant in light of the history of foreign-influence on the education systems in those countries (foreign influence that includes the widespread use of English, which enabled this particular project.)

The convergence of approaches developed independently by Kubow and by Atkinson and Wyatt in South Africa 10 years earlier (this volume, chapter 10) attests to their significance. Kubow elucidates a six-stage data-gathering research process she labels "democratic concept development," or DCD. As with Atkinson's and Wyatt's needs assessment, Kubow's first stage involves intensive data gathering within the relevant contexts in Kenya and South Africa. Similarities and differences are then identified and represented graphically, before a team of representatives is assembled to construct lessons, which are implemented and, with extensive feedback (again like Atkinson & Wyatt), revised collectively a final time.

Kubow shows how five common democratic themes emerged in the focus groups: human and individual rights, values/traits of citizens, gender equality, tensions between cultural practices and democracy, and building community. She then illustrates how each of these themes emerged in the lessons themselves. These early sections of the chapter form the backdrop for a theoretical discussion of democratic culture. Drawing upon a schema developed by Mazrui, Kubow theorizes nine different functions of culture in a democracy. She does this in order to provide a heuristic tool for educators to think about how different aspects of a democratic culture can be fostered through a broad and far-reaching democratic citizenship education. In this articulation, democratic culture includes conceptual, behavioral, relational, evaluative, formative, communicative, purposeful, productive, and consumptive roles. In addition to these nine functions, Kubow draws attention to the temporal component of work in democratic education. Everyone has a past that gave shape to the conditions of the present, which in turn form and constrain the directions we wish to pursue in the future. Such elements, Kubow argues, need to be kept in mind for the educational goals to succeed.

David Landis and Sapargul Mirseitova discuss the past, present and future of international collaboration with the Kazakhstan Reading Association (KazRA) and its extraordinary accomplishments during the past decade. The development in Kazakhstan of the Reading and Writing for Critical Thinking (RWCT) project not only embraces principles of relational theories—the authors specify an ethic of care and of participatory citizenship—but it also showcases the complex interplay of international donors and partners in educational projects. Initiated in Slovakia under USAID support, it developed across the postcommunist world with support from the Open Society Institute and other Soros-supported foundations, only to return to Kazakhstan with additional USAID support, together with money from such groups as Chevron and Shell, the Ministry of Education, and an endorsement from UNESCO (United Nations Educational, Scientific and Cultural Organization). The sustained support from USAID allowed KazRA to maintain focus on its key goals, and thus to avoid the project-hopping that is characteristic of revenue dependent NGOs (see chapter 5).

RWCT does not rely on translators to transmit information from foreign experts to domestic teachers, but instead provides intensive instruction (120 hours in total), including exposure to more than 100 teaching techniques and methods and the underlying democratic philosophy, to teachers in their own language. When the author of this introduction asked a leading Estonian civics teacher from an elite high school which civics program she had found most valuable, without hesitation she singled out the RWCT sessions taught by a fellow Estonian teacher, even though they were not explicitly about civics. This powerful endorsement made me eager to learn more about a program that had reached 50,000 teachers in the postcommunist states. Further, since this teacher, reached through the "train the trainers" approach, spoke no English but nevertheless adopted methods she learned in these seminars, the American influence was diffuse, indirect, and "left no fingerprints." For these reasons, the dialogic format adopted by Landis and Mirseitova, who is executive director of KazRA, is enlightening even as it puts into practice the values it advocates.

The authors' 6 years of participant observation and subsequent research provide a foundation for a deep consideration of the cultural issues at work in their partnership. They immediately bring forth the importance of the language barriers in communication, illustrating in great detail an issue raised by Stevick in chapter 5. Their discussion of the different meanings cross-culturally of seemingly basic words such as "teach" and "evaluation" and "critical" is among the most compelling to be found in the literature. The authors' struggles to understand these differences, and their persistence in working across them, are models of relational theories' aims. The authors conclude that some time spent at the very beginning, in which Kazakhs and foreigners simply had the opportunity to get to know each other and their circumstances—a relational theory tenet—would have been a great boon to the project. It is striking to encounter a genuine dialogue between two people who have worked so closely for so long: their conversation includes thoughtful questions, and they teach each other, as when Mirseitova interprets for Landis the seemingly-obstructive or formulaic behavior of Kazakh school leaders.

The authors do not adopt the approach they advocate only in the format of the chapter; they implement it in myriad ways throughout KazRA's activities. KazRA not only advocates that students and teachers should write and have a voice, they publish and distribute 2,000 or more copies each of journals filled with teachers' and students' writings. A similar process led to radical change in the way the organization ran its national conferences. Most striking is the more recent push to democratize ethnography by teaching it to school age children, so inquiry becomes a tool for teachers and students to research students' funds of knowledge and their community life. This practice is illustrated by a remarkable story of first-graders and their research into the complexities of a department store. Although Mirseitova discusses the challenge of achieving sustainability for KazRA, their cross-cultural dialogue will continue and deepen: Landis left his position at the University of Northern Iowa and is now associate professor of language education and director of the master of arts in TESOL (Teaching English to Speakers of Other Languages) program at the Kazakhstan Institute of Management, Economics, and Strategic Research in Almaty, Kazakhstan.

Payal Shah is also concerned with developing an ethic of care for humanity through her work with mostly American high-school students in a month-long service-learning project in rural India. A reflective practitioner who designed the students' experiences around Nussbaum's conception of cosmopolitanism, and with the tenets of international and global education in mind, Shah explores the extent to which these goals were actually achieved as students returned to the United States and reconsidered their own society in light of their recent experiences in India. The research, which takes the form of a dialogic encounter, continues the pattern of engagement between Shah and the students that characterized their time together in India. In her work, Shah discusses in depth the theoretical concepts of international and global education, cosmopolitanism, and world citizenship, with particular attention to its civic implications. This philosophical examination is grounded by the analysis of 11 U.S. high school students' experiences in the global education program in Rajasthan, and it is used to reflect on the role international and global education programs can play, in conjunction with formal education, towards a reconceptualization of civic education in the United States.

Shah concludes that the students did not make critical, transnational connections between issues that they saw in India (i.e., poverty and inequality), and their similar manifestations within the United States (notably, the fallout from Katrina). What accounts for this absence? Shah explores various explanations—cognitive development, critical race, and white privilege theories—to explicate why these students did not demonstrate the achievement of the most critical and reflective stages of global consciousness development. Although the experience allowed well-off American children to experience both poverty and life as a racial minority, they nevertheless retained their privileged status in India, and their language, English, was also privileged. Although many of the students became critical of material aspects of their own lives and society, the experience may in turn also function to consolidate their privilege. Shah reports that all of the interviewees made the experience the core of their college application essays. Her work points towards a paradox, that the transformation of individual perspectives can occur even while that same transformation functions in a broader system to consolidate their own privilege. As we explore ways to advance the transformative nature of the educational experience we provide, and to expand the groups of individuals to whom we can provide them, we must also be attentive to changes within the systems themselves.

Ron Atkinson and Judy Wyatt conclude the book with just such an account, an international partnership to retrain—or simply to train—South African principals in a way that transformed their practice of leadership roles and brought change to the institutions as well as the individuals. This crucial work to transform the authoritarian school leadership took place during the waning years of the Apartheid regime, when schools were key sites of organization and resistance to the government. The work was conducted with Teacher Opportunity Programs (TOPS), which was South Africa's largest NGO when apartheid collapsed. Atkinson and Wyatt were invited to join the South African effort to improve schooling for Black Africans by providing training for school directors in South Africa. The school system suffered from the double bind of being both a tool of oppression for the racist government and a key site of resistance and solidarity against that same regime. Principals in schools for Black African children often had little or no training. Grassroots reform efforts lacked resources, yet they could lose all credibility if they were perceived as serving government interests or of being co-opted by foreign actors. Atkinson and Wyatt managed to tread this treacherous ground successfully both by spending a tremendous amount of time in the context and by adopting methods consonant with the values of grassroots effort.

Their first task was to produce reliable information about the real needs of school leaders throughout the country. Their needs assessment took an innovative form. While a transmission-orientation approach would simply import foreign values or models, a more democratic approach is open-ended and dialogic. While the question of when an attempt to change someone else's values can be legitimate (one commonly-advanced involves the prevention of physical harm to others) and not oppressive or imperialistic is thorny and unresolved in philosophical literature, few doubted that foreign support for the efforts of oppressed peoples in South Africa could be justified. But how? Instead of advocating foreign priorities, goals or values, Atkinson and Wyatt surveyed the school leaders' perceived needs. But they did not stop there. They also gathered information systematically from the teachers who worked under these leaders, revealing an entirely different set of issues and concerns. These issues and concerns became the basis for developing training materials, thus using domestically generated priorities as a basis for promoting change. Through an extended and collaborative curriculum development process, and a field-testing regimen that gathered helpful data for revisions, the authors were able to produce a textbook that successfully addressed both the school directors' own perceived deficiencies and the issues (such as authoritarian management styles) raised by teachers. This process, both democratic and firmly grounded in the empirical realities of local communities, led to intensive training seminars. These seminars received compelling evaluations, and the authors share the data that demonstrate that a potentially transformative experience was provided to participants, one that produced real changes in the practice of school management. Concerned with sustainability, the authors and TOPS also embraced a "train the trainers" model, in which 50 school directors—half of whom, remarkably, were women—completed a master's degree in educational administration from the University of South Carolina. Together, these programs reached more than 2,000 school directors from across the country. Driven by domestic needs and goals, this partnership was able to raise millions of dollars, with $1.7 from USAID, without falling prey to the common pitfalls of such partnerships.

Together, these 10 chapters provide a rich sampling of the diverse contexts and ways in which American ideas, practices, and policies of education for democracy are spread, encountered, appropriated, rejected, or embraced around the world. While not meant to provide a complete or systematic overview of the American influence on education for democracy around the world, the volume nevertheless introduces concepts, identifies processes, notes obstacles and challenges, and reveals common themes that can help us to understand American influence on education for democracy more clearly, wherever it occurs. Whether they are questions of power, dimensions of structure and agency, the role of interests, how economic concerns can impinge on other priorities, the role of culture, ethical approaches to difference, and so forth, different elements will emerge for each reader. We hope, through this work, to have made a contribution to the appreciation of the complexity, the situatedness, the diversity, and the reciprocal nature of these processes.

NOTES

1. With apologies to the many countries of North, South and Central America, we use this unfortunately ambiguous term to refer to the policies, practices, and cultures of the United States.
2. Buck and the author have had the same racist scourge enter our communities. One of the author's former students was a devotee of the World Church of the Creator, killing two and shooting nine more before taking his own life in a 1999 shooting spree (see Stevick, 2007). The killer's mentor, the "pontifex maximus," now behind bars and held incommunicado for soliciting the execution of a federal judge, used the Somali community in Maine as an opportunity to lead a white supremacist rally. Refugees from Somalia sometimes aggregate with family members or friends in certain locations, such as Minneapolis, despite being settled by the government in a more dispersed fashion. Such communities increase opportunities for cultural maintenance, but can also make them flashpoints for demagogues or racists.

REFERENCES

Agar, M. (1994). *Language shock: Understanding the culture of conversation*. New York: William Morrow.

Baumann, G. (2004). Introduction: Nation-state, schools, and civil enculturation. In W. Schiffauer, G. Baumann, R. Kastoryano, & S. Vertovec (Eds.), *Civil enculturation: Nation-state, school and ethnic difference in the Netherlands, Britain, Germany and France* (pp. 1–18). New York: Berghahn Books.

Brecher, J. (1995). "The National Question" reconsidered from an ecological perspective. In O. Dahbour & M. Ishay (Eds.), *The nationalism reader* (pp. 344–361). Atlantic Highlands, NJ: Humanities Press.

Go, J. (2003a). Introduction: Global perspectives on the U.S. colonial state in the Philippines. In J. Go & A. L. Foster (Eds.), *The American colonial state in the Philippines* (pp. 1–42). Durham, NC: Duke University Press.

Go, J. (2003b). The chains of empire: State building and "political education" in Puerto Rico and the Philippines. In J. Go & A. L. Foster (Eds.), *The American colonial state in the Philippines* (pp. 182–216). Durham, NC: Duke University Press.

Go, J., & Foster, A. L. (2003). *The American colonial state in the Philippines.* Durham, NC: Duke University Press.

Gutmann, A., & Thompson, D. (1996). *Democracy and disagreement.* Cambridge, MA: Belknap Press.

Hampshire, S. (2000). *Justice is conflict.* Princeton, NJ: Princeton University Press.

Levinson, B. A. U., & Sutton, M. (2001). Introduction: Policy as/in practice—A sociocultural approach to the study of educational policy. In M. Sutton & B. A. U. Levinson (Eds.), *Policy as practice: Toward a comparative sociocultural analysis of educational policy* (pp. 1–22). Westport, CT: Ablex.

MacArthur and the Japanese occupation (1945–1951). (n.d.). In *People and Events.* Retrieved May 5, 2008, from http://www.pbs.org/wgbh/amex/macarthur/peopleevents/pandeAMEX99.html

MacDonogh, G. (2007). *After the Reich: The brutal history of the Allied occupation.* New York: Basic Books.

Marsick. V., & J. Mezirow. (2002, November). *New work on transformative learning. Teachers College Record.* Retrieved July 9, 2004, from http://www.tcrecord.org (ID Number: 10876)

Maybury-Lewis, D. (1997). *Indigenous peoples, ethnic groups, and the state.* Boston: Allyn & Bacon.

Motani, Y. (2007). The emergence of global citizenship education in japan. In E. D. Stevick & B. A. U. Levinson, (Eds.), *Reimagining civic education: How diverse societies form democratic citizens* (pp. 271–292). New York: Rowman & Littlefield.

Puaca, B. (2005). *Learning Democracy: Education reform in postwar West Germany, 1945–1965.* Unpublished doctoral dissertation, University of North Carolina, Chapel Hill.

Rosenzweig, B. (1998). *Erziehung zur Demokratie?: Amerikanische Besatzungs- und Schulreform in Deutschland und Japan* (Beitrage zur Kolonial- und Uberseegeschichte) [Trained in democracy: American occupation and school reform in Germany and Japan (Contributions from colonial and international history)]. Stuttgart: Franz Steiner Verlag.

Ross, H. (2002). The space between us: The relevance of relational theories to comparative and international education. *Comparative Education Review, 46*(4), 407–432.

Schwandt, T. A. (1999). On understanding understanding. *Qualitative Inquiry, 5*(4), 451–454.

Stevick, E. D. (2007). The politics of the Holocaust in Estonia: historical memory and social division in Estonian education. In E. D. Stevick & B. A. U. Levinson (Eds.), *Reimagining civic education: How diverse societies form democratic citizens* (pp. 217–244). New York: Rowman & Littlefield.

Stevick, E. D., & Levinson, B. A. U. (Eds.). (2007). *Reimagining civic education: How diverse societies form democratic citizens*. New York: Rowman & Littlefield.

Wedel, J. (2001). *Collision and collusion. The strange case of Western aid to Eastern Europe*. New York: Palgrave.

Wedel, J., & G. Feldman. (2005). Why an anthropology of public policy? *Anthropology Today, 21*(1), 1–2.

Wilson, C., Ford, D., & Jones, A. (2005). The history text: Framing ethno-cultural and civic nationalism in the divided Koreas. In E. Vickers & A. Jones (Eds.), *History, education and national identity in East Asia* (pp. 227-253). New York: Routledge Taylor & Francis Group.

CHAPTER 1

BEYOND NATIONALISM

The Founding Fathers and Educational Universalism in the New Republic

Benjamin Justice

WHISPERED WASHINGTONS

In his widely regarded 1790 essay, "On the Education of Youth in America," Noah Webster sounded a clarion call for a nationalistic American education. Sometimes bordering on xenophobia, the essay decried Americans' tendency to use foreigners as teachers, to use textbooks from other countries, and to teach American children the languages and histories of other countries without first teaching them to treasure their own. He wrote

> Every child in America, as soon as he opens his lips ... should rehearse the history of his own country; he should lisp the praise of liberty and of those illustrious heroes and statesman who have wrought a revolution in her favor. (pp. 64–65)

Advancing Democracy Through Education? U.S. Influence Abroad and Domestic Practices, pp. 1–27
Copyright © 2008 by Information Age Publishing

Webster even went so far as to write a federal catechism for schoolchildren, and to recreate the English language in a distinctly American mode. His efforts have earned him the reputation of the "founding father of American nationalism" (Rudolph, 1965, p. 41). His famous spelling book, first published in 1783, sold 5 million copies by 1818, 60 million copies by 1890, and remains the second-best selling book in American history, after the Bible (Unger, 1998, p. 343; Webster, 1824, p. iv).

In the popular imagination, the Founding Fathers of the United States have become precisely whom Webster had hoped. According to the nation's civil religion, Webster's "heroes and statesmen" of the revolution have become national demigods—geniuses, men of profound vision and wisdom ((Ellis 1997, pp. 3–23; Frisch, 1989). Washington above all has withstood the text of time, aloof and pure, the "First of the Fathers." Yet all the Founders have achieved a collective status that continues to demand not only piety (including expensive monuments and cold portraiture on our currency), but also oracular veneration. Whether or not babes in the young republic once did whisper the name of Washington, men and women who are old enough to know better still lean toward the grave and ask Washington and his fellow founders to whisper back. "What would you think about ___?"

Historians of American education, myself included, are no exception to this Founders fetish, and we embed questions of the moment into our studies of the past (Justice, 2005).[1] Although Jefferson declared that the world belongs to the living and that each generation must reinvent its own government, modern historians, judges, and policymakers continue to pepper him and his fellow Founders, figuratively, with questions such as: What is the relationship between religion and public education? How can schools teach moral values? Does a state-sponsored curriculum violate individual liberty of conscience? Indeed, Webster's nationalism has, until recently, dominated the field of American history. Most studies of the early national period still operate within the framework he implanted in the minds of millions of schoolchildren: the American nation (or its subdivisions) as the unit of analysis. For the most part, scholars of early American education look to the founding generation as a cynosure for "national education" in America, focusing on two issues in particular: the perceived need to homogenize and assimilate the population into a distinctly American mode, and the perceived need to centralize and "nationalize" a system of public schools. It is Webster's view that predominates. The whispered Washington has become a symbol not only of how Americans regard the founding generation as oracular, but also represents the static, immutable idea of American nationalism in education. As an increasing body of recent scholarship shows, however, it is not at all clear that the Founding generation had the same ideas about the nation, nationalism, or national education that historians have willed them to (see Cremin, 1980, pp. 2–3; For an analysis of this historiography see Moroney, 1999).

Lawrence Cremin's (1970) monumental work, *American Education: The Colonial Experience*, offers the most influential example of this nationalistic tendency. Cremin began with the unit of analysis already fixed: the territory that would eventually be the United States. Within that space, he traced what he saw as the development of uniquely American ideas and patterns of education—often, of course, based on outside influences from across the Atlantic. Cremin concluded that it was the unique patterns of American education that led to the American Revolution and the formation of the United States of America. Whether called "multicultural historians" or the new social historians, some scholars have questioned the existence of a static notion of America; they have also plumbed with increasing sophistication the different meanings of nationalism in local, regional, and cultural terms. Ironically, they have explored precisely those tendencies that George Washington once warned against in his Farewell Address: political parties, local and sectional prejudices, and religious conflicts. They have also gone beyond what Washington said to what he did not say—about the racial and gendered boundaries of civic identity, and about capitalism (see Foner, 1997 for a comprehensive, if basic overview of recent scholarship in various fields and time periods).

What educational historians have paid much less attention to—and until recently they have been joined in this omission by their colleagues in mainstream American historical research—is the way in which American educational thought was situated in contexts broader than the nation-state. There was no state, let alone a unified nation, before 1776; arguably there was no coherent state before 1789. If one considers American imperial attitudes toward indigenous peoples, the institutions of slavery and Jim Crow apartheid, and other limitations on civic identity by race, gender, and religion, there may not have been an American nation, defined by a shared and coherent identity, until quite recently, if indeed, there is one today. Beyond the borders of the eighteenth century United States, all people of the Western world were reshaping their political institutions, realigning their identities around different notions of "nationalism" even as they lived in an increasingly interconnected and dynamic world system of trade in people, ideas, goods, and power. (Scholars from many fields converge on this point. See, e.g., Adas, 2001; Boswell, 1989; Wolfe, 1997.) The modes of thought that Americans used when they talked about the project of national education and nation-building were ones inherited not from their unique experience as Americans (as Lawrence Cremin famously argued) but by their cultural experience as part of the Atlantic World of the eighteenth century, and by their political experience as subjects of the

British Empire. Recent scholarship on these themes by Robert Ferguson, Bernard Bailyn, Eliga Gould, Peter Onuf, and others suggests that there is much to be gained by moving beyond the narrow and often anachronistic confines of the American state to understand the development of American history (Ferguson, 1994).[1] The founding fathers wanted education to forge a national identity to stabilize and strengthen their newly formed state; but did they think in nationalistic terms themselves? What were the unique features of this nationalistic education they envisioned?

In fact, in an essay Webster wrote a year before the publication of "On the Education of Youth in America," there is an element of uncertainty about the future of a single American state that suggests a tempered view of nationalism. Before the Louisiana Purchase of 1803, of course, citizens of the United States could not be certain that their country would stretch across the continent. And before 1789, they could not even be certain that their country would be a single entity. Had the Constitutional Convention collapsed, or the states not ratified it, the Unites States could have become a collection of small states, each a former colony, or collections of states in loose federation; the colonies might even have been reconquered piecemeal by England, France, or Spain. In his 1789 essay, "Dissertations on the English Language," Webster revealed this uncertainty when he laid out his argument for standardizing American English. Regional differences in pronunciation, Webster argued, led North Americans to disrespect and misunderstand each other. "Our political harmony is therefore concerned in a uniformity of language." A unity of language would distinguish North America from cacophonous Europe, and would bring stability to society. But Webster (1789) was also aware that the "we" that he implied in his definition of Americans, was by no means a fixed entity. Nor was it anchored, necessarily, in a single nation-state. He explained,

> Within a century and a half, North America will be peopled with a hundred millions of men, all speaking the same language. Place this idea in comparison with the present and possible future bounds of the language in Europe—consider the Eastern continent as inhabited by nations, whose knowledge and intercourse are embarrassed by differences of language; then anticipate the period when the people of one quarter of the world, will be able to associate and converse together like children of the same family. Even supposing that a number of republics, kingdoms or empires, should within a century arise and divide this vast territory; still, the subjects of all will speak the same language, and the consequence of this uniformity will be an intimacy of social intercourse hitherto unknown, and a boundless diffusion of knowledge. (p. 269)

A number of republics? Kingdoms? Empires? Even supposing a different American state, or many American states, Webster argued, common language could promote common culture, ease of trade, and progress. This statement qualified Webster's nascent nationalism with a kind of pan-Americanism that transcended a single form of government, a single region, or the interest of a single country, the United States of America. (The latter is axiomatic among American educational writers of the early national period. See, e.g., Doggett, 1796.)

Webster was not alone. Throughout the educational writings of the early national period there was a strong universalist streak, inherited from the region's former sociopolitical identification as a part of the British Empire, and more broadly, the Atlantic world. Even as they formulated plans to shape and sustain a nation, scholars, clergy, and political leaders demonstrated complex and, at times, catholic understandings of purposes and practice of formal education—they spoke and wrote of universal truths, universal values, and a universal historical destiny. Their educational ideals were not uniquely American, but expressly of, and for, the people of the world. If the project of building a nation was to create a *narrow and unique* sense of shared identity among the disparate peoples, then the founders had a curious approach.

As historical scholarship of the last 30 years has emphasized, America meant many things to many people. It was a unified nation, a collection of states, a local economy, a state of mind, an experiment, a virgin land, Protestant Utopia, a White man's paradise, or a Black woman's hell. Certainly regional, local, and sectarian concerns on the one hand, and narrowly nationalistic concerns on the other, did play an important role in educational theory, policy, and practice in the early republic. But the people who lived in the colonies *cum* states were also part of a broader system of markets, migrations, and ideas that transcended the uncertain notion of what, exactly, the American nation was or would become. In that sense, the project of educational thought in America was not only the education of a nation, for a nation, by a nation, but the beginning of a "novus ordo seclorum," a new order for the ages. It was an education for all nations. As it turned out in later centuries, European and American imperialism made some elements of these "universal ideas" literally universal—especially the use of public education as an instrument of state formation and consolidation across the globe, and the justification of state educational policy in economic, social, and political terms. (The literature on this point is extensive. See, by way of example, Carnoy, 1974.)

Elite intellectuals were not the only people having a conversation about education in the early republic. At the local level, Americans of the early republic continued to educate their children, their servants, and each other at home and, increasingly, in the public sphere in common schools paid for by the community or more formally by a state-sponsored tax. The most popular textbooks were not written in America for a uniquely American audience; and those that were reflected strong regional biases and little in the way of the banal nationalism that would characterize textbooks of later periods (Nash, 2006). Nationalism did not grip American education at the local level in the decades following the American revolution; indeed, it was a strong and deeply cherished localism that insulated American education from the Founding Father's electric educational idealism (Kaestle, 1983). Yet the ideas of the Founding Fathers mattered: in an age of political and intellectual deference, elite discourse did shape politics. Intellectual elites served in positions of power in state and national government. They wrote, enacted, and enforced laws. A few, like Webster and Jedidiah Morse, wrote textbooks. In some cases where their proposals for state policy made only limited headway, their ideas influenced later generations.

The remainder of this essay considers the continuity and evolution of civic educational thought in America between the 1750s, when no one could have imagined the creation of the United States of America, and the 1790s, when Noah Webster and other men and women leaders of the founding generation struggled to define it. The chapter will focus on two educational plans in particular as case studies: one by William Smith in 1754 for the creation of charity schools for German-speaking children in Pennsylvania, and one by Samuel Harrison Smith that won an education essay contest set by the American Philosophical Society in 1795. The two authors offer important bellwethers for the educational ideas among intellectuals, and incorporate themes common to educational writers of their times. In each case, the author aimed to clarify the political and social purposes of formal education; in each case the author cited a body of contemporary scholarship; and in each case, leading thinkers of the day vetted and praised the essay. Indeed, soon after writing each piece, the authors would become leading figures in their own right: William Smith as the Provost of the College of Philadelphia; Samuel Harrison Smith as the editor of the chief Jeffersonian newspaper, the *National Intelligencer*. By the same token, this chapter will also look at the lives and intellectual context of the writers themselves to understand the origins of their ideas within a global intellectual marketplace. In each case, a particular state (The United States of America) or region (British North America) makes a weak unit of analysis. The tale of these two Smiths suggests that the project of forging a national identity through education in the early republic was not, for the Founding Fathers, a story of American exceptionalism, so much as it was a study in educational universalism.

WILLIAM SMITH, THE BRITISH EMPIRE, AND
THE PENNSYLVANIA GERMANS

William Smith's personal story, as well as his involvement with the German Charity schools, exemplifies the international character of American life and thought in the decades prior to the American Revolution. Smith was born near Aberdeen, in the Eastern Highlands of Scotland, in 1727. At that time, Scotland was a recent if ambiguous partner in the British Empire. The 1707 Act of Union had brought Scotland formally into the political and economic fold of England, including representation in Parliament. The union transformed the Scottish economy, but by mid-century much of Scotland remained a semi-independent backwater. Some observers even compared the Highlands to the wilds of America (Richards, 1991, pp. 67–114). Presbyterian Scotland shared Congregational New England's severe view of illiteracy: all people had to learn to read the Bible as a moral, and mortal, imperative. Scotland had a long history of encouraging the elite to be literate, and since the Scottish Act of 1696, the law required each parish to conduct a school, though, as in the case of colonial New England, compliance was irregular (Richards, 1991, p. 83). The Society for the Propagation of Christian Knowledge (SPCK), a missionary society which funded educational efforts throughout the British Empire, formed a special "S" SPCK for Scotland in 1709. The SSPCK supported parishes in meeting the requirements of the school act, especially in the "uncivilized" regions of Scotland—not coincidently those same regions sympathetic to Roman Catholicism. Whether or not the schools were directly responsible, Scots of the mid-eighteenth century could read and write at high rates, with numbers for lowland men comparable to those of New England. (For compilations of data, see Monaghan, 2005, pp. 384–385; Stephens, 1990.) As a child, Smith attended one of these parish schools and a charity school before attending the University at Aberdeen.

After university, Smith pursued a career in education. He secured a job with the Society for the Propagation of the Gospel and began writing educational reform essays (Smith, H. W., 1880, pp. 1–20). In 1750 he published at least three works—a memorial to Parliament on behalf of Scottish schoolmasters, an "Essay on the Liberty of the Press," and a scheme for augmenting the salaries of parochial schoolmasters in Scotland for *Scots Magazine* (p. 20). In 1751, he moved to New York and began writing proposals for education in the colonies, including schools for Native Americans and the formation of a college in New York (p. 21).[2] As did his essays written in Britain, these tracts espoused a strong commitment to the political role that formal education, through schooling, could play in the maintenance of social and political harmony within the

British Empire. He wrote characteristically in his 1752 essay *Thoughts on Education*

> If we look into the Story of the most renown'd States and Kingdoms, that had subsisted in the different Ages of the World, we will find that they were indebted for their Rise, Grandeur, and Happiness, to the early Provision made by their first Founders, for the public Instruction of youth. (p. 1)

Although his various schemes did not catch on, they did attract the attention of Benjamin Franklin, who was seeking a head for his academy (and soon to be college) of Philadelphia. Smith's educational ideology, developed in Scotland and exerted toward so many different targets within the Empire, resonated with the aims of Franklin and the academy's trustees—indeed Smith would soon, for a time, become one of Franklin's closest friends. Franklin offered the job and Smith accepted. The Scotsman returned briefly to London to be ordained in the Anglican Church before taking his new post in Philadelphia in 1754.

The same broad economic and political forces that landed the precocious Scotsman a job in Philadelphia as head of an academy were moving masses of other groups throughout the Atlantic world. In the decade of the 1750s alone, over 120,000 immigrants or abductees reached the 13 colonies that would become the United States, including 50,000 Africans, 30,000 German-speakers, 14,000 Northern Irish, 8,000 Southern Irish and another 20,000 English, Scots, Welsh and others (Fogelman, 1996, p. 2). The most conspicuous group in Pennsylvania was German-speaking people from Northern Europe. Estimates during the mid-eighteenth century put the total number of German-speakers living in Pennsylvania at 60,000 to 100,000, or approximately 1/3 to 3/5 of the colony's population. Franklin estimated that the Quaker and German populations of the state each constituted one third of the total (Franklin, 1776). Early generations of German immigrants tended to be pacifistic and middle class; by mid-century, German-speaking immigrants tended to be peasants with less sophisticated beliefs. These recent immigrants numbered as many as 7,000 annually during the 1750s.

German immigration to Pennsylvania was so extensive that prominent English-speaking colonists complained they were being overrun. From the 1720s onward, the Pennsylvania Assembly considered and passed laws to address the "problem," including a 1727 law requiring all German immigrant men to take an oath of allegiance (Frantz, 1998, p. 21; Cremin, 1970, pp. 256–259). While Benjamin Franklin at first saw the German speakers as a new market for his printing business, and subsequently came to admire their work ethic, their increasing opposition to his own political ambitions led him to join the chorus of criticism in the 1750s. The catalogue of insults Franklin concocted about the erstwhile "brave and steady" German men ran through his private and public writings of the 1750s. He attacked their intelligence, their character, their morals, and even their wives. He concluded that Germans were not really White at all, but "swarthy." As the French Empire expanded into the Ohio Valley (hastening the French and Indian War), Franklin feared that Germans would not only refuse to fight, but that they would be duped by French treachery (Cremin, 1970, pp. 259–264; Frantz, 1998, pp. 21–34). The Pennsylvanian asked rhetorically,

> Why should Pennsylvania, founded by the English, become a Colony of Aliens, who will shortly be so numerous as to Germanize us instead of our Anglifying them, and will never adopt our Language or Customs, any more than they can acquire our Complexion.

Even in his primitive eighteenth century formulations, Franklin (1751) linked his notion of national identity and progress to an immutable racial hierarchy. He warned a friend, "Already the English begin to quit particular Neighborhoods surrounded by [Pennsylvania] Dutch,[3] being made uneasy by the Disagreeableness of dissonant Manners; and in Time, Numbers will probably quit the Province for the same Reason." As modern Americans might put it, "there goes the neighborhood" (Franklin, 1753, 1755, 1750).

Franklin was not alone among English leaders concerned about the German problem. The Colonial Government of Pennsylvania and sympathetic members of the British Parliament considered legislation to curb the immigration threat (Bell, 1955; Cremin, 1970, pp. 259–264; Frantz, 1998). Franklin's friend and member of Parliament, Peter Collinson, considered a series of acts, ranging from establishing schools, to making English the official language, to suppressing German printing presses and banning German books, to the obvious tactic of discouraging further immigration by rerouting Germans to other colonies. Franklin thought some measures were too harsh. Yet he approved of rerouting immigrants, making English the official language and, most significantly, starting schools to Anglicize German youth (Franklin, 1753).

While the other measures came to naught in Parliament and the Pennsylvania Assembly, the idea of using formal education as the solution to the German "problem" bore fruit. Pennsylvania Anglos were not alone— indeed the effort reflected the international nature of American colonial life. Even as English leaders pondered the problem of educating the Pennsylvania Dutch, a real Dutch minister named Michael Schlatter returned home from a 5-year mission among Pennsylvania Germans to launch an aid campaign to provide money for teachers and ministers. The

Synod of North Holland and other Protestant groups across Northern Europe took up collections. The idea spread to Scotland, where the Church of Scotland raised funds as well, and eventually caught the attention of Franklin's friend Peter Collinson. A committee known as the Society Entrusted with the Monies Collected for the Use of Foreign Protestants in Pennsylvania formed in London to manage the growing fund. The proprietor and even the king and queen of England (German speakers and immigrants to England themselves) made large contributions.

William Smith heard of the German Charity School plan while he was in England for his ordination and quickly wrote to the committee for the German Charity School with a proposal. Smith's fascinating plan anticipated much of the language that would later characterize the educational writings of Founding Fathers like Thomas Jefferson, Benjamin Rush, and Noah Webster. Yet Smith was a Scotsman, an Anglican, writing in the context of an international educational effort, for a German population living in a British colony in America. His proposal drew upon popular notions of political theory and philosophy, religion, and history. Overall, Smith's plan had three main points: to encourage the German Society to define the problem as a British one (to the exclusion of the Hollanders and other Protestant contributors); to define the problem as primarily one of the education of youth—and not of the absence of religious institutions and leaders; and to offer a specific plan for forming and maintaining common schools that would Anglicize German Americans, but which they would patronize voluntarily. While Smith's proposal contained much of the language that had come to characterize missionary work, his proposal changed the priority, from one of religion, to one of politics.

William Smith wrote in the midst of an expanding empire; and he knew it. He began the proposal by quoting Joseph Addison's phenomenally popular play, *Cato*. In the play, Cato died a martyr to a virtuous republic, at the hands of the ruthless Julius Caesar. Using Roman history as an allegory, the play explored the effects of empire on domestic politics and society. As they viewed the profound changes wrought by their own expanding empire, English Tories and Whigs alike related to *Cato*, and by the 1770s the play would come to serve as a rallying point for revolutionaries in the American colonies (Litto, 1966). For Smith's purposes, Cato highlighted the burdens of the British Empire in the Americas, and he substituted the word "British" for the word "Roman," lest the point be lost.

> A British Soul is bent on higher views;
> To civilise the rude unpolished world,
> And lay it under the restraint of Laws;
> To make man mild and to man,

> To cultivate the wild licentious Savage
> With wisdom, Discipline and liberal Arts,
> Th' embellishments of Life. (Smith, 1753)

Even without the obvious substitution, few could miss the obvious connection to the problems of the Pennsylvania Germans—cultivation, civilization, law, discipline. Smith would shortly frame the solution in terms of formal education.

If Addison's Cato did not sufficiently stir the souls of the society members, Smith made sure that his ringing appeals to patriotism did. "How much, then, is this unfortunate people obliged to you for commiserating their sad circumstances?" He asked rhetorically. "How much is the whole British nation, nay the whole protestant interest, and the interest of liberty obliged to you for exerting yourselves in such a cause?" The answer lay in the language of Cato. It was a question of responsibility, of national destiny, of economics, and of history. The British Empire was an empire of liberty, of enlightenment. A Protestant empire.

> No; ye noble and worthy patriots! it is the work of no party. It is a British work. It does not regard a handful of men, of this or that denomination, happily escaped from popish tyranny and persecution; but its success is to determine whether a vast multitude of fellow-protestants, of many different denominations (doubling in their numbers perhaps once in twenty years) shall fall into the deepest ignorance, shall be seduced by our indefatigable Foe, shall live in a separate body, shall turn our trade out of its proper channel by their foreign connections, and perhaps at last give us laws and language or, whether, on the other hand, they shall adopt our language, our manners ... and incorporate with us in one happy enlightened Society. (Smith, 1753)

The threats were essentially twofold: seduction by the Popish Empire of Catholic Europe, or disharmony and discord within the British sphere.

This kind of rhetoric was not new, and since Elizabethan times Englishmen had fashioned themselves as an enlightened, vigorously Protestant alternative to Roman Catholic Europe. The religious dissenters who settled New England, for example, had carried this sense of identity with them. They quickly built schools, most notably Harvard, and emphasized formal education as a religious duty. They fretted over the loss of their identity in the New World, and struggled to maintain civilization in the wilderness. But their primary focus was religion itself. Building and maintaining churches, congregations, and competent clergy were their top priorities. Schools played a subordinate role, especially for the education of younger children, which was required by law and enforced by custom, but which occurred in the home. In his proposal to the German Society,

William Smith argued something new: the roles should be reversed. Build schools first and churches second. Put civic and social cohesion before doctrinal purity. Encourage parents to send their children into the public sphere for instruction. It took the power of Enlightenment political theory to pull it off (Armitage, 2000; Axtell, 1974; Canny, 1998).

First, Smith's proposal spelled out the German problem: a mass of Protestant immigrants facing French papists from without and slippage to barbarism from within, with no access to the noble British institutions that could save them from both. Whether or not continued immigration was desirable, German-Americans were already there to stay. They were "strangers,"

> strangers indeed to every thing of ours; Strangers to our Laws and manners; strangers to the sacred sound of liberty in the land where they were born, and uninstructed in the right use [and] Value of it in the country where they now enjoy it; utterly ignorant and apt to be misled by our [un]ceasing enemies, and surrounded by such enemies to mislead them; and what is worst of all, [in] danger of sinking deeper and deeper every day into these deplorable circumstances, as being almost entirely without instructors and unacquainted with out language, so that it is hardly possible for us to warn them to their danger, or remove any prejudices they once entertain[ed]. (Smith, 1753)

According to Smith, the problem was not that the Germans were morally deficient or wicked. Instead, Smith framed the problem in Lockean terms: the Germans' ignorance resulted from their environment. Without proper instruction, rising generations of German immigrants would have no understanding of those political, social, and religious institutions that could integrate them into British society. The Germans were not depraved, but deprived.

Smith conceded that religious institutions were necessary, especially for the German-Americans, and acknowledged to the society that the "service done to religion, in the dark parts of the world, by other pious societies, will sufficiently justify and recommend that part of your design which regards the settlement of clergy among them." Nevertheless, he went on to argue, it was the other part of their mission—to educate the German youth of Pennsylvania—that deserved special attention. Indeed, in the present case, he argued,

> Nothing else can answer the principal design. Clergy as I said before are greatly wanted and must be sent to preserve the present generation from falling off; but it is from a right institution of the rising generation that we are to expect the desired coalition. The old can only be exhorted and warned. The young may be instructed and formed. The old can neither acquire our language, nor change their national manners. The young may do both. The old, whatever degree of worth they may acquire, descend

apace to the grave and their influence is quickly lost. The young, when well instructed, have their whole prime of life before them, and their influence is strong and lasting. (Smith, 1753)

According to this vision, German children were blank slates, upon which English manners, customs, and language might be written. Smith's goals were primarily social, economic, and political, not religious. He imagined integrated common schools for English and German children, where they would form bonds of affection and learn similar "national manners." In terms of economic prosperity, he explained, "Commerce is the child of Industry and an unprecarious Property, but these depend on virtue and liberty, which again depend on knowledge and Religion." In the case of Pennsylvania, these interlocking notions of social harmony, economic prosperity, and political liberty all depended on a populace with a "common" education. As he explained, "A common language and conformity of manners would also be acquired, and [the children] might be taught to feel the meaning, and exult in the enjoyment of *liberty, a common weal and a common country* [original emphasis]."

If these social goals were not enough, Smith drew explicitly on the political theories of Montesquieu (1914), whose 1748 sensation, *The Spirit of Laws*, had just been translated into English by Thomas Nugent the year before. In this landmark book, Montesquieu had argued that, "The laws of education ought to be in relation to the principles of government" (book IV). Smith endorsed this view enthusiastically. Schools would not just Anglicize children culturally and socially; they would prepare them to become full citizens of the British Empire. Through formal education, "such a spirit may be promoted through all ranks as is best suited to the particular genius of every government in our colonies" (Smith, 1753). He wrote enthusiastically, "It is evident, in the present circumstances of the people under consideration, that nothing but a common education of youth can obviate the inconveniences justly dreaded, and incorporate them into one happy whole" (Smith, 1753).

Smith's plan for German schools focused on three issues. For curriculum, he proposed a basic course of reading, writing, and arithmetic, free of charge to all children in the "Township or District." First and foremost, students would learn English, and ideally schoolmasters would be bilingual. Yet the basics were not enough. The curriculum "should be calculated rather to make good citizens than what is called good scholars." Students should learn a "system of truths and duties," in the form of a catechism. Schoolmasters should also offer short lessons in politics and government, including the "general principles of our common Christianity," and "the difference between one sort of government and another." Students should be discouraged, however, from "lingering" in school beyond basic studies, and schoolmasters should charge tuition for those advanced studies, especially in Latin and Greek, "for which the vulgar have neither leisure nor capacity."

For the governance of the schools, Smith proposed that the German Society appoint six to seven "trustees general" living in Pennsylvania, who would oversee the formation and funding of all the schools. These men would be like founding fathers in their own right: encouraging students to apply their academic learning toward defining their civic identity. At least one of these trustees would visit each school annually to award a cash prize, or "premium," to the winners of competitions in English and civics—demonstrating the primary importance of these subjects. "What a glorious sight will it be," he waxed, "to behold the [trustees] enter these schools, in person to perform their part of the visitation, and see that all things be carried out according to the public sense." He continued, "These will indeed be acting like the fathers of their country, and those ancient Lawgivers who deigned in person to superintend the education of youth as the rising hopes of the state." Trustees-general would themselves appoint local deputy trustees to oversee daily matters at each school, and who would themselves award monthly premia to students on various topics. These local trustees should include three Germans and three English-speakers per district. Schoolmasters should speak both German and English, and of great importance, should be native to Pennsylvania. (He hoped his academy in Philadelphia could be a feeder school [Smith, 1754].)

The German Society approved Smith's plan. They appointed the Reverend Schlatter, the real Dutchman who had begun the collections in Holland, as the supervisor and visitor of schools at a salary of a hundred pounds per annum. They also appointed six trustees-general, including the provincial governor, the provincial chief justice, the provincial secretary, the provincial liaison to Native Americans (and the only German appointee), Benjamin Franklin, and of course, William Smith. Naively, the society assumed that Germans would flock to schools where their children would be Anglicized. Benjamin Franklin had predicted it based on his own stereotypes. In a 1753 letter to Peter Collinson, he rhymed, "The Dutch, Wou'd fain save all the Money they Touch. If they can have English Schooling gratis, as much as they love their own Language they will not pay for German Schooling" (Smith, 1754).

In fact, the German-speaking community's reaction to the schools was complex. Resistance to the German Society sprung up almost as quickly as the schools did, mainly from German Baptists and other "plain folk" who were (rightly) skeptical of the political and cultural aims of the Charity School Trustees. Nevertheless, several communities petitioned for schools immediately; despite disruptions of the French and Indian War (1754–

1763; also known as the North American theater of the Seven Years' War), enrollment peaked in 1759 at between 600–750 students, a third of whom were English-speakers (Cremin, 1970, p. 262). To the chagrin of the Trustees, several of the teachers charged with Anglifying the German children were, in fact, teaching German. The end of the war in 1763, on the other hand, contributed to the ultimate demise of the schools. Although disruptions from fighting ceased, financial support for the schools dried up as paranoia over German political allegiance eased. Soon a new crisis would eclipse the "German problem" in Pennsylvania, as the British Crown passed the Stamp Act to help pay for the War; This disastrous legislation pushed Pennsylvania and other colonies down the road to revolution. The German Charity Schools died a quiet death in 1769, when the society donated the remainder of its funds to the College of Philadelphia.

The example of William Smith and the Pennsylvania Germans demonstrates the development of many elements of "American" thought in the context of the British Empire, and more generally, the Atlantic world of the eighteenth century. What Cremin once argued was a characteristically American mode of education was, in reality, much larger and more complex than a single unit of analysis, "America," can explain. The modes of thought that would define the "nationalism" of the Founding generation in the 1780s and 1790s were the inheritance of the experiences of men like William Smith—born of one outpost in the British Empire, landed in another, and a firm believer in the power of formal education to bring social and political cohesion among the disparate people of the Western World. In the subsequent decades, Smith would play a leading role in shaping educational thought and practice in America, as a college president and trustee, as a minister, an essayist, and member of the American Philosophical Society.

SAMUEL HARRISON SMITH, THE AMERICAN NATION, AND THE WORLD

Samuel Harrison Smith (1772–1845), no relation to William Smith, was born in Philadelphia 3 years after the end of the Charity School collapse. Like William Smith, he was precocious, and by the age of 15 had graduated from the University of Pennsylvania. Also like William, Samuel Smith was a prodigious writer. Smith's essay on education was unusual subject matter for him—most of his writings were political, and his first career was as a newspaper editor. At the time that he entered his education essay to the American Philosophical Society's (APS) contest, the 23-year-old Philadelphian was printing a newspaper called, aptly, the *New World* (APS, 1797; Biographical information may be found in Smith, 1973. p. 292). The contest that induced Smith to write his now famous essay shows how the intervening 40 years since the creation of the German Charity Schools had modified, but not fundamentally altered, the global marketplace for educational solutions to the political and social upheavals of the era. Nor had independence erased the international character of eighteenth century educational thought in America.

The Philadelphia of Samuel Smith's youth was a cradle of the American Revolution and became the seat of government for the emerging United States of America. The Continental Congress that met there had little to do with education, with one exception. As settlers poured into the Northwest Territory (now the Midwest), the Congress hastily made plans to organize and sell plots of land, encourage settlement, and lay the foundation for future states. In the Land Ordinances of 1785 and 1787, the Congress set aside parcels of land for the maintenance of New England style common schools, in the hopes of attracting the right sort of settlers and to insure political and social stability. At the state level, several states included provisions for encouraging education in their constitutions, inspired by John Adam's Massachusetts Constitution of 1780. Thomas Jefferson authored a plan for universal elementary education in Virginia that failed in 1779. In the popular American press, writings on education increased dramatically during the 1780s (Berkhofer, 1972; Onuf, 1986; Onuf, 1987; Smith, 1973).

While America did not have educational institutions to rival those of the old world, the APS, founded by Franklin in 1743 to encourage and disseminate useful knowledge, emerged as the most significant outpost of the Enlightenment in America, sharing members and correspondence with similar institutions across the Atlantic. Members of the society included many of the leading men of the period from Washington, Adams, Jefferson, Madison, Rush, and Webster to Linnaeus, Lafayette, Talleyrand, Condorcet, and Crevecoeur (Odgers, 1943; see also www.amphilsoc.org). In its monthly meetings, the society sought to balance lectures and discussions among many fields, from political science and philosophy to agriculture and natural history (Hansen, 1926, p. 106). When in 1795 the APS announced a series of contests for essays or inventions in education, navigation, horticulture, and home heating (to name a few), it was following the precedent and procedure of the Republic of Letters.

Both the form of and substance of the education essay contest that would attract Samuel Smith came directly from a larger, longer-standing discussion about the role of education in the rapidly changing world of the eighteenth century. Academies and learned societies commonly sponsored intellectual contests with a cash prize. Not only did such inducements inspire and sort out merit from mediocrity, but they caused all students to emulate excellence. William Smith had proposed premia for the German Charity Schools for just this reason. In the 1780s and 90s, some prize contests caused such sensations as to become international. The most famous started in the Academy at Lyon in 1780. The question, "Was the Discovery of America a blessing or a curse to mankind?" attracted prominent writers and led, in the case of Condorcet, to a famous treatise on the American Revolution. Other institutions and newspapers in Europe and America copied the contest, including *Boston Magazine* in 1784 (Danzer, 1974). The APS awarded its first prize, the "Magellanic Premium" for discoveries "relating to navigation, astronomy, or natural philosophy," in 1786 (Fay, 1932).

The substance of the APS education essay contest reflected concerns throughout Europe and America. Benjamin Rush wrote famously in 1786 that the "business of education has acquired a new complexion by the independence of our country. The form of government we have assumed created a new class of duties to every American" (Rush, 1786, p. 243). But he was exaggerating. The "business of education" had been changing throughout the century, on both sides of the Atlantic. Rush's argument was, of course, a direct application of Montesquieu's argument in the 1748 *Spirit of Laws*, which had strongly influenced William Smith's plan for the German Charity Schools. Intellectuals across Europe and America considered the "new complexion" of education in the late 18th eighteenth century even before the conclusion of the American Revolution; and nations from Catholic Spain to Protestant Holland enacted educational reforms in the name of national identity and enlightenment theory. (In 1800, Pierre Du Pont de Nemours credited Holland as being the first nation to achieve a "national" system of education. See Du Pont, 1923, pp. iii–iv.) The American Revolution may have intensified the discussion of formal education's role in the new nation, and American writing on education increased dramatically in the 1780s; but it was new bottles for old wine.[4] In the educational credo of Enlightenment thinkers like Franklin, Jefferson, and Rush, the question of the moment was how to create educational institutions adapted to the unique problems of the new state; but they also understood, just as their colleagues in Europe did, that the problem was necessarily a universal one. Indeed, many essays on educational reform in America in the early republic were written by Scottish immigrants (including Witherspoon and Rush) and French expatriates such as Pierre Du pont de Nemours and Amable-Louis-Rose de Lafitte de Courteil, and they applied the same general enlightenment arguments that characterized the seemingly nationalistic arguments of the Americans (Du Pont, 1923; Lafitte, 1797 as cited in Rudolph, 1965, pp. 225–270).

Learned societies and academies throughout the Atlantic world responded to the problem of education's "new complexion" by sponsoring prize contests—even before the end of the American revolution. From 1779–1781, the Chalons Academy sponsored a prize contest on the "best plan of education for the people." Later, from 1797–1803, the class of moral and political sciences of the French National Institute sponsored a series of contests on such questions as: "Is emulation a good means of education?" and "What are the most suitable institutions to establish morality in the people?" (Staum, 1985–1986, pp. 153–179, 155–156, 163). In America, in fact right down the street from the APS building in Philadelphia, Mr. Poor's female academy sponsored an essay contest on the "best essay on education" in 1789 ("A Promoter," 1789).

When the men of the APS decided to offer a premium for an essay on education in 1795, then, they did so in an international context. The challenge, as they saw it, was to apply the universal theories of education known throughout the Republic of Letters to the specific context of the United States. In other words, they were asking the same question that historians have asked since: was there such a thing as an "American education?" If so, what was it, or what should it be? Specifically, APS asked for:

> a system of liberal education, and literary instruction, adapted to the genius of the government, and best calculated to promote the general welfare of the United States; comprehending, also, a plan for instituting and conducting public schools in this country on principles of the most extensive utility. (APS, 1795, entry 1)

In essence the question had two parts: how to fix existing elite or "liberal" education, and how to provide education to the masses. But the question was also specific: it asked writers to make their system national, to make it uniquely American, and to make it "useful."

Samuel Harrison Smith's answer to the question, submitted in December of 1796, accomplished the former but failed in the latter two. It proposed a national system of education, but it did not articulate anything uniquely American, nor did it generate a plan that was practical. Even with his opening sentence, Smith explained the problem as designing a system of education for a particular type of government, a republic, rather than a particular government or nation—the United States. "The man who aspires to the honor of forming a system of education adapted to a republic," he wrote with feigned humility, "should either possess the capacity of original reflection or that of improving, without adopting, the ideas of others." In the following essay, Smith drew on existing writings on education and political theory, most of it European. Nor were his particular proposals unique to educational writings at the time. But it was the length, depth, and prescient quality of the essay that caught the attention of the APS, and of subsequent scholars (Justice, in press; Rudolph, 1965, p. 169).

Smith's loosely organized essay consisted of four parts: a philosophical examination of virtue and wisdom, a discussion of methods and curriculum, a organizational plan for enacting a system from the local to the national level, and a brief speculation on the effects of the plan. The first and most extensive portion of the essay examined the question at the heart of Scottish moral philosophy: were men born inherently good or evil, blank slates, or somewhere in between? As Bacon, Montesquieu, Rousseau, and others had argued, these questions were of the utmost moment in a republic. Smith tried to stake out a middle ground (probably influenced, as Jefferson was, by Lord Kames), arguing that people were born with varying degrees of a moral sense, but that all benefited from its practice through formal education (Smith, 1973, pp. 107–142; Yarbrough, 1997, pp. 271–303). Just as William Smith had done, Samuel H. Smith concluded that the nation should focus on the education of children, whose minds were still malleable and free from prejudice and superstition, rather than on the indoctrination of adults. Samuel H. Smith's goals were not entirely the same as those of the preceding Smith, however—due in part to the different contexts: charity schools for outsiders to the Empire versus a system of national education for nation-building. Whereas William Smith had emphasized the more conservative aims of political and social homogeneity and harmony, Samuel H. Smith saw education as helping each individual citizen secure his rights and happiness, and to enable the government to rule without force.

Ironically, however, Samuel Smith's "liberal" plan for national education rested on the proposition that the state had the right to compel all families to send their children to school, or to provide a comparable education at home. Indeed, Smith endorsed homogeneity of a different sort than the voluntary association at the heart of the German Charity School scheme. Borrowing from a proposal for the new Napoleonic Civil Code in France, Samuel H. Smith argued that, "Society must establish the right to educate, and acknowledge the duty of having educated, all children." The reason, he argued by quoting the Roman poet Juvenal, was to stamp out superstition, bigotry, and false ideas. "Error is never more dangerous than in the mouth of a parent…. Hence prejudices are as hereditary as titles, and you may almost universally know the sentiments of the son by those of the father (Rudolph, 1965, pp. 190, 206). Instead, from the ages of 5–18, boys should attend state schools, supported by property tax, where they would learn an increasingly complex curriculum resting on basic instruction in the three Rs, as well as the memorization of key passages exemplifying universal civil ideals. At higher levels, children should learn U.S. history, natural philosophy (science), and geography. Students would study from state-approved texts, and would learn only those things that were either "true" or "probably true," including universal political beliefs and values. Smith sought to expunge all superstition, intolerance, and specifically religious instruction. After two levels of primary education, some students could go on to college or a national university, at the state's expense. In a radical move, Smith removed the study of dead languages from all but the university curriculum. In a more conservative vein, he refused to take a stand on girl's education, but suggested tepidly that "the improvement of women is marked by a rapid progress and that a prospect opens equal to their most ambitious desires" (Rudolph, 1965, p. 217).

Among his approximately two hundred paragraphs, Smith did devote one to American exceptionalism. What American education could do specially, he argued in a vein similar to Webster, would be to bring educational materials in line with the new form of government. "The radical ideas we have already established and which are in a great measure peculiar to us claim a new and entirely different exposition from that which they have yet received" (Rudolph, 1965, p. 216). In particular, the absence of medieval institutions allowed Americans the opportunity to achieve an enlightenment too much encumbered in the old world. Americans needed to produce home-grown educational materials. Smith saw no contradiction between freedom and a compulsory, censored and prescribed curriculum based on "truth" and "reason."

The price of failing at universal education, Smith argued, was to follow the fate of other republics in history. "It is true that some nations have been free without possessing a large portion of illumination," he wrote, "but their freedom has been precarious and accidental, and it has fallen as it rose" (Rudolph, 1965, p. 219). Savagery, stupidity, and disharmony sprang from ignorance and passion unrestrained. Indeed, Smith even pleaded with his colleagues engaged in the bitter politics of the day to stop "denouncing [one] another for equivocal political crimes," and "attest to their patriotism by their cooperating in efforts in so great a cause." He warned that,

> Should avarice, prejudice, or malice frustrate this great object, and should a declension of knowledge, gradually…be suffered to triumph, the prospect is gloomy and dreadful. Gigantic power misapplied, towering ambition unsatiated [sic] with criminal gratification, avarice trampling property underfoot, mark but a few of the dark shades which will, in all probability, envelop our political horizon. On such an event, we must expect the miseries of oppression at home and conquest abroad. (Rudolph, 1965, pp. 219–220)

This fate resembled the fears inspired by William Smith's German Charity School plan … a descent into savagery and depravity, political disunity, and the threat of external foes unchecked. History proving that America was not exceptional would be the price of failing at educational reform.

Speculating optimistically on the results of his proposal, Samuel Smith looked to its effects on individual citizens, the state, and the world. His observations provide yet another example of how the narrow nationalism proposed by Noah Webster, which would come to characterize nineteenth century educational thought, did not yet obtain at the end of the eighteenth century. For the individual citizen, education would enhance freedom and happiness. "Too well informed to be misled, too virtuous to be corrupted, we shall behold man consistent and inflexible." In fact, education in enlightened principles would transcend politics. "Not at one moment the child of patriotism, and at another the slave of despotism, we shall see him in principle forever the same." For the United States, universal education would ensure the "perpetuity" of the political principles embedded in the Constitution, it would improve the economy by encouraging invention and improvement, and such a state would in turn free men to take time to pursue happiness. Through universal education, American could become a model enlightened nation.

Finally, Smith understood the destiny of the United States in universal terms—though not stated explicitly as such, as the inheritance of the imperial legacy of Britain. While he predicted (perspicaciously) that immigration and natural increase would cause explosive population growth, he did not speak of uniquely American virtues, nor with the rhetorical nationalism of Noah Webster. In his conclusion, he pondered the role of an enlightened United States educating the world:

> but more important, still, will be the example of the most powerful nation on earth, if that example exhibit dignity, humility, and intelligence. Scarcely a century can elapse before the population of America will be equal and her power superior to that of Europe. Should the principles be then established, which have been contemplated, and the connection be demonstrated between human happiness and the peaceable enjoyment of industry and the indulgence of reflection, we may expect to see America too enlightened and virtuous to spread the horrors of war over the face of any country and too magnanimous and powerful to suffer its existence, where she can prevent it. Let us, then, with rapture anticipate the era when the triumph of peace and the prevalence of virtue shall be rendered secure by the diffusion of useful knowledge. (Rudolph, 1965, pp. 222–223)

The educational institutions of the new nation, then, needed to reflect this imperial, global identity. This was Cato's burden.

In September of 1797, the APS announced that Smith and another essayist, a Baltimore Scotsman named Samuel Knox, had won the essay contest. The blind review committee reading Smith's essay had been chaired by none other than William Smith, the aged architect of the German Charity Schools. (When the elder Smith did not follow through on his duties, possibly for ill health, his close colleague Samuel Magaw, a former teacher in the Charity Schools, took over as chair.) All the membership in attendance voted in the selection. Among seven entries, only three of which were serious contenders, Smith and Knox had impressed the members with their "superior merit." Nevertheless, the secretary of the organization noted with regret that "none of the Systems of Education under review appeared to them so well adapted to the present state of Society in this Country, as could be wished" (As cited in Hansen, 1926, p. 139). In the opinion of the APS, neither Smith, nor Knox, nor any of the other contestants, had offered a vision of American education uniquely suited to the United States. What they had done was to demonstrate the way in which most intellectuals in the newly created United States failed to articulate a distinctive educational vision adapted to the American nation, except by arguing that America was the place where the universal truths of the enlightenment could be realized.

CONCLUSION

The line of thought connecting William Smith's plan for German charity schools to Samuel Harrison Smith's shows continuity and change. Obviously, the specific context of each differed—one planned a small collection of privately-funded charity schools in Pennsylvania; the other a national system of publicly-funded education. Each also addressed a different political reality. William Smith glorified the British Empire, Samuel Smith saw the United States as a new order for the ages. William Smith saw the French Empire as a threat (even as he drew extensively on French philosophy), while Samuel H. Smith quoted admiringly from the Napoleonic Civil Code.

Yet both also show a progression of very similar ideas. First, both saw universal, formal, public education of youth as an engine for political and social cohesion; and identified the education of youth under a single set of ideas as being in the best interest of all people—not just those of one particular nation or religious creed. (Each was silent on the education of Africans.) Indeed, each saw the need for social and political cohesion as necessarily trumping the traditional role of specific churches taking responsibility (or not) for mass education, and each insisted on native-born teachers and materials. Second, both had similar ideas about the details: the rudimentary curriculum of the three Rs plus a smattering of universally accepted aphorisms, the exclusion of divisive issues like sectarian religion and politics, and the use of emulation to excite and motivate students.

Finally, and most significantly, each saw their project as transcending the narrow needs of a particular community or even nation-state, but instead, as hastening the birth of a harmonious empire of reason, civility and freedom by realizing the universal truths of the Enlightenment.

Obviously these two essays were not representative of all educational thought in eighteenth century. As historians Margaret Nash, Siobhan Moroney, and others remind us, the ideas of elite intellectuals did not necessarily represent those of average people in local contexts, or of the intermediaries between the two worlds—the makers of textbooks. Even among the Founding Fathers (and indeed among the other anonymous essayists in the APS contest) there was disagreement about some of the specifics. Benjamin Rush argued that churches should be at the heart of universal education, Noah Webster fretted that teaching the Bible in public schools would be blasphemous, and Thomas Jefferson saw no role for religion at all. Other debates centered on the importance of dead languages, the education of girls, and the responsibility of state governments for educating the poor. On other issues, however—that an educated citizenry was desirable for political and social stability, that education should be in the public sphere, and that the curriculum should emphasize common culture—the movement from the British Empire of the 1750s to the American nation was not as radical as it might seem.

In the early nineteenth century, as Americans turned to conquering and consolidating their western empire in North America, the sophisticated philosophies of the Enlightenment gave way to more homegrown notions of Protestant millennialism and democratic localism. Yet the imperial legacies of educational thought endured. The British burden that William Smith cited in 1753 still resonated with the American's burden felt by Noah Webster 43 years later. Anxious to forge a distinctly American identity, civic culture, and even language, Webster wrote schoolbooks to form American children out of the vast empire that Americans liked to call a unified nation. Generations of American schoolchildren could open Webster's reader to page 181 and read the following stirring words (re-spelled in American English):

> A Roman soul is bent on higher views;
> To civilize the rude unpolished world,
> And lay it under the restraint of Laws;
> To make man mild and to man,
> To cultivate the wild licentious savage
> With wisdom, discipline and liberal arts,
> Th' embellishments of Life.
> (Webster, 1796, from Addison's Cato, pp. I, iv, 30–36)[5]

The language of Cato, that of empire, resonated in the American context of the nineteenth century as strongly as it did in the British context of the eighteenth century. Washington may have proclaimed the nation; but if we listen closely, he whispers the world.

NOTES

1. Ferguson (1994) criticizes Bernard Bailyn and other historians of 18th eighteen century American thought for their "nationalistic orientation." Ferguson writes that "Above all, as Enlightenment thinkers, [the founding fathers] believe[d] in the global sphere of connections and the promise of republicanism throughout the world" (p. 34).
2. These proposals include, "Some Thoughts on Education" (1752), "Indian Songs of Peace" (1752), and "The Idea of the College of Mirania" (1753).
3. By "Dutch," Franklin meant German speakers.
4. Readers may refer to the *American Periodicals Series*, which allows for keyword searches online. The number of articles containing the word "education" jumps dramatically over the course of the 1880s (www.proquest.com/products_pq/descriptions/aps.shtml)
5. I thank Frederick Litto for this delightful discovery.

REFERENCES

A promoter of female education. (1789, January). Essay on education. *Massachusetts Monthly Magazine*. Retrieved March 10, 2008, from American Periodicals Series Web site: www.proquest.com/products_pq/descriptions/aps.shtml

Adas, M. (2001, December). From settler colony to global hegemon: Integrating the exceptionalist narrative of the American experience into world history. *American Historical Review, 106*(5), 1692–1720.

American Philosophical Society. (1795, May 1). *Minute book of the American Philosophical Society. Archives.* Philadelphia: Author.

American Philosophical Society. (1797). *Archives of Samuel Harrison Smith minutes as editor of New World.* Philadelphia: Author.

Armitage, D. (2000). *The ideological origins of the British Empire.* Cambridge, England: Cambridge University Press.

Axtell, J. (1974). *The school upon a hill: Education and society in colonial New England.* New Haven, CT: Yale University Press.

Bell, W., Jr., (1955). Benjamin Franklin and the German Charity Schools. *Proceedings of the American Philosophical Society, 99*(6), 381–387.

Berkhofer, R. F., Jr., (1972). Jefferson, the Ordinance of 1784, and the origins of the American territorial system. *The William and Mary Quarterly, 3rd Ser., 29*(2), 231–262, 243.

Boswell, T. (1989). Colonial empires and the capitalist world-economy: A time-series analysis of colonization, 1640–1960. *American Sociological Review, 54*(2), 180–196

Canny, N. (Ed.). (1998). *The origins of empire.* New York: Oxford University Press.

Carnoy, M. (1974). *Education as cultural imperialism.* New York: D. McKay.

Cremin, L. (1970). *American education The colonial experience.* New York: Harper & Row.

Cremin, L. (1980). *American education: The national experience.* New York: Harper & Row.

Danzer, G. A. (1974). Has the discovery of America been useful or hurtful to mankind? Yesterday's questions and today's students. *The History Teacher, 7*(2), 192–206.

Doggett, S. A (1796). *Discourse on education, Delivered at the dedication and opening of Bristol Academy, the 18th Day of July, A.D.* New Bedford, MA: Spooner.

Du Pont de Nemours, P. (1923). *National Education in the United States* (B. G. Du Pont, Trans.). Newark: University of Delaware Press.

Ellis, J. J. (1997). *American sphinx: The character of Thomas Jefferson.* New York: Knopf.

Fay, B. (1932). Learned societies in Europe and America in the 18th century. *The American Historical Review, 37*(2), 255–266, 261.

Ferguson, R. (1994). *The American Enlightenment: 1750–1820.* Cambridge, MA: Harvard University Press.

Fogelman, A. S. (1996). *Hopeful journeys: German immigration, settlement, and political culture in Colonial America, 1717–1775.* Philadelphia: University of Pennsylvania Press.

Foner, E. (Ed.). (1997). *The New American History.* Philadelphia: Temple University Press.

Franklin, B. (1750, March 20). *Letter to James Parker, Philadelphia.* Benjamin Franklin Papers. New Haven, CT: Yale University. Retrieved May 16, 2006, from www.franklinpapers.org

Franklin, B. (1751). *Observations on the increase of mankind.* Benjamin Franklin Papers. Retrieved May 16, 2006, from www.franklinpapers.org

Franklin, B. (1753, May 9). *Letter to Peter Collinson, Philadelphia.* Benjamin Franklin Papers. New Haven, CT: Yale University. Retrieved May 16, 2006, from www.franklinpapers.org

Franklin, B. (1755, May 15). *Pennsylvania Assembly: Reply to Governor.* Benjamin Franklin Papers. New Haven, CT: Yale University. Retrieved May 16, 2006, from www.franklinpapers.org

Franklin, B. (1776, February 13). *Examination before the Committee of the Whole House of Commons.* Benjamin Franklin Papers. New Haven, CT: Yale University. Retrieved May 16, 2006, from www.franklinpapers.org.

Frantz, J. B. (1998). Franklin and the Pennsylvania Germans. *Pennsylvania History, 65,* 21–34.

Frisch, M. (1989). American history and the structures of collective memory: A modest exercise in empirical iconography. *Journal of American History, 75*(4), 1130–1155.

Hansen, A. O. (1926). *Liberalism and American education in the eighteenth century.* New York: MacMillan.

Justice, B. (2005). *The war that wasn't: Religious conflict and compromise in the common schools of New York, 1865–1900.* Albany, NY: State University of New York Press.

Justice, B. (2008). The Great Contest: The American Philosophical Society Education Prize of 1797. *American Journal of Education, 114*(2), 191–213.

Kaestle, C. (1983). *Pillars of the Republic.* New York: Hill & Wang.

Litto. F. M. (1966). Addison's Cato in the colonies. *The William and Mary Quarterly, 3rd. Ser., 23*(3), 431–449.

Monaghan, E. J. (2005). *Learning to read and write in Colonial New England.* Amherst: University of Massachusetts Press.

Montesquieu, C. (1914). *The spirit of laws* (Thomas Nugent, Trans.) (J. V. Prichard, Rev. ed.). London: G. Bell & Sons.

Moroney, S. (1999). Birth of a canon: The historiography of early Republican educational thought. *History of Education Quarterly, 39*(4), 476–491.

Nash, M. A. (2006, October). *Contested identities: Nationalism, regionalism, and patriotism in early American textbooks.* Paper presented at the History of Education Society annual meeting, Ottawa , Canada.

Odgers, M. (1943, July 14). Education and the American Philosophical Society. *Proceedings of the American Philosophical Society, 87*(1), 20–23.

Onuf, P. S. (1986). Liberty, development, and union: Visions of the West in the 1780s. *The William and Mary Quarterly, 3rd Ser., 43*(2), 179–213, 187.

Onuf, P. S. (1987). *Statehood and union: A history of the Northwest Ordinance.* Indianapolis: Indiana University Press.

Richards, E. (1991). Scotland and the Uses of the Atlantic Empire. In B. Bailyn & P.D. Morgan (Eds.), *Strangers within the realm: Cultural margins of the first British Empire.* Chapel Hill: University of North Carolina Press.

Rudolph, F. (Ed.). (1965). *Essays on education in the Early Republic.* Cambridge, MA: Harvard University Press.

Rush, B. (1786). Plan for the establishment of public schools and the diffusion of knowledge in Pennsylvania. In W. Smith (Ed.), *Theories of education in early America, 1655–1819* (p. 243). New York: Bobbs-Merrill.

Staum, M. S. (1985–1986). The Enlightenment transformed: The institute prize contests. *Eighteenth-Century Studies 19*(2), 153–179, 155–156, 163.

Stephens, W. B. (1990). Literacy in England, Scotland, and Wales, 1500–1900. *History of Education Quarterly, 30*(4), 545–571.

Smith, W. (1752). *Some thoughts on education: with reasons for erecting a college in this province, and fixing the same at the City of New York: To which is added, a scheme for employing masters or teachers in the mean time: and also for raising and endowing an edifice in an easy manner.* New York.

Smith, W. (1753, December 13). *William Smith to Benjamin Franklin and Richard Peters (unpublished) Will[iam] Smith to the Society Entrusted with Monies Collected for the Use of Foreign Protestants in Pensylvania.* Benjamin Franklin Papers. New Haven, CT: Yale University. Retrieved May 16, 2006, from www.franklinpapers.org

Smith, W. (Ed.). (1973). *Theories of Education in the Early America, 1655–1819.* New York: Bobbs-Merrill.

Smith, W. (1754, February). *Smith to society; William Smith to Richard Peters and Benjamin Franklin.* Benjamin Franklin Papers. New Haven, CT: Yale University.

Smith, H. W. (1880). *Life and correspondence of the Rev. William Smith, D.D., with copious extracts from his writings.* Philadelphia: Ferguson Bros.

Unger, G. H. (1998). *The life and times of Noah Webster, an American patriot.* New York: Wiley.

Webster, N. (1796). *An American selection of lessons in reading and speaking* (13th ed.). Hartford, CT: Hudson & Goodwin.

Webster, N. (1789). *Dissertations on the English language: With notes, historical and critical. To which is added, by way of appendix, an essay on a reformed mode of spelling, with Dr. Franklin's arguments on that subject.* Boston: Isaiah Thomas. (Reprinted in Wilson Smith (Ed.). (1973). Theories of Education in Early America 1655–1819. New York: Bobbs-Merrill).

Webster, N. (1824). *The American spelling book; containing the rudiments of the English Language for the use of schools in the United States.* Brattleborough, Vermont: Holbrook and Fessenden.

Webster, N. (1790). *On the education of youth.* Reprinted in F. Rudolph (Ed.), *Essays on Education in the Early Republic* (pp. 43–77). Cambridge: Harvard University Press.

Wolfe, P. (1997). History and imperialism: A century of theory, from Marx to postcolonialism. *American Historical Review, 102*(2), 388–420.

Yarbrough, J. M. (1997). The moral sense, Character formation, and virtue. In G. L. McDowell & S. L. Noble (Eds.), *Reason and Republicanism: Thomas Jefferson's legacy of liberty* (pp. 271–303). New York: Rowman & Littlefield.

CHAPTER 2

BECOMING AMERICAN IN TIME?

The Educational Implications of Binary Discourse on Immigration

Patricia Buck with Rachel Silver

INTRODUCTION

Rachel and I taught an entry level English for Speakers of Other Languages (ESOL) class at the Milltown Adult Education Center (MAEC) in a small city in northern New England. Our class, which fluctuated between 6 and 12 students, was largely made up of Somali refugee women who had recently resettled in Milltown. After teaching the class for a couple of months, I sat down one day to talk with Sue, the center's coordinator. She asked how the class was going and who was attending. I explained that there was a core group of regulars and that others came and went. Some students were there waiting at 8 a.m.; others came in at various times throughout the class. Sue nodded knowingly and suggested I tell students that class starts at eight, meets every day, and that they are expected to be there on time and to attend regularly. "If you can't do

Advancing Democracy Through Education? U.S. Influence Abroad and Domestic Practices, pp. 29–54
Copyright © 2008 by Information Age Publishing

that, you can't come to the class anymore" she instructed me to tell them. I paused at the thought of excluding women from class based on their use of time. One woman in particular came to mind.

Fardous was a 70-year-old Somali refugee who came to the United States after a temporary stay in France, where she was denied permanent residency. She had six children, only one of whom had made it with her to the United States. Amina, her daughter, reportedly attended law school in France but sacrificed the legal credentials she gained there in order to accompany her mother to the United States. In Milltown Amina attended nursing classes at the local community college. Fardous walked six blocks to the center every morning regardless of the season and, once there, cajoled her frustrated classmates to accept that they were "children" all over again and needed to learn how to speak, walk, and survive in a new world. She had an indomitably patient and loving spirit. But, she never came to class on time.

As I pictured Fardous and ran her story through my mind, Sue continued on to say that Somalis have a different sense of time than we do in the United States. "They are still on African time." If they are to become employable, she advised, seeming to sense my hesitance, "they need to adapt to American expectations."

In her words Sue ceded authority to affect change in newcomers' practices. She did so in light of my status as a teacher, U.S. citizen, White person, and native English-speaker. Internally, I resisted the invitation to regulate students' movement to and from the classroom, which I understood as an imposition of normative ways of spending time in the U.S. upon Somali students. From a poststructuralist-anthropological perspective, I interpreted the desire to amend the women's use of time as a reinscription of dominant cultural ideals and practices. As a friend, I believed Fardous, a 70-year-old woman who had lost children to war and yet managed to evoke joy in others, deserved to sleep late and walk slowly to school. Pragmatically speaking, I wondered whether a regimented approach to schooling was appropriate for many of the Somali refugee women who, like Fardous, may never be employable in the postindustrial town into which they had settled. All face cultural, language, and religious barriers to availing limited employment opportunities. The vast majority of the women who enrolled at MAEC had little, if any, formal schooling experience. At MAEC, they were learning to read and write for the first time, even as they struggled to attain English. When they were able to acquire the minimum language and literacy skills necessary for available jobs in the region, few had the experience necessary to make them attractive candidates. Additionally, as mothers with multiple young children and an extended family and social network, many had significant responsibilities outside of school that consumed their time and energies. Further, work in local grocery stores, restaurants, and many other service industries would bring them in contact with pork or alcohol, both of which are prohibited in Islam. On top of these limitations, job developers serving the Somali refugee population reported that many local employers blatantly refused to hire Somalis when there were many unemployed long-term Maine residents who also needed work.

As obstacles to the prospect of teaching Somali women to be desirable workers passed through my mind, it struck me that, even beyond Sue's and my differences in perspective, educators at the MAEC held an array of ideas about apt uses of time among newcomers at the school. Educators' standpoints regarding newcomers' punctuality and attendance reflect equally diverse perspectives on what comprises an appropriate education for newcomers to the United States. While insistence upon promptness and regular attendance is commonly exercised in schools, in the case of MAEC making this familiar expectation strange reveals implicit, multilayered intercultural relations and power dynamics between refugee students and educators, refugee students and surrounding community members, and educators and surrounding community.[1] In what follows I propose that desire to regulate newcomers' use of school time is not simply a matter of common pedagogical sense, but rather, needs to be viewed in light of a localized binary in discourse on immigration.

As is the case across the United States, in Milltown low income newcomers of color are commonly talked about either as needy others with a still-as-yet undeveloped potential to contribute to the vibrancy of the economy and culture or undesirable burdens upon scarce resources (Chavez, 2001; Katerberg, 1995; Vecoli, 1996). In the former case the discourse of immigration emerges out of a liberal political philosophy that sees merit and equal access to opportunity (regardless of race, class, gender, and national origin) as pillars of political stability within pluralistic societies (Stevens, Wood, & Sheehan, 2002). In the latter case discourse echoes a nativist strain present throughout American history and routinely adapted to fit the circumstances associated with changing populations of newcomers (Chavez 2001; Katerberg, 1995; Thomas & Murr, 1993; Vecoli, 1996; Waldinger, 2001).

Given the longstanding notion that schooling serves as a primary mechanism for the incorporation of newcomers into the national community (Fass, 1989), educators who serve newcomer populations are compelled to stake a position in relation to these two pervasive and highly polarized outlooks on immigration and immigrants. Wishing to advocate for their student body, many educators align their practice with liberal discourse in a strategic effort to implicitly counter nativist portrayals of newcomers as opportunistic and disloyal interlopers. In California educators made up a major block of the anti-Proposition 227 campaign in the state. After the proposition passed, The San Francisco Board of Education voted to unanimously continue bilingual programming regardless of the legal implications (Alarcon, 1998). Nationwide, teachers stand at the forefront of multiculturalism and routinely implement curriculum meant to promote tolerance for cultural diversity. While educators' proimmigrant efforts are intended to positively influence popular opinion about immigrants, educators' frequent appropriation of liberal discourse has unfortunate repercussions for school culture. In what follows I explore the implications of educators' appropriation of liberal discourse on immigration and argue that educators' consequent efforts to regulate the school environment newcomers inhabit reveal larger dynamics of power at play with regard to schooling's functionality as a primary mechanism for the incorporation of newcomers from the Global South into the U.S. national community.

While the current examination focuses in upon the relationality between educational leaders' policy and practice and local response to recent immigration, it draws upon a larger, in depth 4 year ethnographic study of the ESOL program at the MAEC. Rachel and I joined a liberal arts college community located within Milltown at roughly the same time Somali refugees arrived in significant numbers to the area. Rachel enrolled at the college in the fall of 2001 and I joined the faculty in the fall of 2002. Individually, we followed local events and reactions to the cultural and demographic changes brought about by the influx of refugees. We each attended relevant community gatherings, demonstrations, and meetings organized by both Somali and longtime Milltown residents. In the fall of 2002, Rachel enrolled in one of my classes. Aware of MAEC's unique presence as a gathering place for many new Somali community members, Rachel requested to complete the service-learning component of the course at the center. Rachel tutored and wrote journal entries that depicted vivid scenes from MAEC. She described adult learners who used their time at the center to practice reading and writing, exchange valuable information about local employment and housing opportunities, and share their experiences and frustrations as Muslims and Africans in the post-September 11 United States. Captivated by these images, I also began to make regular visits to the center. Soon the two of us envisioned an ethnographic study that would capture the rich texture of this newly diverse institution set within one of the most racially homogenous states in the country. Our resulting ethnographic study spanned 3 years of extensive participant observation during which we maintained a steady presence and occupied various roles at MAEC.

After first tutoring for a year and a half, Rachel offered the center's first organized citizenship course while I observed the center's upper level

ESOL 4 class. Together, we attended the center's informal weekly women's group in which a diverse gathering of immigrant and refugee women voluntarily met to discuss a range of issues of concern in their daily lives. During the summer of 2004, I began teaching the center's entry level ESOL class. Rachel joined to co-teach the course from the fall of 2004 through the summer of 2005.

Rather than look at both Somali men and women, early in our study we elected to focus exclusively on Somali women's experiences in school, a decision that emerged out of a confluence of theoretical and methodological factors. According to Sue, approximately 70% of the center's Somali population are women. While our ESOL classes were composed almost exclusively of women,[2] our social and personal interactions around the center occurred primarily with women, a dynamic resulting both from gender segregation within Somali communities as well as our positionalities as unmarried women. As women, we were able to broach topics and build friendships with Somali women that may or may not have been possible with Somali men. Additionally, our relationships with female students at the center carried over into our homes and personal lives, something that would certainly have been impossible or deemed inappropriate with men.

The group of women with whom we worked in this study was not bounded. Rather, like the population of Somalis in Milltown at large, the women at the center came and went as jobs, family, and social responsibilities dictated. Our study focused mostly on roughly 20 women, many of whom had spent varying amounts of time in our own ESOL class as students or observers. Participants came from varying regions within Somalia (i.e., rural, urban, northern, and southern) and had differing family compositions, educational backgrounds, and trajectories since leaving Somalia. They also spanned a wide range of English proficiency levels. We often relied upon those with stronger English skills to translate conversations between us and entry level English language learners.

As a researcher and practitioner, I approach the study of newcomer education from a particular positionality. I am a White woman from a working class family and have used educational opportunities to attain professional status and credentials. In the process I have learned to see and question implicit relations of power that organize our everyday school lives and become committed to working toward the realization of the democratic potentiality of education.

As is widely known, over the last 3 decades the United States and other nations of the Global North are experiencing an increasing flow of immigrants from the Global South. According to the U.S. Census Bureau (2004), in March of 2003 11.7% of the U.S. population was foreign born. Only 13.7% of the U.S.'s foreign born emigrated from Europe.

Accordingly, the demographics of the westward flow introduce a particular set of challenges to the incorporation process given newcomers' status as racial, language, and religious minorities. Newcomers from the Global South tend to have lower than average income and educational levels as compared with more long term U.S. citizens (Borjas, 1990; Burke, 1995; Kemnitz, 2006; Thomas & Murr, 1993). Finally, those within the current demographic of newcomers from the Global South are perceived to be less familiar with meritocratic and democratic governance traditions, an impression that raises concern about the continued wellbeing of structures of reward, discipline and governance in the Global North. While, as Vecoli (1996) writes that "the danger posed by foreigners to American values and institutions" (p. 13) has been a constant theme throughout American history. Most recently, such xenophobia has been focused on a presumed incompatibility between Islam and liberal democracy (Fukuyama, 2006).

Each of the enumerated characteristics describing immigrants from the Global South applies to Somalis. Somalis, who represent the African nationality with the highest number of refugees resettled to the United States (Singer & Wilson, 2007), are Muslims from the Horn of Africa. Prior to the current prolonged period of civil disorder, Somalia had a history of autocratic governance (Adam & Ford, 1997; Besteman, 1999; Cassanelli, 1982; Laitin & Samatar 1987; Mazrui, 1997; Samatar, 1994). Traditionally pastoralist goat and camel herders, Somalis have among the lowest literacy rates in the world ("Countries With the lowest," 1999). Fleeing Somalia in desperation and fear, most refugees come to the United States with scarce economic resources. Given the representative nature of the Somali population (of newcomers from the Global South at large), examination of Somalis' school experiences provides an opportunity to interrogate some of the relations of power brought to bear as educators work to facilitate the incorporation of newcomers from the Global South into the national community.

As members of the Global South enter the cultural, economic, and political space of the Global North, disparate understandings and practices come in contact with one another and do so across a range of venues. Actors labor to organize these spaces of cultural intersection according to both implicit and explicit arrangements of power. As postmodern theorist David Harvey (1993) contends,

> [t]here is, then, a politics to place construction ranging dialectically across material, representational, and symbolic activities which find their hallmark in the way in which individuals invest in places and thereby empower themselves collectively by virtue of that investment.... And it is precisely in this realm that the intertwining with place of all those other political values of community, of nation, and the like, begins its work. (p. 21)

As publicly sponsored institutions that have traditionally borne key responsibility for the incorporation of newcomers into the national community, emerging power relations within public schools serve as salient indicators of larger relations between newcomers and members of the receiving nation. Relations between newcomers and educational practitioners reveal areas of convergence, conflict, and negotiation and create a portrait of the positionality into which newcomers are invited to incorporate into the civic, economic, and social spheres of the U.S. national community.

I employ cultural production theory in my examination of the policy and practices institutionalized at MAEC. Cultural production theory, which emphasizes the exercise of bounded agency within structurally determined parameters, offers a means to articulate the ways in which understanding and action reflect the specificities of time and place. Debra Skinner, Dorothy Holland, and Alfred Pach III (1998) write that such treatments,

> avoid a simplistic portrayal of people's actions and resistance as freewheeling agency. Instead, they offer a complex and nuanced account of how people struggle and make hard choices in ambiguous worlds, with outcomes that are open-ended and often unresolved. (p. 7)

In the present study, bounded agency is evident in educational leaders' orientation to dominant discourse on immigration in the local community. Additionally, educational cultural production theory explores the interplay between actors' positionality or perspective and the communication of cultural knowledge and beliefs via the institutionalized mechanism of schooling. "[W]e see schools as sites for the formation of subjectivities through the production and consumption of cultural forms" (Levinson & Holland, 1996, pp. 13–14). In the present study, I examine the ways in which key educational leaders at the MAEC use schooling as a space and process through which to convey a message about the ways Somalis may suitably enter the larger Milltown community.

I begin the ethnographic examination with a brief introduction to three perspectives on newcomers' use of school time held by an array of educators at the center. As I detail, each of the educators' viewpoints speak to particular ways of thinking about immigrants, the immigrant experience, and the purpose of (newcomer) education. I then proceed to place the policies and practices of those educational leaders who most strongly influence the organizational culture of MAEC within the discursive context of the surrounding Milltown community. In my investigation of the local community I detail the ways in which immigrants from the Global South are commonly regarded. Such local talk demonstrates that the binary according to which local views of immigration and immigrants are organized reflects a similarly bifurcated orientation present at the national level. The very pervasiveness of the dualism characterizing talk of immigration and immigrants suggests its significance to educators who, in working with newcomer populations, find themselves caught between its opposing polarities. I conclude with an analysis of the implications of educators' subsequent alignment with liberal discourse on immigration.

PERSPECTIVES ON TIME

Sue, the ESOL program administrator and Jacqueline, the head ESOL teacher, were long term leaders within the Milltown community and at the MAEC. The two women understood their role in relation to new-comer students as that of guides. In words and action, they worked to symbolically shepherd students from one culturally-derived positionality (as unskilled refugees) to another (as skilled members of the local econ-omy and community). From their point of view, schooling provided new-comers with the ability to attain self-sufficiency, acceptance by the local community, and ultimately, social mobility. Because they viewed entry into the low skilled work force as an essential element of newcomers' "sur-vival," they focused on training students to demonstrate punctuality and regular attendance.

Sue and Jacqueline were not alone in their desire to reorder students' use of school time. Each of the full-time ESOL permanent staff spoke of the need for students to be more punctual and reliable. However, the reasoning behind this shared sentiment varied. Alley and Robin were in their 20s, had done grassroots community development work either abroad within the Peace Corps or in the local Milltown community. Respectively, they had taught for 1 and 3 years at MAEC. They explained that their desire to regulate students' use of time derived primarily out of pedagogical concerns: they wanted the content of their instruction to develop cumulatively, which demanded students' regular attendance. They described a desire to "create a structure" for the school day so that they could progressively "build upon" content and skills within class. Robin reported telling her students, "That is fine. (If you need to be late) I understand. You just need to call or tell me ahead of time." While both tried to communicate sensitivity to the variety of factors that can account for students' lateness, they were firm about students' obligation to operate within the framework of the class. In order to impress the need to be punctual upon her students, Alley locked her classroom door ten minutes after the scheduled start time. Robin asked those who used class time to speak Somali to leave the classroom.

Alley and Robin's perspective contrasted with Sue and Jacqueline's in that it was less directed toward cultural assimilation on the part of students and more aligned with the notion that schooling should provide accessible and practical lessons on the surrounding community. In their case, the main content of lessons concerned learning the vocabulary necessary to understand the expectations of and effectively communicate with health care providers, landlords, employers and perspective employers, neighbors, and K–12 teachers.

As an instructor at the MAEC, my orientation to students' use of school time emerged out of theories of progressive education. In our classroom Rachel, who had graduated with a minor in education from the liberal arts college where I teach and so had a similar fluency in progressive educational philosophy, and I fostered a free flow of people and perceived the ebb and flow of student attendance as a form of "voting with the feet." When large numbers of students attended class, and new faces came to join more familiar ones, students assured us that word-of-mouth had it that we were "good teachers." When attendance waned, we considered whether we were off track, and we worked with students to reassess the value of what we were currently working on together. We hoped our practices would reflect a respect for student agency, students' right to act upon culturally derived notions of time usage. We believed that the expression of student agency was fundamental to the creation of an engaged learning environment. For, in our estimation the main purpose of schooling for newcomers was to realize the democratic potential of schooling. Ideally, we sought to include multiple voices and cultural practices within a collaborative learning environment that fostered a sense of belonging, care, and flexibility.

While a number of sometimes overlapping and in other ways contradictory, ideas about newcomers' use of school time and purposes of schooling were at play within the ESOL program, in the main, it was the educational leaders' perspectives that became institutionalized. As long term leaders, Sue and Jacqueline strongly influenced policy and practice. Sue was the head of personnel, fund raising, and programming. As the teacher with the most seniority and in whose classroom ESOL students spent considerable amounts of time (often multiple hours on a daily basis), Jacqueline, too, made a strong impression upon the student body.

In addition to the degree of influence they held at MAEC, Sue and Jacqueline's perspectives are particularly compelling. Although there was not unanimous agreement about the best methods and purposes of newcomer education among MAEC staff, as long term members of the Milltown community, Sue and Jacqueline's viewpoints were sensitive to the workings of the larger community and lent a nuanced reading of the particularities of educating newcomers in Milltown during the current time period of rapid community change. Alley, Robin, Rachel and I were simply not as invested in or informed about life in Milltown. Each of us lived outside of the community; none had established a history as key players in local politics or were involved with the ins and outs of community life to nearly the same degree as Sue and Jacqueline. Both Sue and Jacqueline were deeply engaged in the civic sphere of community life and were well versed in the worldview and proclivities of fellow community members. From this position, they enjoyed a "bird's eye view" of the environment into which the resettled newcomers entered and had insight into the developing relations between the newcomers and other members of Milltown's largely working class, White, politically conservative and Catholic community.

Because they were attuned community members, Sue and Jacqueline's decision making in regard to educational practice was deliberately responsive to local contextual factors. They justifiably worried that their students would not find success in the economically struggling city whose dying textile industry was dealt a final blow with the passing of NAFTA (North American Free Trade Agreement). The Maine Department of Labor reports that between 1993 and 2005, the Lewiston-Auburn area alone lost 1,685 trade-related manufacturing jobs ("The Dangers of," 2007). Sue and Jacqueline felt an urgent need to prepare students to meet the challenges that faced them: to compete in the economic sphere and find acceptance in the social. Their desire to change students' culturally derived ways of being emerged out of an earned appreciation for the misgivings newcomers faced within the larger community and reflected on-the-ground realities associated with the schooling of newcomers in the current neoliberal and global era.

Local Discourse on Immigration

While all educators working with newcomer populations stand at the intersection of discourses of education and immigration, Sue and Jacqueline's positionality was a particularly public one as local realties of underemployment and xenophobia propelled Milltown into the national spotlight.

Beginning with the influx of Somali refugees to the city in 2001, Milltown and, often, the MAEC itself was routinely featured in the local newspaper and appeared in multiple stories run in national journals and newspapers. Between 2001 and 2003 approximately 1,200 Somali refugees came to Milltown, which as of 2005 had a total population of 36,050 (Maine State Planning Office, 2005). In May of 2001, the city sponsored a public forum regarding what was commonly referred to as the "Somali situation." The local paper describes this event: "About five hundred, mostly Whites, filled the Milltown Armory Tuesday night to listen to the city's panel of immigration experts—from State Department of Human Services officials to representatives from Catholic Charities Maine and the Somali community itself" (Taylor, 2002, p. C1). The majority of questions broached that evening focused on the distribution of social service benefits between refugees and native residents, as well as the migration's impact on employment levels in the area.

In addition to logistical questions, intolerant sentiments were voiced both subtly and explicitly. Skepticism about the new Somali refugees permeated the Milltown community. In the fall of 2002, within weeks of moving to Milltown myself, I spoke with an elderly man at a local Laundromat about the "Somali situation." He described the "primitive" practices of newly arrived Somalis, who, he reported, moved into government provided housing that featured new oak cabinetry. "They removed the cupboard doors so they could raise chickens in them!" he exclaimed. He concluded that, "This always was a good place to live, not anymore. That's all over now." Over the next few years I encountered this oft-repeated rumor about chickens being raised in cabinets, along with other equally disquieting ones, that convey a widespread perception of Africans as culturally backward and as a drain upon an overly generous state welfare system.

The undercurrent of resentment flowing through Milltown peaked in the fall of 2002 with the publication of the mayor's controversial letter titled, "Maxed Out." In his letter, the mayor asked leaders of the Somali community to "stem the tide of migration," in order to lessen the economic strain on Milltown. He wrote, "[P]lease pass the word: We've been overwhelmed and have responded valiantly. Now we need breathing room—our city is maxed out physically, financially, and emotionally" ("Mayor Raymond's Letter," 2002). The controversial rhetoric of the mayor's letter put Milltown in the national spotlight, receiving coverage in various newspapers and media sources around the country, including the *New York Times, Washington Post, CNN,* and *National Public Radio.*

The letter also attracted the attention of national White-supremacy groups, including the National Alliance and the World Church of the Creator, which planned and held a controversial hate rally in Milltown on January 11, 2002. One such event speaker characterized Somalis as "the enemy" who, if given the chance "will probably slit your throat" ("4,500 People Rally," 2003). More frequently echoed rhetoric described Somalis as leaching off of the welfare system or taking already scarce jobs from locals (Bouchard, 2002; "4,500 People Rally," 2003). A hugely successful counter rally occurred at the same time. In this latter event various Somali, local, and state leaders offered words of praise for the newcomers and called attention to the responsibility of long term members of the community to extend a welcoming hand to the newcomers. Former Lewiston Mayor John Jenkins announced, "We are many, we are one—one community that welcomes all. We say "no" to hatred. We say "yes" to safety. We support full membership in the community for everyone" ("Maine Town's Diversity Rally," 2003). Together, they described an imagined future in which Somali newcomers were fully incorporated into the local schools, neighborhood, and marketplace.

The two gatherings symbolize a starkly divided community. On the one hand there were those reacting in fear and aggressive intolerance to newcomers from the global South. Those on the other side wished to open doors of opportunity and to celebrate Milltown as a city united in its increasing diversity and called attention to the vulnerability, gratitude, and resiliency of Somali newcomers.

The duality of response to Somali refugees' entrance into the Milltown community, while reflecting the particularities of a small post industrial northeast U.S. city, is not unique. On the contrary, they were local instantiations of the liberal and nativist binary that characterizes national discourse on immigration and is a keystone of American national identity and identity work. Accordingly, talk about newcomers in Milltown community signifies a localization of discourse that is in fact national in scope.

National Discourse on Immigration

In a recent report on immigrants' opinions about life in the United States, Farkas, Dufer, Johnson, Moye, and Vine (2003) argue that immigrants are "thankful and appreciative" for the opportunity to live and work in the United States. Immigrants' sentiments, they claim, are "anchored in the view that the U.S. holds the comparative advantage over their home countries, and these are not limited to economic considerations" (Farkas et al., 2003, p. 28). Indeed, the authors call repeated attention to newcomers' esteem for the United States.

> The focus group conversations with immigrants would typically follow this pattern: an initial outpouring of affection for this country would be followed by candid talk about the nation's shortcomings and would end with a bottom line assessment—its problems notwithstanding, there is no place better than the U.S. in which to build their home. (p. 28)

Through the act of sympathetic portrayal, Americans position themselves to be seen as noble caretakers, a move that has become fundamental to

American self-identity. In his examination of the significance of immigration in the early formation of American national identity Vecoli (1996) writes,

> The notion of America as an asylum for the oppressed of the world has exerted a powerful influence on [American] minds and hearts.... And let it be said that it was flattering to the national ego the United States was the Promised Land to the poor and persecuted of the old world. (p. 12)

In his account of more recent history, Chavez (2001) demonstrates that Americans continue to generous immigration policy as a bulwark of the national self image. Describing media portrayal of Vietnamese immigrants of the 1970s, Chavez writes,

> Refugees came to symbolize how we thought of ourselves as a nation that helps the world and the uprooted in their times of need.... By generously receiving Vietnamese refugees, America was acting in character, at least the part of our national identity that welcomes immigrants. (p. 84)

Commonplace liberal portrayal of newcomers as industrious, vulnerable, and appreciative and of Americans as generous caretakers stands in opposition to an equally familiar nativist image of newcomers as lazy, devious, and ungrateful. Lytle (2003) describes this phenomenon as the "criminalization not only of migration, but of migrants" (p. 2). Looking as discourse emerging in response to immigrant activity along the U.S.-Mexico border, Lytle notes that border crossers are commonly referred to as "border violators" and "criminal aliens." Such talk is coupled with increased regulation, both official and vigilante, of the border under the auspices of a war on drugs.

> Therefore, the way that the War on Drugs has transformed border spaces and filled prisons has fueled the general panic about race and migration that is simmering in the United States. It is the collision of discourses of the criminal alien with the incarceration structures of the War on Drugs during this specific period of racial panic that has awoken the vigilante spirit along the U.S.-Mexico border at the turn of the twenty-first century. (p. 8)

As the race-laden fear Lytle describes suggests, opposing representations of newcomers are rooted in particular utopia visions of U.S. nation identity. On the one hand nativist political philosophy imagines a homogeneous, White Anglo-Saxon nation-state and thereby perceives the immigrant (racial and religious) other as a threat to national well being and as undeserving of protection or inclusion (Chavez, 2001; Katerberg, 1995; Higham, 1955; Perea, 1997; Vecoli, 1996). Alternatively, the liberal political tradition idealization of individual rights is being used to promote equal access to opportunity in response to sociocultural pluralism. In this context liberalism translates into a discourse that foregrounds the contribution newcomers make to the U.S. economy, celebrates U.S. self-characterization as a nation of immigrants, and boasts that equality of opportunity afforded by the U.S. social and economic system distinguishes it as a morally advanced nation. While anti-immigration discourse focuses on immigration as a drain upon our economy and a threat to our civil order and cultural unity (see Chavez, 2001), the liberal "system of relations" positions native citizens as benefactors to the needy immigrant other, who longs to integrate into American society. Rahnema and Bawtree write that,

> The system of relations establishes a discursive practice that sets the rules of the game: who can speak, from what point of view, with what authority, and according to what criteria of expertise; it sets the rules that must be followed for this or that problem, theory or object to emerge and be named, analyzed, and eventually transformed into a policy or a plan. (2003, p. 87)

Liberal discourse suggests an exchange in which the U.S. extends welcome in return for gratitude and service. In this arrangement, the U.S. appears as an accommodating host while maintaining its position of power and ownership. Those who welcome immigrants and refugees often expect newcomers to shout the loudest about the freedom and opportunity that life in the U.S. provides and, then, to get to work. Given extant relations of power, this schema presents a seemingly fair trade: the U.S.'s existing assets (social order, services, educational opportunity) in exchange for immigrants' and refugees' efforts to become American through obsequiousness, accommodation, and labor.

Negotiating the Intersection

The binary in popular discourse on immigration establishes a framework for thinking and talking about newcomers that educators must respond to in their work with immigrant students. Educators need to choose between pro and anti-immigrant sentiment could not have been more starkly demonstrated than in regard to California's Prop 227 in which the elimination of bilingual education in the state was proposed. In the controversy that ensued, educators and immigrant rights groups served as the main vanguard against the passing of the legislation. After Prop 227 did in fact pass into law, the San Francisco Board of Education voted unanimously to continue bilingual programming in its schools regardless of the legal implications. Perhaps not surprisingly, as citizens who work closely with newcomers, educators often chose to align policy and practice with liberal, proimmigrant discourse. For Sue and Jacqueline, liberal discourse offered both a language in which to respond to strident, local anti-immigrant sentiment and a framework to structure the rapidly expanding adult education program.

Sue and Jacqueline saw the MAEC as carrying forth a proimmigrant agenda in the face of local, nativist anti-immigrant sentiment. At a celebration of student achievement at the MAEC, Jacqueline spoke to an assembled crowd, "Those people who say our students are lazy should come in any day and watch them. They work for hours every day to learn English, and it is not easy to learn a language." Even as Jacqueline's words of praise implicitly countered derogatory characterizations of Somali refugees prevalent in the community, both Sue and Jacqueline also explicitly pushed back against racist, anti-immigrant sentiment in Milltown. Both attended the large counter rally against the hate group that came to Milltown in 2002. (The main organizer of this counter rally was a popular teacher at the MAEC until the summer of 2005). They were also frequently quoted in local, regional, and national media covering the story of Somali resettlement where they always offered words of admiration and empathy regarding newcomers. As reported in the local newspaper, Sue described Somalis as "among the most interesting, engaged and appreciative students [Sue] has met." She continued to say, "These immigrants, who have come from terrible situations in their home country, can begin to build their lives here" and finished to explain that "every student she's worked with wants a job and wants to learn English so that they can get a job" (Washuk, 2006).

While Sue and Jacqueline made their allegiance to newcomers evident, they were also sensitive to the perspective of members of the White working class community, which was often identified by the media as the source of anti immigrant sentiment. Sue was careful to point out that the vast majority of those who attended the rally and continued to be involved in an advocacy coalition that subsequently formed, "do not represent your average Milltown resident. Most are from out of town." In a depiction of the racial and ethnic tension that flow through Milltown, she stated,

> I am not going to talk badly about Milltown because it is the same everywhere. When you bring a group of people into a community who are different, people have a hard time with it. They want them all to be the same and when they see how they are different, different skin, different clothes, different food, what have you, they want them to change. I deal with it myself. We all do. The same rules just have to apply to everyone, that's all. That's what I think.

As adult educators, Sue and Jacqueline were called upon to serve members of both the White working class and newly arrived refugee communities and spoke regretfully about the decrease in working class White student enrollment following the influx of Somali students at MAEC. Sue reported that, before withdrawing in large numbers from classes, working class Whites had become resentful of the sheer number of newcomers enrolling at the MAEC. White students felt pushed out of the very classrooms they had occupied for years both physically, by the sheer number of new students making use of the facilities, and symbolically, as their interests and needs were no longer reflected at the center of the curriculum. As Sue explained, "it is easier for the middle class to embrace newcomers because we are not poor and scrambling for the same finite resources."

As her words suggest, Sue believed that the best way to balance diverse students' varying interests and needs was through assurance of fair access to opportunity. For Sue, the classically liberal orientation to the challenge of grappling with difference offered a manageable and fair solution: apply the same rules and processes regardless of difference. Accordingly, Sue and Jacqueline worked to produce hardworking, economically independent citizens who could compete on a level playing field with their working class White counterparts. Indeed, the wish to transform newcomers into desirable community members was responsive to the heightened hostility non-assimilationist immigrants and refugees were likely to face. The everyday practices and interactional dynamics between students and teachers within the MAEC conveyed the message that in order for students to gain equal access to economic and social opportunity, they not only needed to learn to read, write, and speak English; they also needed to learn to behave like workers and neighbors who would be desirable in the local context. Implicit in the liberal promise of equality to which Sue and Jacqueline subscribed lies the conviction that in order to enjoy its rewards immigrants should assimilate to the demands of the local economic and social spheres. According to this reasoning, immigrants and refugees must change culturally-informed values and routines in order to mirror the grateful immigrant of liberal imagination. Sue's efforts to facilitate the transformation of newcomers' into desirable workers and community members took many forms. She worked to secure grants and take advantage of a service-learning partnership with a local college in order to gather the resources necessary for newcomers' to acquire communication skills. She labored to supply students with watches and proper interview attire. She sought and received funding for a course in preemployment in which students were introduced to vocabulary that conveyed workplace expectations about punctuality, alongside terms for the hierarchy of power, such as "boss," "employee" and "time clock." She proposed that students wear color coded tags that would signify their class schedule so that they might be admonished if found in the hallways when they ought to be in class. She monitored the hallways herself coaxing entry level students into short conversations in English, loudly praising the "quick learners," and berating (sometimes jokingly, other times not) those who were frequently late or absent.

Jacqueline's leadership in the classroom expressed a similar liberal orientation to schooling. She positioned herself as a pseudoemployer responsible for inculcating her charges with workplace practices and values. While there were roughly seven classrooms available for use, "Jacqueline's room" dominated the landscape of the ESOL program and served as a homeroom of sorts. All ESOL students work individually in Jacqueline's room, cycling out at different points of the day for direct instruction sessions from other ESOL teachers. Jacqueline's room featured a large, rectangular table. Students filled the chairs around the table as well as the small desks scattered in the room's pockets of free space. Each student had his or her own assignment to complete, workbook to finish, or old textbook to read as Jacqueline circled around the room correcting, directing, and scolding.

Jacqueline not only helped students with language and literacy acquisition but also instructed students on "proper" manners and codes of conduct. She often scolded students for having drinks in class, talking too loudly, writing in books, or displaying behavior or conversational dynamics she deems inappropriate. On one particular morning, Fathia, who until this moment had been working by herself, called Jacqueline over to ask for help with her work. Jacqueline, who had been with another student when Fathia called, reprimanded her for interrupting. "When a tutor [is] working with students their time is valuable. It is very rude, very rude." Fathia responded several times, "Okay teacher, I am sorry."

On this occasion, Jacqueline used Fathia's request for attention to convey a lesson on proper interactional dynamics between teacher and student. In our work with Somali women in and out of the school environment, Rachel and I consistently noted the employment of overlapping and collaboratively constructed oral narrative form. Judging from this observation, while Fathia probably addressed Jacqueline in a way that she would have spoken to any one of her family members or friends, Jacqueline made it clear that these informal, or more typically "Somali," conversational dynamics were simply not appropriate in the classroom.

In her mention of time as valuable, Jacqueline re-invoked the ever-present notion that time in the United States has monetary value. This principle also resonated in the use of attendance logs: The many students who received state aid were required to record hours of school attendance in order to maintain eligibility. Jacqueline supplemented such authentic documentation with forms that mimicked time sheets used in the workplace.

In addition to discouraging particular conversational styles, Sue and Jacqueline have banned Somali language itself from the classroom. The English-only language rule limited some of the newer English learners from communicating with one another either about personal matters or schoolwork. One morning as Rachel entered Jacqueline's room to greet students, Jacqueline communicated Sue's newly enacted rule that "if students speak Somali, they go into the hall."[3] On another morning, Jacqueline chastised a student for speaking Somali by saying, "English is green. The Somali language is worthless in America."

Jacqueline's enforcement of a hierarchy of authority in her tutoring room reflected and reinforced the class inequalities that exist between her and students. Indeed, English-only language instruction has been theorized as a limiting pedagogical technique that actually hinders language acquisition (Auerbach, 2000, as cited in Warriner, 2003; Roseberry-McKibbin & Brice, 2000; Taylor, 1997; Warriner, 2003). As a result, English-only instruction reinforces structural inequalities. As Warriner (p. 31) describes, "the real aim of monolingual ESL instruction is 'functional *illiteracy*' that will 'maintain a class of unskilled, non-English speaking workforce who are marginally literate and thus willing to take minimum wage jobs which others are unwilling to accept'" (p. 31).

Like a workplace manager, Jacqueline regulated who could enter and leave her classroom, as well as the sorts of language and behavior condoned within that space. One morning Rachel was working with Saba, who painstakingly copied word for word out of a book so she would have a duplicate to take home and study. To expedite the process and save Saba the pain of hand-copying the entire chapter, Rachel asked Jacqueline if she could photocopy the sheet for Saba. "No!" Jacqueline responded emphatically, as she then informed Rachel that Saba needed to copy every word she could because her writing is "what's the worst."

On a different day, when our ESOL class was having a seminar-like discussion on the situation in Sudan, Jacqueline walked in to use the copy machine in the room's corner. During our class's conversation, Fathia had been participating verbally, while simultaneously finishing an assignment that she had started in a workbook. Though we had decided not to say anything and allow Fathia to continue with her independent work, Jacqueline, interrupting the discussion, demanded that Fathia stop, pulled the book away from her, and left the classroom. Anyon (1980) writes,

> One characteristic of most working-class jobs is that there is no built-in mechanism by which the worker can control the content, process, or speed of work. Legitimate decision making is vested in personnel supervisors, in middle or upper management, or, as in an increasing number of white-collar working-class (and most middle-class) jobs, by bureaucratic rule and

regulation. For upper-middle-class professional groups there is an increased amount of autonomy regarding work. (p. 71)

In these incidents, Jacqueline's interactions with students replicated power relations between employers and employees. Jacqueline, acting with a large measure of autonomy, overrode the students' abilities to decide which learning styles and schoolwork activities were best for them. Students were given little latitude to determine how they would spend their time at school.

Revisiting Liberal Discourse on Immigration

The schooling of newcomers at MAEC reflected the complexity of local social relations between members of the Milltown professional class, White working class, and resettled Somalis. Sue and Jacqueline's desire to turn out newcomers who are more palatable to the local, largely White, working class population and prospective middle class employers was prudent in light of the heightened hostility immigrants and refugees were likely to face in the local community. While the intent behind the alignment of educational policy and practice with liberal discourse on immigration was both benevolent and pragmatic and most certainly preferable to nativist articulations, a closer look at liberal discourse itself exposes significant internal contradictions.

Liberal discourse envisions needy and grateful immigrants who have been pushed from their homelands due to various forms of disaster and suffering but remains silent in regard to those factors contributing to instability in the Global South. In truth, countries of the Global North have capitalized on their advantaged positionality within global geographies of power in ways that contribute to the destabilization of nation-states within the Global South. Individual nations, coalitions dominated by governments of the Global North, and supranational organizations operating within the neoliberal paradigm have long acted to the detriment of the South (Chossudovsky, 2003; Stromquist, 2002). Colonialism, establishment of puppet regimes, staging of proxy wars, post- Cold War abandonment of peoples made dependent by strategic use of wealth and power, self-interested development strategies, and outright military aggression have all served as mechanisms through which the Global North exerts influence at the expense of nations in the Global South.

The story of Somalia's decline into civil war echoes patterns of deleterious Northern involvement in the South. Somalia, like the majority of Africa and much of the global South, was subject to European colonial rule and exploitation for decades and continues to bear its significant consequence. By 1885, territory that would later become known as Somalia was divided under British, French, and Italian colonial rule into five Somalilands. The north was controlled by Great Britain; the east and southeast, which now make up Djibouti, were governed by France; the south was occupied by Italy. Colonial boundaries, which later translated into political borders as African countries gained independence and formed nation-states, were designed by and for Europeans without reference to preexisting ethnic or clan-based communities. Indeed, 3 million ethnic Somalis presently live outside of the borders of the Somali state in northern Kenya and eastern Ethiopia (Hussein, 1997). During the colonial era, such externally imposed boundaries seldom remained static but rather shifted in reflection of power struggles between European nation states.

While Somalia gained independence from colonial powers in 1960, subtler, enduring forms of neocolonialism including economic imperialism continued to shape Somalia's political climate. In the 1970s and 1980s, the United States and the Soviet Union competed to control Somalia's strategic location on the Horn of Africa because of its physical proximity to Middle Eastern oil reserves. Due to the USSR's alignment with Ethiopia in Somalia's 1977 Ogaden War, the United States allied itself with Siad Barre's regime, collaborating in the massive buildup of armaments in the region. Post-Cold War withdrawal from the region left the country vulnerable to clan-based insurgents. The ensuing violent civil war, which continues some 16 years later and in which the United States has periodically interceded without advancing peace, has been directly fueled by the weaponry provided by both multiple sources including the United States.

The collapse of the Somali government following the withdrawal of cold war American military presence reflects a much larger pattern in which the United States and other nations of the global North play a destabilizing role in the governance and development of post colonial countries. A perhaps ironic outcome of such foreign policy has been an increase in the flow of immigrants and refugees from the global South to North (Issa-Salwe, 2000).

Neoliberalism has had an additional impact upon Somali refugees' entrance into the U.S. national community. In the past, immigrants and refugees filled industry positions in the United States, and thereby entered the multigenerational storyline of upward mobility that frames the American dream narrative. While the reality of the immigrant story of old often differed from such Horatio Alger stories, low skilled workers who arrive in Western countries now find that they often cannot even write themselves onto the first page of the script. The dismemberment of the social welfare system in the U.S. means that just as jobs disappear so, too, do the (always weak) safety nets once provided the poor (Rodgers, 2000).

As evidenced in the case of Somalia, critical analysis of overall patterns of human movement from the Global South to North effectively fractures binary discourse of immigration. Given the North's interventions, it is no more accurate to portray (Somali) newcomers as the victims of unfortunate but perhaps inevitable hardship and expect untempered gratitude in return for asylum than it is to view (Somali) newcomers as lazy and disloyal opportunists who weigh down the national economy and threaten civil order. Even more specifically, it is difficult to see the preliterate, middle aged to elderly Somali women in our class as poised to "become American" through timeliness, hard work, and appreciative demeanor.

When describing the war in Somalia, women students at the center report seeing family members killed before their eyes, being raped by rebels from differing clans, and becoming disconnected from remaining family members in panicked flight to safety. Before coming to the United States, most of the women were refugees at camps in Kenya, where they fled when their country fell into civil disorder. At these camps the women were dependent upon the hosting government and humanitarian relief agencies for survival. Women who spent periods of time in Kenya told stories of repeated victimization at the hands of the local police. They reported that their names were put on waiting lists, and when called they were given the choice between going to a country currently accepting refugees or waiting longer for a country of their choice to provide hostel. Some of the countries accepting refugees that they mention include the United Kingdom, Canada, Denmark, the United States, and Australia.

As part of the application process, they sometimes needed to present what remained of their families as monogamous, when they were in fact often polygamous. The result was a further destruction of culturally established family order, and the abandonment of many women and children by husbands forced to select only one from among the multiple wives they had promised support. Many of these abandoned women came to the U.S. legally determined to be "divorced." In other cases, the move to the U.S. cultural context precipitated the break-up of long term monogamous marriages. As a result, the majority of women that we taught were single, with multiple children to support.

In short, Somali women's lived realities contradict the terms of the bartering arrangement implicit within liberal immigration discourse. Rather than evoking gratitude, Somali women's experiences bring into focus a group of student newcomers with histories of personal trauma for which the U.S. shares responsibility.

CONCLUSION

In this chapter I set out to explore the relationality between local and national discourses of immigration and the policy and practice shaping newcomer education. In the case of Somali newcomers who have resettled in the United States, the predominance of polarized discourse on immigration has profound educational implications. In an examination of everyday school policy and practice at MAEC there is: an emphasis upon the production of low skilled workers; an invoking of authoritarian relations between newcomers and longer term residents; a patronizing portrayal of immigrants as culturally naive and vulnerable; an exclusion of newcomers from decision making regarding their schooling; and, finally, a silencing of critical analysis of the very patterns of global movement of which newcomers are a part.

Because one of the main missions of the U.S. public education system is to produce an informed, engaged, and civic-minded citizenry capable of serving as custodians to our democratic ideals, these are unacceptable implications that invite educators to explore territory beyond the traditional polarities that mark liberal and nativist immigrant discourse. The interactional dynamics and organizational structure in place at MAEC in light of the global geographies of power at play in the transnational movement of people both highlights the contradictions inherent in liberal discourse and points to the need for a form of schooling that would better facilitate newcomers' incorporation into the national community.

The U.S. looks to schooling to nurture a national commitment to equality of opportunity, representation, and appreciation for pluralism. As articulated by Deborah Meier (1995), a leading voice among proponents of democratic education, the " 'details' of what goes on in our schools matter" (p. 9). Schooling, as an institution and a process, is inextricably bound-up in the production of ways of being and, as such, its habits, commitments, and ordering principles have profound repercussions. William Tierney, (1993) another spokesperson for democratic schooling, writes,

> Education concerns the ability of people to come to terms with their own and others' identities, and to understand how the world shapes and is shaped by social interaction. And such knowledge is not merely to be learned for learning's sake: rather, it is to be employed in the work of building democracy-in our organizations, in or communities, and in our nation. (p. 158)

Meier's (1995) and Tierney's (1991) words indicate the realization of the democratic potential of schooling encompasses a range of activities including the ability to involve school community members in educational decision-making and the critical telling of their own personal and national history. It also entails interactional dynamics that diminish rather than accentuate power differentials. Finally, schooling that is democratic in nature invites students' to purposefully consider ways of acting as members of the U.S. national community.

I end, then, with a proposal that educational leaders and practitioners join in looking critically at the flawed polarities of discourse on immigration and work toward staking out a third, alternative space. In the envisioned third, democratic school space, newcomers are included as partners in educational decision making; various members of the local community—including members of the White working class, newcomers, and the middle professional class—are brought together to pursue critical inquiry into the realities of transnational migration; and, together, members of the school community iron out the details of day-to-day school policy and practice in ways that give voice to multiple experiences and perspectives. Whether or not we collectively agree upon such a vision, as the U.S. moves toward an increasingly diverse national community, we need to complicate our discussion of immigration in order to make nuanced and well informed choices regarding newcomer education.

NOTES

1. See Noel Gough's 2006 paper titled, *Changing Planes: Toward a Geophilosophy of Transnational Curriculum Inquiry* for a etymological tracing of the phrase "making the familiar strange."
2. Though the population of our ESOL classes was constantly in flux as students came and went from the center, our classes were composed exclusively of women with very few exceptions. While some men dropped in for one or two mornings, in our years of teaching we only had two men maintain steady attendance in our class, both of who ended up leaving the center entirely. While this trend is not uncommon for MAEC, with a disproportionate number of Somali women to Somali men, why our class so steadily remained sex/gender segregated is not entirely clear.
3. Despite Jacqueline and Sue's recommendation/rule, Rachel and I made the decision to continue to not only allow Somali in our classroom but to also incorporate it in our actual curriculum. Even more, the women themselves continue to speak Somali both in hallways, during breaks, and even quietly in Jacqueline's class. While I occasionally hear scolding from Jacqueline or Sue, I quite often continue to hear Somali conversations occurring between students.

REFERENCES

4,500 people rally in support the Somali community of Lewiston, Maine Against Neo-Nazi Rally. (2003). *Democracy Now.* Retrieved May 17, 2007, from http://www.democracynow.org/article.pl?sid=03/04/07/0316235

Adam, H. M., & Ford, R. (Eds.). (1997). *Mending rips in the sky: Options for Somali communities in the 21st century.* Lawrenceville, NJ: The Red Sea Press.

Alacron, E. (1998). Fight against prop. 227 not over. *People's Weekly World.* Retrieved March 10, 2008, from http://www.pww.org/archives9/98-06.13-1.html

Anyon, J. (1980). Social class and the hidden curriculum of work. *Journal of Education, 162,* 167–192.

Auerbach, E. R. (2000). When pedagogy meets politics: Challenging English only in adult education. In R. D. Gonzalez & I. Melis (Eds.), *Language Ideologies: Critical perspectives on the official language movement: Education and the Social Implications of Official Language* (Vol. 1, pp. 177–204). Mahwah, NJ: Erlbaum.

Besteman, C. (1999). Unraveling Somalia: Race, violence, and the legacy of slavery. Philadelphia, University of Pennsylvania Press.

Borjas, G. J. (1990). *Friends or strangers.* New York: Basic Books.

Bouchard, K. (2002). Lewiston's Somali Surge. *Portland Press Herald.* Retrieved May 17, 2007, from http://pressherald.mainetoday.com/news/immigration/020428lewiston.shtml.

Burke, M. (1995). Mexican Immigrants shape California's fertility, future. *Population Today, 23*(9), 4–7.

Cassanelli, L. V. (1982). *The shaping of Somali society: Reconstruction of the history of a pastoral people 1600–1900.* Philadelphia: University of Pennsylvania Press.

Chossudovsky, M. (2003). *The globalization of poverty and the new world order.* Oro, Ontario: Global Outlook.

Chavez, L. R. (2001). *Covering immigration: Popular images and the politics of nation.* Berkeley: University of California Press.

Countries with the lowest rates of literacy. (1999). LinguaLinks Library Version 4.0. *SIL International.* Retrieved May 16, 2007, from http://www.sil.org/lingualinks/literacy/prepareforaliteracyprogram/countrieswiththelowestratesofl.htm

Farkas, S., Dufer, A., Johnson, J., Moye, L., & Vine, J. (2003). Now that I'm here: What America's immigrants have to say about life in the U.S. today. *American Educator, 27,* 28–36.

Fass, P. (1989). *Outside in: Minorities and the transformation of American education.* New York: Oxford University Press.

Fukuyama, F. (2006). Identity, immigration, and liberal democracy. *Journal of Democracy, 17*(2), 5–20.

Gough, N. (2006, May). *Changing planes: Towards a geophilosophy of transnational curriculum inquiry.* Draft paper presented at Meeting International and Global Challenges in Curriculum Studies, The Second World Curriculum Studies Conference, Tampere, Finland

Harvey, D. (1993). From space to place and back again: Reflections on the condition of postmodernity. In J. Bird, B. Curtis, T. Putnam, G. Robertson, & L. Tickner (Eds.), *Mapping the futures: Local cultures, global change* (pp. 3–29). London: Routledge.

Higham, J. (1955). *Strangers in the land: Patterns of American Nativism 1860–1925.* New Brunswick, NJ: Rutgers University Press.

Hussein, I. (1997). *Teenage refugees from Somalia speak out.* New York: The Rosen Publishing Group.

Issa-Salwe, A. (2000). *Cold War fallout: Boundary politics and conflict in the Horn of Africa.* London: HAAN.

Katerberg, W. H. (1995). The irony of identity: An essay on Nativism, Liberal democracy, and parochial identities in Canada and the United States. *American Quarterly, 47,* 493–524.

Kemnitz, A. (2006). Immigration as a commitment device. *Journal of Population Economics, 19*(2), 299–313.

Laitin, D. D., & Samatar, S. S. (1987). *Somalia: Nation in search of a state.* Boulder, CO: Westview Press.

Levinson, B. A., & Holland, D. C. (1996). The cultural production of the educated person: An introduction. In B. A. Levinson, D. A. Foley, & D. C. Holland (Eds.), *Cultural production of the educated person: Critical ethnographies of schooling and local prac*tice (pp. 1–54). Albany, NY: State University of New York Press.

Lytle, K. (2003, October). *Constructing the criminal alien: A historical framework for analyzing border vigilantes at the turn of the 21st century.* Paper presented at the Center for Comparative Immigration Studies, the University of California, San Diego.

Maine State Planning Office. (2005). *Frequently requested Maine Data.* Retrieved March 1, 2004, from http://www.maine.gov/spo/economics/census/frequent.php

Maine town's diversity rally outdraws hate group gathering. (2003). *Southern Poverty Law Center.* Retrieved May 17, 2007, from http://www.splcenter.org/center/splcreport/article.jsp?aid=28

Mayor Raymond's letter to the Somali community. (2002). *Portland Press Herald.* Retrieved December 1, 2004, from http://pressherald.mainetoday.com/news/immigration/021005raymondletter.shtml

Mazrui, A. A. (1997). Crisis in Somalia: From tyranny to anarchy. In H. M. Adam & R. Ford (Eds.), *Mending rips in the sky: Options for Somali communities in the 21st century* (pp. 5–11). Lawrenceville, NJ: The Red Sea Press.

Meier, D. (1995). *The power of their ideas: Lessons for America from a small school in Harlem.* Boston: Beacon Press.

Rahnema, M., & Bawtree, V. (Eds.). (2003). *The Post-Development Reader.* New York: Zed Books.

Rodgers, H. R., Jr. (2000). *American poverty in a new era of reform.* Armonk, NY: M. E. Sharpe.

Roseberry-McKibbin, C., & Brice, A. (2000). Acquiring English as a second language. *ASHA Leader, 5,* 4–7.

Samatar, A. I. (1994). *The Somali challenge.* London: Lynne Rienner.

Singer, A., & Wilson, J. H. (2007). Refugee resettlement in metropolitan America. *Migration Information Sources.* Retrieved May 16, 2007, from http://www.migrationinformation.org/Feature/display.cfm?id=585

Skinner, D., Pach, A. III, & Holland, D. (1998). *Selves in time and place: Identities, experience, and history in Nepal.* Landham, MD: Rowman & Littlefield.

Soysal, Y. N. (1994). *Limits of citizenship: Migrants and postnational membership in Europe.* Chicago: University of Chicago Press.

Stevens, E. G., Wood, H., & Sheehan, J. J. (Eds.). (2002). *Justice, ideology, and education*. Boston: McGraw Hill.

Stromquist, N. (2002). *Education in a globalized world: The connectivitiy of power, technology, and knowledge*. Landham, MD: Rowman & Littlefield.

Taylor, D. (Ed.). (1997). *Many families, many literacies: An international declaration of principles*. Portsmouth, NH: Heinemann Trade.

Taylor, S. (2002, May 15). Roomful, earful. *Lewiston (Maine) Sun Journal*, C1, A8.

The dangers of "Free Trade." (2007). *PICA*. Retrieved March 15, 2007, from http://www.pica.ws/fairtrade/index.html

Tierney, W. G. (1993). *Building communities of differences: Higher education in the twenty-first century*. Westport, CT: Bergin & Garvey.

Thomas, R., & Murr, A. (1993). The economic cost of immigration. *Newsweek, 122*(6), 18–20.

U.S. Census Bureau. (2004). *The foreign-born population in the United States: 2003*. Retrieved December 8, 2005, from http://www.census.gov/prod/2004pubs/p20-551.pdf

Vecoli, R. J. (1996). The significance of immigration in the formation of an American identity. *The History Teacher, 30*, 9–27.

Waldinger, R. (Ed.). (2001). *Strangers at the gates: New immigrants in urban America*. Berkeley: The University of California Press.

Warriner, D. S. (2003). *"Here Without English You are Dead": Language ideologies and the experiences of women refugees in an adult ESL program*. PhD dissertation, Department of Education, University of Pennsylvania.

Washuk, B. (2006). Learning to thrive. *Lewiston Sun Journal*. Retrieved May 17, 2007, from http://www.sunjournal.com/index.php?storyid=175935

CHAPTER 3

HIGHER EDUCATION AND CIVIC ENGAGEMENT IN THE UNITED STATES

Budgetary, Disciplinary, and Spatial Borders

Kathleen Staudt

Higher education generally has assumed a role in what is termed "citizenship" education in both historical and contemporary eras. By citizenship, many meanings are evoked, from active leadership and service ethics to productive, law-abiding, tax-payers. This chapter focuses on the *new* mobilization of citizenship education, known under the broad rubric of civic engagement programming. Such programming is present in a quarter of U.S. higher education's 4,000 institutions, including 2-year community colleges, undergraduate and graduate comprehensive research universities.

This chapter draws insights from organizational theory on higher education, utilizing ethnographic data and vantage points both from national networking "encounters" among civic engagement faculty and staff leaders and from the deep, thick knowledge that comes from

Advancing Democracy Through Education? U.S. Influence Abroad and Domestic Practices, pp. 55–74

participant observation in civic engagement leadership at a medium-sized, public comprehensive, doctoral granting university on the U.S.-Mexico border. Engagement programs facilitate many border "crossings," but the focus herein is on budgetary, disciplinary, and spatial borders.

University departments have long had their token faculty community activists, who involved themselves and their students in what educator-theorist John Dewey (1938) would call experiential, active, or democracy learning. In the last decade, this isolated activism has blossomed into multiple activisms under program umbrellas with different names, herein referred to as civic engagement. In the 1990s, a major shift occurred, broadening and systemizing engagement and activism with the rationale of responsiveness to the "community." The word community tended to refer to issues, constituencies, and neighborhoods that many universities had previously ignored: social justice, immigration, and battered women, along with public schools and nongovernmental organizations (NGOs) in economically distressed neighborhoods. For partial course credit, students learn individually or collectively in teams with nonprofit NGOs. Civic engagement programming is different from pre-professional programs which make community-based, individual internships part of licensing requirements in nursing, social work, and teaching. Civic engagement programming is strictly voluntary, and not typically tied into the degree requirements of a particular program.

Studies on institutional change make it seem as though higher education presidents need do little more than declare their interest and adjust the language of key institutional documents in order to transform civic engagement practices throughout campus culture (Astin & Astin, 2000; Eckel & Kezar, 2003). In reality, such transformation represents complex political and organizing challenges at the academic "grassroots" of universities: faculty members and students in undergraduate courses— the core mission of most higher education. Several questions emerge here: To what degree can such programs, organized within complex higher education bureaucracies, enhance democratic citizenship? And importantly, what is the meaning of "democracy?" Lappe and DuBois (1994) contrast "representative democracy" with "living democracy." Representative democracy focuses on free and fair procedures and elections where informed voters delegate decisions to elected, appointed, and bureaucratic officials. Living democracy is a broader definition that expands from the citizen-government interaction to include attention to social justice in market, workplace, and household settings. I am political scientist, steeped in disciplinary traditions that focus on representative democracy, but my own commitments lean toward a socially just, living democracy. However, I work in settings with multiple views of democracy and I do not seek to impose my own views on programs and students. I have hope and faith that students who are critically aware of multiple options will make their own choices and carve their own pathways.

If higher education were to foster healthy citizenship and democracy, the fruits of its work could begin to counter trends in turn-of-the-millennium U.S. society. Influential writers have commented on the decrease of social capital (that is, relationships of trust for public problem solving) over the last quarter century, and the increase of radical individualism (Bellah, Madsen, Sullivan, Swidler, & Tipton, 1985; Putnam, 2000). Progressive politics have been on the decline (Hart, 2001).

The chapter is organized around the following topics. The first section draws on organizational and historical concepts of higher education. Then a typology of engagement programs is offered in the second section, drawing on analysis of documents from research, advocacy associations and funding sources that supply technical assistance and incentives for different types of programs. The aim here is to understand the reasons behind some of the strategic styles in civic engagement. The third section contextualizes engagement at a particular public higher education institution along with the dynamics of building a program, securing resources, and blending what Boyer (1990, 1996) calls the "scholarship of engagement" with institutional missions (also see Bringle, Games, & Malloy, 1999; Ehrlich, 2000; Lynton & Elman, 1987).

The author utilizes an ethnographic approach that incorporates vantage points that emerged from participant observation. The analysis also draws on document analysis, such as studies, the publications and missions of funding sources, and advocacy materials, the latter from higher education associations. Participant observation occurred at 30 national encounters, wherein associations and funders facilitated "networking" among engagement-oriented faculty and staff, and in organizing and leadership roles for an engagement program at a medium-size public university with nearly 20,000 students on the U.S.-Mexico border.

The border region, as the section below on context indicates, represents a crossroads where deeply rooted authoritarianism and fledgling democracy meet, as its largely Mexican-heritage residents experience patron-client type politics whether from the south or from the peculiar hybrid of U.S. individualism and machine-style representative democracy of the twenty-first century (Staudt & Coronado, 2002, pp. 24–37). Thus the context is one in an authentic borderland of nations, cultures, and languages. Other borders also emerge, relating to crossing institutional lines (community organizations and higher education) and disciplinary lines, and procuring multiple sources of grant funding. Can a powerful and useful democratic education emerge in this cauldron of higher education bureaucracy and flawed political institutions?

CONCEPTUAL AND THEORETICAL PERSPECTIVES

In *The Knowledge Factory*, Stanley Aronowitz (2000) criticizes the trends toward corporatization and centralization in U.S. higher education administration.

> Some [universities] have become big businesses, employing thousands and collecting millions in tuition fees, receiving grants from government and private sources, and, for a select few, raising billions in huge endowments.... With these funds, the universities construct buildings, help pay their CEOs (presidents) handsomely, and retain a small army of administrators and fundraisers. (p. 11)

The knowledge factory concept, Aronowitz argues, captures key tasks of the university in late twentieth century America: to advance scientific and technological discoveries for economic development and to prepare students for vocational, technical, and professional occupations, including its internships and practice orientations (pp. 38–57). He questions whether universities can prepare students for citizenship and critical thinking in the new corporate era, when they must contend with ongoing fiscal crisis aggravated by reduced public subsidies. Aronowitz defends a type of democratic education related more to individualist critical thinking rather than including within that approach skill-building in service, applied, and/or experiential education.

Privatization has been the market fundamentalists' mantra for governments and administrative enterprises, including public higher education, in the last 30 years around the world. This trend occurred in the United States as well. The percentages of higher education budgetary appropriations from the federal (national level), state (regional level), and local government levels have been in decline since 1980, while the proportion of funding from tuition and fees, gifts, restricted grants and contracts, and sales and services have all increased, according to the U.S. Department of Education's National Center for Education Statistics (n.d.). This phenomenon is not unique to the United States, as a study of European and Australian universities documents (Slaughter & Leslie, 1997).

U.S. higher education has become entrepreneurial, with internal bureaucratic units that generate external grant funding, gifts, and revenue from technical assistance and inventions. Aronowitz's (2000) foundational analysis is therefore not disputed here. Yet higher educational institutions are not monolithic hierarchical, command-control systems, but are rather pluralist, consisting of units that compete for authority, budget, and space. Higher education in the United States, moreover, fosters more individual professional autonomy than other organizations. Academic faculty members are socialized to become autonomous professionals, responding primarily to their disciplinary based departments and associations. Internal organization hierarchies involve discipline-based faculty members interacting primarily within, rather than across disciplines. These organizational features pose challenges to interdisciplinary and community collaboration.

Higher educational incentive systems pose yet another challenge. Incentives that reward research and teaching have yet to incorporate the idea of community-based research and teaching, the base of civic engagement. Faculty members are socialized to privilege research and publication over, or on a par with, effective teaching, rather than service, leadership, and community activism. Annual evaluation forms, tenure, and promotion guidelines, and course assessments often ignore interdisciplinary collaboration and community engagement, resulting in faculty-perceived *dis*incentives to change. Faced with the opportunity to pursue long-term, collaborative engagement approaches to their research and teaching, many faculty members will pass on such opportunities until incentive systems change. Of course, the semipermanence that tenure provides can liberate faculty members from adherence to historic incentive systems and enable them to alter incentives, for themselves and their own departments.

Discipline-based higher education, along with its autonomous tenured faculty members, has led some organizational theorists to conceptualize U.S. higher educational structures as "organized chaos" (Cohen & March, 1974). They bemoan organized-chaos challenges for higher education presidents. Despite growing centralization trends, higher education presidents cannot wave magic wands that evoke automatic compliance with their policies, visions, missions, and strategic plans—the wide array of organizational tools assembled to transform institutions. Moreover, the cast of characters is constantly changing in higher education, with presidents, provosts, vice presidents, and deans usually serving terms of 5 or fewer years.

What do these organizational and incentive challenges mean for civic engagement leaders? The higher education associations that promote civic engagement and service learning direct their primary attention to presidents who may instigate new policies, but who rarely control the implementation of new policies and the transformation of long institutionalized incentive systems. Later the chapter analyzes engagement leader strategies to deal with these organizational challenges, including the challenge of facilitating new directions amid fiscal crises, faculty disincentives to change, and specific budgetary commitments to organize civic engagement programs.

Civic engagement leaders, unless blessed with generous benefactors or endowments, develop and employ entrepreneurial skills. They network with faculty across disciplinary lines and across institutional lines at national networking encounters to learn change strategies. They generate external grant and contract funding, offer technical assistance for revenue, and struggle to obtain internal budgetary commitments, the seeming solution for program sustainability. With these monies, engagement leaders can do many things to facilitate change: instigate faculty development seminars; offer faculty with material incentives to change courses, to award exemplary coursework, and to encourage community action or applied research; hire and groom students; and collaborate with staff and students who facilitate community connections, a labor-intensive process. Effective engagement leaders are like community organizers, but organize on and off campus while simultaneously building bridges across those borders, all of which take precious time—the limited commodity in academic labor.

As outlined, engagement leaders pursue activities that Aronowitz (2000) might criticize. To obtain external funding, they become entrepreneurs. They use discourse that prizes experiential and applied learning, and could fall prey to Aronowitz's critique on that, for through engagement programs, students acquire vocational and professional orientations. After all, engagement programs involve leadership, organizing, nonmaterialist service, and nonprofit/NGOs, themselves tainted with the need to raise funds rather than look to public support or subsidy in the era of privatization.

This chapter offers a more nuanced view than Aronowitz's (2000). In this view, engagement leadership is considered to be compatible with democratic citizenship. Yet when engaged faculty members and leaders move toward the delicate border that crosses conceptions of democracy from service and procedural skills to leadership for social justice, they create political risks for the corporatized CEO/president. For this reason, the language and discourse of engagement are crucial. Service language is less threatening and seemingly politically safe to administrators, yet less interesting to faculty, primarily concerned with teaching and research in higher education incentive systems. Therefore, advocates of civic engagement programming must learn to craft a message that seems palatable to university administrators, even as it energizes and attracts a broader variety of faculty involvement.

A TYPOLOGY OF CIVIC ENGAGEMENT PROGRAMS

A triad of engagement programs has emerged since 1990 across the United States. The most common type focuses on **service and volunteerism**, with the discourse of "service-learning" as its mantra. For private schools, Historically Black Colleges and Universities (known as HBCUs in the United States), and those with religious origins, service discourse often resonates with particular higher education missions.

Another type of engagement program focuses on **technical assistance**, primarily for nonprofit NGOs. Such programs, entrepreneurial at local levels, offer courses and workshops, for a fee, to build NGO capacity in the region. Universities also offer revenue-generating short-term contracts to business and government for policy and survey research.

The third type of engagement program has a more radical and potentially risky edge to it, stressing **leadership, advocacy, community-based research, and social justice**. It comes closest to the "public work" that Harry Boyte and others have used to criticize pure volunteerism and service: those potentially "feel good" or patronizing programs that do not challenge the root causes that generate service needs in the first place (Boyte & Karr, 2000). Volunteerism alleviates symptoms, but does not address causes because it is politically safe and noncontroversial.

Beyond the typological triad, some urban universities aim to do "all of the above," and they are large enough to do so. They offer structured service-learning opportunities in the community, technical assistance through engagement or continuing education programs, and opportunities for faculty and students to engage in systemic change through leadership, community-based research, and advocacy that responds to social justice intentions seeking a redistribution of resources and voices from the privileged to the many. These universities have been called **comprehensive urban institutions**.

Advocacy associations and funders play key roles in fostering certain types of programs. By and large, most advocacy and funding support **service learning**, and advocacy associations at the national level foster conferences, network exchanges, and technical assistance to broaden service-learning programs. Among large, national nonprofit organizations, Campus Compact (2003) is a leader with nearly 900 higher education institutional members, as well as 30 state campus compact chapters it helped spawn. Campus Compact sponsors many studies, drawing on its memberships; it makes an annual service-learning award, and it produces useful newsletters (www.campuscompact.org). It offers conferences, books, workshops, and lists of consultants to mobilize service learning movements, a veritable cottage industry unto itself. The American Association of Higher Education celebrated the engagement theme in summer academies, panels at its multiple annual conferences, and a book series that focuses on service-learning in the disciplines (Rhodes & Howard 1998). The Association of American Colleges and Universities organizes conferences to "practice" liberal education and deepen knowledge, pursue justice, and take action, to paraphrase their language.

These organizations disseminate ideas widely through Web sites, LISTSERVS, and collaborative encounters, whereby higher education "activists" network and bond with one another across institutional boundaries, sharing ideas about what works and where to find the next rounds of funding. Among many other foundations, Kellogg, Pew, Carnegie, Kettering, and even pension-giant TIAA-CREF funded and published reports with a higher education change agenda (see Eckel & Kezar 2003; Leslie & Fretwell, 1996). The author had multiple opportunities to participate in and host several encounters at the border university which is the object of the current study.

Beyond advocacy, funding sources are also pieces of the engagement mobilization puzzle. Public institutions have long depended on funding from their state legislatures, noted earlier. Moreover, higher education faced and continues to face political criticism for its isolation and seeming disinterest in public problems, a reason why Boyer's call for universities to contribute to problem solving and social justice resonated well. Engagement can also be good public relations for universities in communities (see Zimpher, Percy, & Brukardt, 2002).

Along with the 1980s-era privatization and government downsizing generally was an associated "bureaucrat bashing" of educational institutions, from K–12 through higher education (Kimball, 1990). Popular opinion treats professors with a 6-, 9-, or 12-credit-hour teaching load per semester (generally referring to contact hours with students) as living lives of leisure, not recognizing the labor that goes into preparation for those 6, 9, or 12 contact hours in classrooms or other academic responsibilities in research, publication, and service.

Opportunities opened up for higher educational funding through public and private sources, with bipartisan Congressional support. Beginning in 1992, the U.S. federal government legitimized and authorized funding for the Corporation for National Service (CNS), two large stipend-provided programs which included AmeriCorps (volunteerism) and Vista Volunteers (community activism). (CNS has recently been renamed the Corporation for National and Community Service/CNCS.) Universities apply for and receive a critical mass of this funding. As political times changed, so also did programs within CNCS, such as more recent emphases on homeland security. Moreover, the U.S. federal government offers work-related financial aid to students (the "work-study" program).

By Congressional mandate, at least 7% of work-study students at any given institution of higher education are to be placed in community settings.

These funding sources and more have offered public policy incentives to initiate or expand higher education engagement programs. Another key program, especially to fund the comprehensive urban universities, has been the Office of University Partnerships in the cabinet-level Department of Housing and Urban Development begun in 1994. The idea behind this was to tap higher educational resources to respond to long-term urban crises.

As is clear, a bundle of factors influence civic engagement programming on campus, including its service learning, technical assistance, and social justice orientations. More than university presidents influence the character of programs, although presidents can facilitate or constrain the sort of political risks that campus cultures will allow in civic engagement. The chapter now moves to analyze engagement program strategies in a border university, one that reflects many of the trends previously outlined. The university is part of the public Texas higher education system. Texas is a state long known for its conservatism under moderate Democratic Party rule. It has become even more conservative, and suffered from further cuts in state spending, under Republican Party rule. The border region has been called a "limited democracy," a result of historical exclusion and discrimination against its majority Mexican-heritage population, poverty, modest educational levels, and patron-client politics (Staudt & Coronado, 2002). Voter turnout is low (lower than in Mexico)—in general elections, one-third or fewer registered voters usually participate, while in school board elections, the turn-out can be as low as one percent. Historically, the Border University operated with lean budgets and limited discretionary resources, thus impelling its entrepreneurial faculty and administrators to seek external funding for new initiatives. Such was the case with its civic engagement program.

ENGAGEMENT PROGRAM STRATEGIES: ACADEMIC INCENTIVES, DEMOCRATIC LEARNING?

The Border University and a local community college are the only higher education institutions in this large metropolitan area with a diverse population and student body. Until the 1980s, the university's student body did not mirror the demographic characteristics of the city. But administrative leadership from that time onward celebrated its unique region, demographics, and mission to serve and to reflect the border community. The institution prides itself on facilitating both "access and excellence," with nearly open admissions policies, but relatively low graduation rates, as measured through traditional formulas. The president supports civic engagement programming through affirming its worth in various speeches and conversations with administrative and community members.

Many programs within the university pursue outreach in its more traditional, historic forms. The College of Business interacts with chambers of commerce, small and family businesses. The College of Engineering works with technology issues that affect the region. The College of Education prepares teachers for K–12 schools. And the College of Nursing prepares professionals for the health sciences. Additionally, several centers and collaborative organizations generate grant proposals for research and contract work in economic development, environmental affairs, and educational reform. Short, noncredit bearing workshops are offered in a "continuing education" program that operates like a separate business within the university.

In this university, as at many others in the United States, the great bureaucratic divide occurs between Academic Affairs and Student Affairs, each with its own vice president, deans, departments, and other divisions. At the Border University, an assistant vice president for Student Affairs has built extensive outreach programs with students in K–12 education, based on federal funds that encourage pathways to college among wider, more diverse populations. At this and many other universities, however, student affairs leadership in service learning or engagement programming rarely is able to connect well with faculty members, courses, and students, except for those in registered student organizations. Student affairs staff members do not network much with faculty and/or understand fully the incentives that impel faculty to do what they do (or don't do). As such, student affairs-led civic engagement programs at other universities tend to focus on volunteerism and service or service-learning approaches.

Beginnings of Civic Engagement at the Border University

In 1998, a major philanthropic foundation funded a consortium of four universities nationally to transform university-community relationships through "community-based teaching and learning." The Border University was one of the four institutions, and it named the new initiative the Institute for Community-Based Teaching and Learning (hereafter called the "Institute"). The author became its faculty coordinator, with a one-third course release, and the external funding permitted a professional community-minded person to be hired as its staff coordinator. Both coordinators did considerable labor-intensive community collaboration and outreach in order to identify NGOs and public schools with which faculty members might collaborate and engage their students, in exchange for partial course credit. For example, a course syllabus might offer options to students: 20% of the grade will be based on one of the following, a traditional research paper, or a 20-hour experiential learning project with an NGO, working individually or in teams.

Engagement Courses

The array of engagement opportunities is wide, with the Institute acting as "matchmaker" between faculty members and NGOs, or monitor of student time-contribution logs in NGOs. Ultimately, faculty members decide what to offer in courses, how to connect it to readings, examinations, writing, and learning overall, and how much community-based learning will account for in course grades. Examples are plentiful. Computer Information Systems courses connect teams of students with NGOs that seek Web site development but lack funds for that. Accounting courses do likewise, for NGOs without bookkeepers, accountants, or software. Students in writing classes locate grant opportunities for specific NGOs and write drafts in collaboration with them. Women's Studies classes connect students with NGOs that deal with family violence, giving presentations at high schools or observing courts for fair process. Teacher Education students work with K–12 students well before their student teaching experiences. History and government students tutor immigrants in citizenship courses, learning and teaching the answers to the 100 questions that U.S. naturalization procedures require new citizens to know. Students make (carefully nonpartisan) presentations on voting and civic action in high schools, encouraging voter registration. Students organize conferences about public affairs, build audiences, write press releases and reports. They testify before city council. The list could go on and on.

As is clear, civic engagement at the Border University combines service learning, advocacy, leadership, and public work. The aim is to build a comprehensive urban university in which increasing numbers of students experience active learning in their community. Students deepen their professional interest and expertise, learn public speaking skills, occasionally discover teaching and organizing talents, and gain insight about the NGO world in the region. The city has hundreds of what, in the United States, is called a 501c3 tax-exempt nonprofit organization established for public purposes (In this chapter, I call these NGOs). At least a third of students indicate in course evaluations for engagement classes that they might consider futures in the nonprofit/NGO sector.

Faculty Incentives and Interests

The Institute offered workshops, training, and retreats to faculty members to meet one another and community partners. It sought to involve faculty based on prospects for teaching innovation and enhanced student learning that responded to the considerable needs in this border metropolitan area. The existence of external funding also allowed modest awards to faculty offering exemplary community partnership courses, wherein syllabi and student-community outcomes could be evaluated. Moreover, the external funding permitted several students to be hired as research/community assistants. Initially, these opportunities appealed to faculty in the social sciences, humanities (especially history and languages), and education, and less to faculty in engineering, science, and business. Each college has its own distinctive academic culture that may place priority on research funding or consultancies, making the engagement appeal more challenging in some compared to others.

The overall proportion of female tenured or tenure-track faculty hovers at a third in the university generally. Yet women faculty members constitute more than half of the engaged faculty. Part of this imbalance has to do with the disciplines in which women are concentrated: for example, more women teach in social sciences and interdisciplinary studies than in engineering. Some may interpret female faculty as more amenable to complex pedagogy and labor burdens (Bauer, 2002; see other selections in Weigman, 2002). Whether male or female, the faculty members who became involved with at least one community partnership course, numbering over 50 faculty members after 5 years of engagement programming, tended to be student-centered and concerned about the community. The rise of border studies as an interdisciplinary and theoretical interest, from the social sciences to literary theory, made border engagement a possible regional research niche as well.

At the Border University, annual faculty evaluations and stringent tenure and promotion guidelines produced anxiety among new faculty members about their participation in civic engagement. The evaluation criteria privilege research and teaching, each constituting about 40% of overall assessment, but downplay service (20% of assessment). Traditionally, service had been viewed as internal committee work and occasional speeches in the region. The Institute leaders made an early strategic decision to avoid the association of community-based teaching and learning with service, given the annual evaluation, tenure and promotion guidelines structure. At the time, the concept of "service learning" was known to few faculty members, except those who studied teaching pedagogy. Even the large philanthropic foundation that provided funding for the Institute's early years recognized these dynamics and downplayed the service language. (By 2005, service-learning terminology has become far more common, so civic engagement programming uses it more. With hindsight, civic engagement leaders consider these early strategic decisions as wise.)

Given faculty anxiety about evaluation, civic engagement leadership looked for opportunities to value community-based teaching and research and to educate administrators in the process. In 2000, the Institute was able to add new lines under research and teaching criteria for the official promotion and tenure guidelines. The Institute did not seek to replace peer-reviewed research and publication expectations with community-based reports or other deliverables, conducted with students and community partners. Rather, it sought to add value to community-based syllabi and peer-reviewable documents (regional research and grant proposals), under research and teaching criteria, which would also "count" in evaluations. The administration, from deans through vice president and president, supported and approved the revised guidelines.

ENGAGEMENT LEADERSHIP:
THE DILEMMAS OF ENTREPRENEURIALISM

After coordinating faculty for the Institute, a group of strategically placed mid-level active faculty and staff proposed to establish a university-wide civic engagement center (hereinafter called the "Center"). The author became its director and chief fund-raiser. The Border University did not allocate any internal budgetary funding, except for faculty released time from a course each semester, until 2004. The author writes several external grant proposals annually, usually half of which result in awards. The Center managed technical assistance for NGO capacity building, although this task was difficult to manage in a public institution, burdened with numerous state government rules that create knots and delays. The Institute, then and now Center, became an umbrella organization for what amounted to several million dollars of external funding. Some of the grants facilitated or required attendance at conferences and networks wherein engagement leaders would learn from one another, share strategies and best practices for possible adaptation and replication. At these cross-university collaborations, funders hope that institutional representatives (mostly faculty) will bond, build social capital, get grant leads, and share ideas for potential replication. Movements grow and grow quickly in such circumstances.

The world of external grant funding has its good, bad, and ugly aspects. The goodness involves generating resources of use to multiple faculty, students, community partners, and the university as a whole.

Funds facilitate new initiatives and job creation. They enable new regional research and outreach. Funds validate civic engagement as valuable public work. They make the administration notice one program among scores of other programs in pluralist universities, all struggling for resources, recognition, and a paragraph in a presidential speech.

There are other sides to external grant funding that are not so pleasant. Grants generate large internal bureaucracies wherein staff jobs are dedicated to control all aspects of money movement through multiple levels of oversight. For grant recipients, whole and halftime staff must devote extensive time to creating documents, moving them through the bureaucracy, and keeping records. Multiple evaluations and reports are required for external funders in tight deadlines. Federal grants allow universities to charge high rates for the "indirect costs" for infrastructure like space and electricity. At the Border University, the rate is 48%, as high as many universities, but only minute amounts of indirect costs trickle down to those who write the grant proposals and generate the funds. With a $400,000 grant, about half goes for civic engagement programming, and half dissipates elsewhere in the university. External grants can prolong the university's dependency and create structural reluctance to make internal budgetary commitments to sustain programs. Some programs could wait forever, and thus die unless other incentives for sustenance have taken hold.

External funders drive agendas and discourse. If funders issue Requests for Proposals (RFPs, in the lingo of grant writing) for service learning, then engagement programs will respond with that language, however incompatible with the institutional contexts and incentive systems. If funders insist on rigid, blueprinted approaches to community development, then grant writers will comply, even after community dynamics have changed a year or more later when the funding arrives. Worse yet, failed grant attempts result in dashed expectations and hopes, or cynicism and suspicions.

One way engagement programs might calculate their worth in the historically specific entrepreneurial university is to calculate ratios of internal investments to costs generated. In universities that release a faculty member from a course, the internal investment can be calculated in two ways: the cost of a part-time replacement instructor, as little as $2,000 per semester, or a portion of the salary and fringe benefit package. At the Border University, for the first 6 years of existence, for every $1 invested, the university gained 20 to a hundredfold. Yet in a university that aspires to a $100 million external funding rate annually (but achieves less), engagement programming would generate less than 1% of overall external funding. Most large grants go to engineering and science, where expensive machinery and equipment rack up costs. Engagement programming will never approach funding levels like those.

There are other gains and costs to engagement programming. The university earns good will from its responsiveness to community concerns. In the border city, the media focus on controversy and crime instead, so civic engagement rarely becomes public news. Occasionally, civic engagement programming entails costs, including political costs and controversy. These costs are the true tests of engagement viability and sustainability in higher education bureaucracy, and of its democratic potentials. However, these costs are not without some agony, discomfort, and anxiety for engagement leaders.

COSTS AND BENEFITS:
THE STIRRING AND ENHANCEMENT OF DEMOCRACY?

As a semimature civic engagement program, aiming for a comprehensive university approach, the Border University's diverse faculty, students, and engagement leadership facilitate many types of behaviors and consequences associated with democratic "citizenship." In a country obsessed with counting and outcome measure, over 5 years, the engagement program tallied the involvement of over 8,000 students and more than 300,000 hours invested in the region. And those hours are just from affiliated civic engagement programs, not the sum total of all Border University outreach.

By and large, these service-learning, advocacy, civic education, and leadership experiences have produced noncontroversial, nonpolitically charged consequences with which few would disagree: tutoring; voter registration; Web site development, grant searches/drafts, and accounting strategies with and for REAL organizations, not hypothetical cases in a $100 textbook from and on mainstream U.S. society. The region is thus a better place for civic education programming, in both general and incremental terms. However, the region has serious economic and environmental marginality issues caused by forces far stronger than civic engagement programming can fully address.

Engaged students acquire insights and skills based on active learning experiences. Thus, civic engagement programs tap many types of learners, and not merely the reading/listening (more passive?) learners who respond to faculty-centered lectures. Many students will join, or are already part of, the region's community leadership. Yet some students will exit the region to abjure its low wages, high unemployment rates, and limited opportunities.

However much optimism the above analysis conveys, civic engagement programming also poses political controversy and risks, even in service learning and certainly in advocacy and leadership for social justice. For example, some community residents do not seek higher naturalization rates for immigrants involved in citizenship class tutoring, despite their own heritages of immigration. Neither do some community members relish a more active, voting citizenry. When activists call attention to violence against women on both sides of the border, some feel that the negative publicity hurts business. And struggles inside the university, among its plural and occasionally competing units, are a constant source of concern for leaders. Several case vignettes illustrate these issues.

Vignette: Interfaith Organizing

The Border University's initial grant from the philanthropic foundation sought the goal to foster long-term multi-semester, interdisciplinary collaboration with NGOs and schools. One of the region's largest NGOs uses the faith-based, congregation-coalition based organizing model for changing power relations and enabling formerly voiceless and marginalized to derive policy and program benefits. The Institute partnered with the NGO, involving multiple faculty members who connected with particular schools in which NGO parents were "engaged," not simply "involved" as volunteers, in campus and district policymaking, to open up pathways to college for their children. The university president was frequently involved in meetings and public assemblies, part of the organizing strategy of the NGO.

The NGO itself, with more than 2 decades of history in the region, had organizational structure and strategy issues that made collaboration difficult and risky. Its goals were worthy, but its strategies and tactics produced occasional tension with school district administrators who also partner with the university on other worthy goals. Some faculty might perceive their use as an NGO organizational tool, despite positive outcomes for engaged student learning and parental involvement. In good courses, this issue was itself part of the discussion agenda.

Interfaith organizing strategy moved away from parental engagement, but university collaborators were merely in alignment rather than leaders in this decision-making process. However, university collaboration continued with the particular schools along with others, for universities cannot and should not form permanent or exclusive alliances. Although the NGO changed, the collaboration allowed university faculty and students to learn a great deal about the potential of campus climates to become friendly and open to parental voice and engagement in "pathways to college" initiatives. The standardized testing regimes in K–12 education, begun in Texas and then spread to the United States under the No Child Left Behind Act, crowded out space for parental organizing given the structural obsessions to prepare students successfully for standardized tests.

Vignette: Internal Struggles

In an entrepreneurial university, units carve out niches for writing grant proposals and supplying revenue-generating technical assistance (TA). Unlike many TA units, civic engagement involves pro bono work, seasonally based and thus somewhat time-consuming, yet generally work of quality that earns trust and good will from community partners. Some partners, when they control resources, seek to work with trusted university units for technical assistance they need. When this occurs, competition arises among units that generate revenue for their bureaucratic livelihood in an entrepreneurial institution.

One might ask a general question of whether and what sort of technical assistance can and should come from public university bureaucracies, saddled with rules and regulations that delay quick response to entrepreneurial opportunities. Universities are perceived as "honest brokers" with good credentials and accounting practices. Yet, as noted earlier, they are not the monolithic institutions that residents often perceive them to be.

Civic engagement was temporarily involved in technical assistance for NGO capacity building, after some tension with a TA unit that sought to control this niche. Ultimately, the Center decided to co-birth a community-controlled nonprofit resource center absent in this border city, an absence unlike other major cities around the country. The president was consulted and cleared this activity. From short-term perspectives, this move toward community control meant less revenue for the university, yet it has the long-term consequences for civic health and power sharing with NGOs.

Free Speech Vignette: Controversy Tests Democratic Political Will

The Center maintains LISTSERVS for students, faculty, and community members with information about public events, job and volunteer/service opportunities. Opportunities and events that are noncontroversial are rarely challenged. But controversial events, films, speakers, and issues are potentially upsetting to the status quo.

The Center was involved in two free-speech events that polarized people. In one, the public showing of movies were announced on the LISTSERV that had titles critical of current politics. A complaint was made to the monopoly city newspaper which pressed for an "investigation." Yet that same newspaper gave a quarter-page of attention to the very same films (an example of the nonmonolithic character of newspaper businesses!). The Center had never gotten coverage for its many activities in service and engagement, even events with photo and good will opportunities. It would not print an OpEd (opinion editorial) response from the engagement leader. Ironically, the newspaper seemed aligned with forces against free speech.

In the subsequent semester, a student organization organized a public protest on the campus. Higher education institutions grapple with the spaces and places for "free speech" and the rules and regulations for their use. The Border University had changed its policy, from free-speech zones to general free speech. However, the policy required forms to complete on equipment, outside speakers, and other matters.

Several student organizations concerned about environmental pollution organized an event, but checked the wrong box on the form. The students also walked to the administration building and a complaint was made that they blocked the doorway, after which they dispersed. Students filmed the event and its public, civil dialogue. They were cited for noncompliance, and a formal investigation ensued.

A large, critical mass of faculty members expressed concern about free speech and assembly procedures on campus. The Center's faculty director was involved in the process. They wrote a letter to the administration, asking for the faculty senate to review free speech procedures and for the investigation to cease. The administration agreed to support the faculty senate committee and to drop the existing investigation in order that public testimony be taken for the faculty senate review.

CONCLUDING REFLECTIONS

Civic engagement programming has developed momentum at universities throughout the United States. This is a progressive trend in higher education, moving away from instructor-centered approaches to those that offer multiple learning opportunities for diverse students with multiple learning styles. The approach, beginning to be institutionalized at sizeable numbers of U.S. universities, contains the promise to address the historic balance of individualism and community and to renew the idea and practice that higher education ought to respond to the communities in which it is situation.

Civic engagement programming offers the promise of democratic citizenship education, but in the growing pains to achieve this promise, strategic decisions are made about the type of civic engagement programs to offer, the language of such offerings, and the entrepreneurial challenges of raising money from inside and outside the university in order to obtain staff for these labor-intensive efforts and the incentives that would motivate increasing numbers of faculty members to change their classes so that students can choose among civic engagement options. The bureaucracy and funding structure of U.S. higher educational institutions are infertile grounds in which such innovative approaches can grow.

Nevertheless, this analysis shows that democratic education is compatible with higher education bureaucracy. That compatibility has associated risks that university presidents and civic engagement leaders must be prepared to face—risks that are acute in polarized and flawed democratic contexts and communities. The language of "service-learning" is one way to deal with such risks, especially with administrators, but not necessarily with faculty members. Service language, however, should not displace other types of and approaches to civic engagement, including leadership, advocacy, and social justice. Students should have the options to choose among orientations.

The three vignettes offer tentative support for the democracy education potentials of civic engagement programming at the Border University. The vignettes illustrate controversy amid what is good, solid, and innovative student-centered pedagogy. Most civic engagement programming is non-controversial: it engages students with NGOs and nonprofit organizations through service, research, and leadership that have consequences for deeper learning, whether critical thinking or professional training. It generates external funding, with all the dilemmas associated with such labor. Yet occasionally political tensions emerge. These tensions offer tests of university commitment to comprehensive engagement that prepares students for public work and democracy, however messy that process in "limited" democracies like the border region.

REFERENCES

Aronowitz, S. (Ed.). (2000). *The knowledge factory: Dismantling the corporate university and creating true higher learning.* Boston: Beacon.

Astin, A. W., & Astin, H. S. (2000). *Leadership reconsidered: Engaging higher education in social change.* Battle Creek, MI: W. K. Kellogg Foundation.

Bauer, D. M. (2002). Academic Housework: Women's Studies and Second Shifting. In R. Wiegman (Ed.), *Women's studies on its own: A next wave reader in institutional change* (pp. 245–58). Durham, NC: Duke University Press.

74 K. STAUDT

Bellah, R. N., Madsen, R., Sullivan, W. M., Swidler, A., & Tipton, S. M. (1985). *Habits of the heart: Individualism and commitment in American life*. New York: Harper & Row.

Bringle, R. G., Games, R., & Malloy, E. A. (Eds.). (1999). *Colleges and Universities as Citizens*. Needham Heights, MA: Allyn & Bacon

Boyer, E. (1996). The scholarship of engagement. *Journal of Public Service and Outreach 1*(1), 11–20.

Boyer, E. (1990). *Scholarship reconsidered: Priorities of the professoriate*. Princeton, NJ: Carnegie Foundation for the Advancement of Teaching.

Boyte, H., & Karr, N. (2000). Renewing the democratic spirit in American colleges and universities: Higher education as public work. In T. Ehrlich (Ed.), *Civic responsibility and higher education* (pp. 37–61). Phoenix, AZ: Oryx Press.

Campus Compact. (2003). Retrieved January 4, 2004, from www.compact.org

Carnegie Corporation of New York and CIRCLE. (2003). *The civic mission of schools*. New York: Author.

Cohen, M. D., & March, J. G. (1974). *Leadership and ambiguity: The American college president*. New York: McGraw-Hill.

Dewey, J. (1938). *Experience and education*. New York: Macmillan.

Eckel, P. D., & Kezar, A. (2003). *Taking the reins: Institutional transformation in higher education*. New York: American Council on Education/Praeger.

Hart, S. (2001). *Cultural dilemmas of progressive politics: Styles of grassroots activists*. Chicago: University of Chicago Press.

Kimball, R. (1990). *Tenured radicals: How politics has corrupted our higher education*. New York: HarperCollins.

Lappe, F. M., & Martin Du Bois, P. (1994). *The quickening of America: Rebuilding our nation, remaking our lives*. San Francisco: Jossey-Bass.

Leslie, D., & Fretwell, E. K., Jr. (1996). *Wise moves in hard times: Creating and maintaining resilient colleges and universities*. San Francisco: Jossey-Bass.

Lynton, E., & Elman, S. (1987). *New priorities for the university: Meeting society's needs for applied knowledge and competent individuals*. San Francisco: Jossey-Bass.

Putnam, R. (2000). *Bowling alone: The collapse and revival of American community*. New York: Simon & Schuster.

Rhodes, R. A., & Howard, J. P. K. (Eds.). (1998). *Academic service learning: A pedagogy of action and reflection*. San Francisco: Jossey-Bass.

Slaughter, S., & Leslie, L. L. (1997). *Academic capitalism: Politics, policies, and the entrepreneurial university*. Baltimore, MD: Johns Hopkins University Press.

Staudt, K., & Coronado, I. (2002). *Fronteras no Más: Toward social justice at the U.S.-Mexico Border*. New York: Palgrave.

U.S. Department of Education. (n.d.). *National Center of Educational Statistics*. Retrieved January 4, 2004, from www.nces.ed.gov

Wilson, J. Q. (1989). *Bureaucracy: What government agencies do and why they do it*. New York: Basic.

Zimpher, N., L. Percy, S. L., & Brukardt, M. J. (2002). *A time for boldness: A story of institutional change*. Bolton, MA: Anker.

CHAPTER 4

DISCOURSE VERSUS PRACTICE IN CIVIC EDUCATION FOR DEVELOPMENT

The Case of USAID Assistance to Palestine

Ayman M. Alsayed

INTRODUCTION

Civic education is an increasingly important part of donor programs of
assistance to developing countries. Programs of civic education are
intended to promote democratization, which donors believe is essential for
strong development in these countries. Goals of these programs include
encouraging participation in formal political processes such as elections
and referenda, developing democratic participatory norms in institutions
of civil society, and reinforcing the internalization of these norms across
communities. Donor agencies argue that these processes will, by raising
awareness and promoting citizen action, reduce corruption and encourage
transparency and accountability. As components of so-called "good
governance," these changes are deemed essential to development.

*Advancing Democracy Through Education? U.S. Influence Abroad and
Domestic Practices*, pp. 75–96
Copyright © 2008 by Information Age Publishing

This discourse of democratization and development is very attractive and presents donors as supporters of the interests of the countries in which they are promoting change, indeed often as saviors of citizens who have lived for years under corrupt or authoritarian governments. However, the good governance discourse is an essential part of a development agenda which is neither always entirely positive nor disinterested. Actually, it reflects the softer side of the neoliberal approach to global economic development,[1] and is closely tied to the goals that the donor countries have for themselves, rather than to the priorities of the recipient nations. The kinds of democracy supported, the choice of organizations for development, the content and focus of civic education programming, and the conditions placed on its implementation all shape the political-economic systems that are developed in recipient countries. Such outcomes, not surprisingly, reflect the interests primarily of the donors and their partners in recipient-nation elites.

Ultimately, these programs are often not particularly democratic themselves. They dictate rather than empower participation; they support stability and small changes rather than thorough reform in corrupt or authoritarian but friendly governments; and they may actually encourage government oppression of some groups and individuals, as I discuss below. They promote a global order that requires sameness across societies, and their most appealing principles are often largely superficial. Indeed, their vision of "development" is narrow, economically-focused, and self-interested—rather than bettering life for all, it broadens the gap between the powerful and the powerless within countries and around the world.

In contrast, I argue that development, rather than focusing on increasing macroeconomic prosperity, must increase human well-being more generally. As Goulet (1996) puts it, "[s]ocieties are more human or more developed, not when men and women '*have* more' but when they are enabled 'to *be* more' " (p. 17). Indeed, development's "ultimate goals are those of existence itself: to provide all humans with the opportunity to live full human lives. Thus understood, development is the ascent of all persons and societies in their total humanity" (p. 9).

From this perspective, social justice must be a priority, at both the national and the international levels. Democratization and civic education can thus be an important part of development efforts if they increase people's self-determination, their ability to "influence their future, both individually and collectively" (Thomas-Slater, 2003, p. 13). As Lebret (1959) notes, "[t]he problem of the distribution of goods is secondary compared to the problems of preparing men [sic] to receive them" (as cited in Goulet, 1996, p. 9). However, for civic education to fulfill these purposes, programs must be designed and conducted in ways that "harmonize with the society's spiritual and cultural values, with the exigencies of solidarity with others, with the demands of wise resource use, and with the aspiration of all individuals and groups to be treated by others as beings of worth independent of their utility to those others" (p. 9).

The Palestinian case is a particularly complex example of the politics of donor involvement in democracy and governance,[2] and clearly reflects the critiques of civic education and democratization for development that I have noted above. Aid that supports civic education in Palestine[3] is high on the agenda of many donors. This aid is promoted as a support for peace and stability and the basis for a strong democracy in the future Palestinian state. While donors speak of empowering the Palestinian people and supporting the growth of their democratic institutions, however, they also—to varying extents—impose conditions and agendas on those institutions that in fact are not democratic and not in Palestinian interests for the long term.

This chapter explores the extent to which USAID, through its Tamkeen civil society development program, actually promotes democratic development in Palestine. First, I provide a framework for understanding donor approaches to democratization through civic education, and some basic background on civil society development in Palestine. I then examine Tamkeen's implementation, paying particular attention to the nature of the civic education programming supported, the participants in and audiences for civic education, and the ways in which it supports or limits Palestinian democracy. I focus in particular on the requirement that Palestinian organizations receiving USAID funding certify that they have not and will not support terrorists or terrorist organizations, and explore how this requirement has affected the program and by extension Palestinian civil society. I ask in whose interests this program, and donor-supported civic education in general, really work, and make some suggestions about ways to encourage more genuine donor support for democracy and development, regardless of their own interests.

This chapter draws primarily on documentary sources, including primary source material from USAID and the Tamkeen program office; external evaluations of that effort; and a range of literature on similar activities and civic education theories internationally. It also reflects my own experience and observations as a Palestinian, an educator, and a scholar working in donor-supported initiatives and interacting with donor representatives. This piece reflects my deep personal engagement with these issues, and my commitment to the development of dynamic and relevant democracy both in Palestine and internationally.

DEMOCRACY, GOVERNANCE, AND CIVIC EDUCATION— LINKS AND CONTRADICTIONS

Since the 1990s, donors have provided increasing support to developing and newly democratic countries to implement programs of civic education. This investment is justified as support for democratization, which is believed to be key to development. From donors' perspectives, democracy is essential for developing countries to make better use of their public resources and to achieve their development goals. Even the World Bank, which historically has claimed that it does not interfere with politics, now favors democracy. As Sen (1999) describes the bank's new vision of development, "A country does not have to be judged to be fit for democracy, rather it has to become fit through democracy" (p. 8)USAID's Democracy Specialist Jerry O'Brien (2004) represents the general donor position when arguing that "liberal democracy ... is the fundamental building block of good governance, which, in turn, fosters and sustains broad-based development" (pp. 4–5).

Indeed, governance has become a core issue for many donors. Defined as "the way in which power is exercised in the management of a country's economic and social resources for the public good" (O'Brien, 2004, p. 2), or as "the traditions and institutions by which authority in a country is exercised for the common good" (World Bank, 2004), good governance has four elements: public policy and decision making; transparency and information sharing; enhanced state performance; and improved social justice, rights, and the rule of law (Institute for Development Studies, 1999, p. 8). Poor governance, on the other hand, is characterized by corruption and mismanagement—which drain a country's resources and present a significant barrier to development—and by a lack of information exchange with citizens, which prohibits public participation in and oversight of development.

Donors often describe the civic education programs they fund as intended to address issues of governance by promoting democracy. However, this understanding of how democracy, civic education and governance are linked is simplistic. Not all democracies demonstrate good governance, and not all countries with good governance are democratic. For example, Indonesia has some elements of democracy, but suffers from bad governance, which is reflected in very high levels of corruption. In Singapore, by contrast, the government restricts freedom of speech and association, but is greatly respected for its otherwise good governance and low levels of corruption (O'Brien, 2004). Clearly the relationship between governance and democracy is more complicated than is often presented. Donors interested in civic education programming need to be aware of the nature of the relationship between governance and democracy in the countries they are supporting, and develop programs that support strengths in each area.

In addition, the nature of the "democracy" that donors are hoping to support is unclear. While emerging theory in civic education (Boggs, 1992; Galston, 2003; Mabe, 1993; Patrick, 2002; Tyack, 1997) generally supports a notion of democracy that is broadly participatory and highly engaged, donors often support forms of democratization that are more representative and superficial, focusing more on the mechanics of political choice than on fundamental change in political systems. Indeed, much of donors' support for civic education concentrates on educating people around issues related to the national or to the formal systems of governance, such as elections, judiciaries, legislatures, and political parties, which are often artificially viewed as culturally-neutral and transportable (see Stevick & Levinson, in this volume). These activities promote what Golub (2000) refers to as "big D" democracy, where the process becomes more important than the product. Golub argues that this form of democratization is largely ineffective, and that "small d" democracy (which relates to local-level problem-solving around issues of daily concern to the disadvantaged) is more important because it achieves a concrete product, reaches a broader base, and provides people with experience and confidence that they can use to try to effect change at higher levels. Such an approach is also more likely to take advantage of cultural specifics that are conducive to the development of relevant, contextualized democracy.

In fact, donor efforts seem to be concentrated in what Patrick (1997) refers to as the civic knowledge domain of civic education, which closely parallels Golub's "big D." Civic knowledge covers basic political concepts (e.g., rule of law; limited, representative government; individual rights; popular sovereignty; political participation and civil society) and an understanding of their institutionalization. Patrick, however, also identifies two other core civic education domains, which he refers to as civic skills and civic virtues. Civic skills are tools of reflection, analysis and action related to public issues. Civic virtues are what he calls "traits necessary to preserve and improve democracy." These include self-discipline, civility, compassion, tolerance, and respect for the worth and dignity of all individuals (p. 3). Civic skills in many donor programs are more technical than they are analytical, and civic values are discussed more than they are practiced.

As donors' primary clients are state governments, radical change that might undermine those governments is not in their interests. Therefore, the typical choice to focus on the technical side democracy is not surprising. However, such a focus limits the range and spirit of civic education, and reduces its potential effect.

Donor support for civic education takes two primary forms: school-based programming and non-school programs for adults provided by institutions of civil society. USAID's Tamkeen project supports adult civic education through its focus on nongovernmental agencies (NGOs), so I will therefore restrict this general discussion of civic education's nature, goals, and outcomes to that realm.

Ideally, "the purpose [of adult civic education programs] is to both develop understanding and judgment about public issues and to contribute to guided and informed decisions and actions through deliberation, public talk, and dialogue" (Boggs, 1991, p. 5). However, these programs appear to suffer from some basic problems with the assumptions about democracy that underlie them, as well as being strongly influenced by internal political tension between governments and civil society.

To deliver nonschool programs of civic education, donors often choose civil society organizations that do not challenge the government. Yet such organizations are frequently poorly rooted in local social structures, and lack a broad public base for their activities. As McGowan (1997) mentions, foreign donors have always funded Western-style organizations that are elite-oriented and urban-biased—organizations that do not really represent the majority of the citizens in a particular country. In order to tap into donor money, leaders of these organizations are often willing to shape their priorities to match donor needs or conditions, regardless of the actual needs of their society. As Ottaway (2001) puts it, they are "more interested in speaking to donors than in speaking for, and to, their societies" (p. 2). Using these organizations to deliver programs of civic education limits the reach of the programs, and reduces the extent to which they address long-term, substantial change.

When donors do support organizations that are not sympathetic to the current government, different problems result. Research indicates that when "the civil society groups who conduct civic education are antagonistic towards incumbents and existing political institutions, civic education produces greater levels of mistrust" in participants than before they entered the programs (Finkel, 2003, p. 13). This mistrust is not helpful in getting people to participate in democratization. It is also more likely that governments will respond to these activities by reducing rather than increasing rights and freedoms of expression, which is the opposite of civic education's desired effect on governance.

In addition, "many of the civil society organizations that are supported by donors in the name of democracy are themselves not internally democratic" (Sabatini, 2001, p. 5). Indeed, these institutions remain largely authoritarian, even when speaking about democratization. This is problematic when delivering civic education, because actions speak louder than words. Organizations which are teaching democracy but are not themselves democratic are unable to build the trust of citizens in those organizations or in a democratic system.

It is also not clear that out-of-school civic education programs contribute significantly to democratization. For example, we may be able to assess how much people acquire civic knowledge, but it is more difficult to tell with the same reliability which values they have internalized. Since values are the core of democracy, this gap is a matter of concern. Indeed, "[t]he success of democracy depends ultimately on the emergence, sustaining and strengthening of values that make responsible democratic practice effective and consequential" (Sen, 1999, p. 9). If these values are not being strengthened, the impact of civic education efforts, limited as they are, is further reduced.

Finally, research seems to show that civic education's influence on people is positively correlated with such factors as levels of formal education, previous participatory orientation or membership in civic society organizations, and age (Finkel, 2003). In other words, civic education tends to reach and affect people who already have access to political resources, not the poor and marginalized. This impact pattern means that "the result of civic education is to reinforce existing levels of political stratification" (p. 15) rather than to expand freedom and participation.

These concerns about the nature and effects of civic education programs are particularly pertinent in the case of Palestine. In a context where civic education, as a means of building a strong and democratic civil society and supporting popular empowerment, has the potential to significantly contribute to national development, there is also a strong tendency for programs to be designed and operated more in the interests of donors and other external parties than in the interests of Palestinians. In the remainder of this paper, I examine the context for donor-supported civic education efforts in Palestine, present the case of USAID (the bilateral donor currently providing the highest level of funding to Palestine) as an illustration of the tensions around issues of justice and development, and suggest some ways to relieve these tensions.

CIVIL SOCIETY AND DEMOCRACY BUILDING IN PALESTINE

The development of civil society in Palestine is a major focus of donor aid in the area of democracy and governance, and is considered to be an essential component of Palestinian development. Here, as in other contexts, donors argue that civil organizations provide an important counterbalance to government power, and offer an opportunity for citizens, particularly the disempowered, to mobilize and participate in decision making, thus increasing both the capacity for and the performance of democracy (a foundational condition for development). Civic education is seen as a key contributor to and component of civil society development.

Before addressing specific programs of civil society support in Palestine, however, it is important to understand what the civil sector looks like in that context, how it has developed over time, and how that history may affect donor success in programming for civic education through civil society. The Institute for Development Studies (1999) defines civil society as "an intermediate realm situated between state and household, populated by organized groups or associations which are separate from the state, enjoy some autonomy in relations with the state, and are formed voluntarily by" members of society to protect or extend their interests, values, or identities (p. 4). Brouwer (2000) contrasts civil society in the Arab world with that in the West, noting that although there are similarities between Western and Arab civil societies (including volunteerism, significant religious influence, and ideological bases, as well as sometimes strong political uses for associations), and although modern professional NGOs are increasing in Arab states, there are also important differences. For example, some kinds of organizations that are thought of as civil society in the West (like trade unions or cooperatives) are often established or directly controlled by governments in the Arab world. Arab civil society legislation also typically restricts organizations' autonomy much more than in the West, and limits the space in which they can operate.

Palestinian civil society is a mix of these Western and more Arab features. Palestinian organizations are extremely political, highly ideological, and often religious in origin. The sector, including modern professional NGOs, has steadily increased in size since the 1970s, with estimates as high as 1,500 organizations in 1996 (Sullivan, 1996). However, Palestinian organizations are more separate from the state than those in other Arab countries, because until 1994 there was no indigenous Palestinian government to organize or oversee them. In fact, Palestinian organizations for many years have provided the services that a state would have provided, as well as grassroots political action and human rights advocacy under Israeli occupation. As a result, they have real power in the society (Christina, 2004; Hammami, 2000). Indeed, Palestinian organizations and their donor supporters were successful in preventing the Palestinian National Authority (PNA), when it was established, from modeling its new NGO law on Egypt's extremely restrictive Law 32 of 1964 (Himal, 1999), with the result that the Palestinian Nongovernmental Organizations Network (PNGO) law established the most liberal framework in the Arab world (PNGO, 1996 and 1999).[4]

Civil society in Palestine is thus very sensitive to the political situation, and its health depends on pressure from both outside and inside, from the government, from donors, and from the ongoing conflict with Israel.

The establishment of the PNA in 1994 had a particularly significant influence on the nature of the civil society and of the activities in which civil society organizations engage. Government ministries took over many NGO or civil society services, and there was a sense of "demobilization" (Brouwer, 2000, pp. 30–32) in the service sector of civil society now that the government was in place.

At the same time, NGOs took on the role of government critics. They resisted restrictive legislation, pointed out and mobilized against government corruption, and pushed for democracy building at the community level. At times this has led to conflict that has been so hot it was described as "war" between the government and the civil society (Himal, 1999, p. 1). Donors have played an ambiguous role in this conflict, at times supporting NGOs, but at other times remaining silent on important issues of democracy and governance.

Interestingly, although developing the civil sector has been a stated donor priority, funding for Palestinian civil society has actually declined since 1990. First, donors reduced funding because of Palestinian support for Iraq in the first Gulf War. Then, after 1994, funding was redirected to the PNA and away from NGOs and civil society organizations, in an effort to strengthen the new government. The $140–220 million that Palestinian civil society received in 1990 was reduced to $60 million in 1996[5] (Brouwer, 2000, p. 31).

Finally, much of the Western funding that went to the civil sector after 1994 has been limited to those organizations that publicly supported the 1993 and 1994 "Oslo Agreements" between the PLO (Palestine Liberation Organization) and the government of Israel, as well as the "peace process" built around these agreements. These requirements have become even more restrictive since September 11, 2001. As many of the social service providers in Palestinian civil society have been affiliated with groups that do not support the Oslo agreement (both Islamist groups and leftists), this has meant that their funding has dramatically decreased. Others have been closed by the government altogether in its efforts to reduce political opposition, under the justification of donor pressure (Brynen, 2000).

These changes have limited the health of the Palestinian civil society, but not completely disabled it. The sector has become narrower in its participants, but those participants still challenge the government and have some effects on change. What their shape and contribution will be in the future is currently under negotiation, both within the sector and in tension with the government. The strongest groups, as Brouwer (2000) notes, are currently the service providers, many of which are Islamic in nature, and the professional advocacy organizations (pp. 31–32).

DONORS AND DEVELOPMENT CONTRADICTIONS IN PALESTINE

There are two types of donors that have supported Palestinian civil society organizations and their civic education efforts. Arab donors, especially some wealthy Gulf countries and private individuals from those states, have supported service delivery, particularly in health, education, and social welfare and relief. They have for the most part stayed out of politics. Western donors, on the other hand, have supported service delivery, but have also supported advocacy. After 1994, the Western donors shifted their approach to focus on this advocacy work, hoping to leave service delivery mostly to the government. Their efforts, as they describe them, promote democratization, the rule of law, elections, good governance, transparency and accountability, human rights, and the development of a strong and sustainable civil sector (see, for example, European Council, 2003; Friederich-Ebert-Stiftung, 2003; Sida, 2001; Youngs, 2004). It is within this realm that civic education support is particularly strong.

However, as Brouwer (2000) points out, the donor definition of a strong civil society may not be the same as that of the Palestinians, and donor goals are not really as broad as they claim. In Palestine, real donor priorities are: "safeguarding Israel, providing a solution acceptable to most Palestinians, and promoting economic reform, in that order, while democratization is lower on the list" (p. 44). To be sure, a wide variety of civil society organizations may in fact prevent the achievement of these donor goals. So, too, might rapid or extreme democratization, because opposition voices would have more power in such cases. In fact, as Brouwer notes, it is in donor interests (as well as the interests of the Palestinian government) to restrict civil society, particularly to exclude the Islamists and the leftists, who provide the strongest challenge to the government and have extremely strong grassroots connections built through years of service provision.

Unfortunately, donors often actually support the authoritarian government in Palestine. As Brouwer (2000) notes, "[t]he governments of Israel, the United States, and some other Western countries encourage[d] [former] Palestinian Authority Chairman Yasir Arafat to take a tough stance against those who resort to violence in their opposition…. As a result, major violations of human rights and undemocratic rule are tolerated in Palestine" (p. 28). These undemocratic activities included the closure of many organizations providing services in health, education and other sectors, and the arrest and harassment of civil society leaders too critical of the government.

Ultimately, Western donors have a "narrow interpretation of democracy promotion" (Brouwer, 2000, p. 44), and a view of the Israeli-Palestinian conflict that is more favorable to Israel than to Palestine. Their agenda for development, based on stability and a particular kind of economic growth, sometimes conflicts with the needs and desires of the Palestinian people, and privileges elites over the general population. As I discuss below, their definition of terrorism penalizes Palestinian organizations, and limits the extent to which real democratic development can occur.

USAID AND CIVIC EDUCATION IN PALESTINE

Perhaps the most problematic of donors, in all of the respects discussed above, is the USAID. As part of its democracy and governance programming, the agency supports civic education through organizations "whose work is fundamental to building a modern democracy that can support a market economy." USAID's support includes "technical assistance, capacity building, and grants to CSOs [civil society organizations] whose aims support the same goals." As USAID notes, these organizations provide civic education both directly and indirectly: "[s]ome of the CSOs incorporate promotion of democratic values into their work. Others focus almost exclusively on democratic activities, e.g., helping communities stay informed about government policy, or making or changing policies that affect them" (USAID, 2004b, p. 1).

USAID's budget for democracy and governance activities in Palestine has grown significantly over the past decade, from $16 million overall ($5 million of which was earmarked for civil society activities) from 1996–98 (Brouwer, 2000, p. 33) to an overall budget for 2003 alone of nearly $19 million (USAID, 2004a). Clearly, USAID is making a significant effort to influence the development of the Palestinian civil sector. However, it is also among the most controlling of civil society development efforts, particularly through its processes of inclusion and exclusion of organizations in its projects.

The agency's major current effort to support civil society and educate about democracy is a program called "Tamkeen" (Arabic for "empowerment"), which is a 5-year effort (2000–2005) "aimed at preserving the 'political space' occupied by Palestinian civil society organizations and promoting their crucial role in public discourse" (Tamkeen, 2004a, p. 1). According to USAID, Tamkeen "helps civil society organizations survive, grow, and educate vast numbers of Palestinians—particularly marginalized groups like children, youths, women and the poor—on the election process, the rule of law, and other aspects of democratic political systems" (p. 2). The project is designed to promote "peace and prosperity" through a "flourishing" civil society (p. 2).

Tamkeen had a 5-year budget of $33 million, of which $30 million had been spent by March 2004 (Tamkeen, 2004g). The program was managed by three international firms and one Palestinian partner. Chemonics International, AMIDEAST, and CARE International were the international partners, and Massar Associates, a Palestinian consulting firm, was the local partner. It is unclear what percentage of the budget mentioned above for democracy activities actually made it into the field, however, and how much paid for the salaries and administrative costs of the foreigners involved with the project (only $16 million in grants were funded over the period 2000–2004 [Tamkeen, 2004g]). As Brouwer (2000) notes, "[i]t should be kept in mind that large amounts of money are never spent in the recipient country but are usually paid to expatriate consultants. In addition, a large portion of U.S. assistance is spent for administrative overhead" (p. 33). USAID policies that require the use of American contractors and services for overseas projects raise these costs even higher.

In contrast to the 1996–98 period, in which half the USAID civil society budget was spent on one program, the Civic Forum (Brouwer, 2000, p. 33), 93 organizations have received grants since 2000 (Tamkeen, 2004g). These include large and small organizations in both the West Bank and Gaza, service providers, and specialized organizations that provide democratic training and civic education. Several of these organizations have also partnered with international or American organizations, like the NDI (National Democratic Institute) or the IRI (International Republican Institute), to conduct civic education and democratization activities.

Tamkeen (2005) grants took two forms. Simplified grants provided up to $150,000 for projects lasting up to 18 months, while fixed obligation grants provided up to $25,000 for smaller, clearly defined projects or to support organizations through the provision of computers and/or information technology. One hundred and seventy-seven simplified grants and 170 fixed obligation grants were awarded over the 5-year project span, many of which were repeat grants to successful organizations (Tamkeen, 2005).

Tamkeen also provided a range of capacity building services to the NGO sector. These included specialized training in media relations, NGO management, accountability, and financial transparency to groups of NGO staff, with a particular focus on governance and monitoring. Tamkeen also provided training to journalists on how to report on civil society activities and issues, and to advocates on how to lobby for their particular issues of concern. Organizations getting funding through the initiative were also able to obtain one on one support in proposal writing to assist them with their submissions.

Tamkeen also developed a specialized needs assessment tool for PNGOs, and encouraged organizations to use it to examine their operations. This tool, known as PONAT, assisted organizations in examining their services, budgeting, external relations, human resources, and administration. In 2005, Tamkeen planned to implement special capacity building efforts focused on particular organizations, as identified by this needs assessment.

Organizations funded by Tamkeen engaged in a variety of civic education activities. Many provided democratic training as part of service delivery. Al-Lod Charitable Society, the Maghazi Community Rehabilitation Society, and Atfaluna Center for the Deaf are examples of small organizations that work with marginalized groups in areas of immediate need that also provide opportunities for related training in democracy and rights issues (Dajani, 2003; Tamkeen, 2004f). These efforts are indirect, building an awareness of needs and rights, and encouraging people to act to achieve them. As one staff member at the Jabalya Rehabilitation Center put it, "When I help children to improve themselves and allow them to communicate their needs to their families or teachers, isn't this democracy?" (Tamkeen, 2005). Another disability service provider noted that "You cannot just tell people that they have rights to do such and such; they have to see it through service delivery, which is more effective" (Eid-Alldredge, 2003). These examples of people learning to behave democratically and to participate are examples of Golub's (2000) "small d" democracy building.

Other grantees provide more direct training in democratic processes (Golub's "big D" democracy building). In these cases, the focus is directly on building civic participation and action. The Civic Forum and the Arab Thought Forum focus on providing opportunities like community meetings, seminars, training sessions, and outreach to help people learn to behave more democratically. Other organizations like Ashtar Theater Company use theater and arts to teach democratic values and raise issues of rights in Palestinian society (Dajani, 2003; Tamkeen, 2004f).

In 2005, Palestinian elections provided an additional important outlet for Tamkeen activities. Tamkeen provided consultation to NGOs on how to design voter education materials and campaigns (which were held in 70 of the 84 districts where local elections were to be held in the spring of 2005 [Tamkeen, 2005]), assisted four organizations in incorporating election training into their ongoing grants, and provided new grants to 27 organizations to facilitate direct voter education activities (Tamkeen, 2005, p. 14). The organization also recruited international advisors to help local organizations train Palestinians about elections and their rights and responsibilities. A particular focus of these efforts was on having women teach other women about voting rights and the goals and benefits of the elections. These activities were directly focused on democracy promotion and building an educated citizenry for civic action.

Tamkeen was evaluated in 2003, with a special focus on its service delivery programs that incorporate democracy and governance activities, as well as its services to people with disabilities (Dajani, 2003; Eid-

Alldredge, 2003). In general, the findings support Golub's 2000 argument that small d democracy building is the most effective, and that organization around issues of immediate concern can encourage people to participate in civic activities in a broader sense, as well. Dajani notes that these service delivery programs reach the grassroots and the marginalized in ways that the direct democracy and governance training programs, which tend to serve and focus on the more privileged and educated, do not. Service delivery programs also provide actual evidence of improvement in people's lives, which gives them more credibility. As Dajani (2003) puts it, "people ... do not want 'talk;' they are more receptive to democracy and governance activities when these are tied to tangible benefits" (p. iii). In particular, the programs appear to have had the most significant effect on youth, which is a Tamkeen focus and therefore a success.

Problems do exist, however. One important concern is the growing imbalance of Tamkeen support by region. In the West Bank, for example, Tulkarem, Tubas, Qalqilya, Salfit, Hebron, and Jericho had no disability service grantees (a significant subset of Tamkeen-supported programs) as of 2003 (Eid-Alldredge, 2003). Services were also much more likely to be concentrated in cities than in villages or refugee camps, raising questions about the extent to which the target marginalized groups have been reached. Political deterioration and a USAID decision to prohibit expatriate staff from traveling to Gaza in 2004–5 also raised costs and negatively effected Tamkeen's "ability to provide high-quality training to Gaza participants" particularly in key areas of elections training and impact assessment training (Tamkeen, 2005, p. 9).

The depth of Tamkeen's impact is also uncertain. As Brouwer (2000) notes, values and behavior-related outcomes are much harder to measure (and achieve) than numerical outputs, such as the number of persons trained (p. 41). Dajani (2003) found that, for Tamkeen, "there is increased knowledge about democracy and governance issues, as well as increased public participation on certain issues. However, apart from youth, Tamkeen-funded projects appear not to be highly effective in transmitting values or changing attitudes" (p. 39). Typically, people are happy to attend workshops where they get free lunches, certificates of participation, and some financial incentives, but they are less interested in applying or able to apply what they have learned to their own lives.

This problem has a number of causes, including project design issues and bureaucratic barriers. Tamkeen funding is limited both in amount and in duration,[6] and many funded programs are not sustainable (Eid-Alldredge, 2003), which raises serious questions about long-term impact. Funded organizations also complain about the reporting and monitoring requirements, which place heavy technical burdens on those with limited staffing and resources (Dajani, 2003, and Eid-Alldredge, 2003). Further, as

Eid-Alldredge notes, "[a]lthough Tamkeen requires that democracy and governance be incorporated into the delivery of services by grantees, there does not appear to be a requirement that the grantees themselves operate on democratic values" (p. 24). Where organizations are not practicing what they preach, credibility gaps undermine the lessons in democracy that they are supposedly providing. Most importantly, however, the ongoing crisis in Palestine "leaves [people] with little time or energy to engage with such values" (p. 40). Doing so is particularly challenging when USAID and its sponsor, the United States government, are not seen as implementing these democratic values themselves.

Under U.S. Executive Order (EO) 13224, organizations receiving grants from USAID through Tamkeen are required, as a condition of funding, to sign a document certifying that they have not and will not "provide material support or resources to any individual or entity that [they] know or [have] reason to know is an individual or entity that advocates, plans, sponsors, engages in or has engaged in terrorist activity" (USAID, 2002). This certificate is seen as oppressive, and signing it presents significant challenges for Palestinian organizations. Both in 2003 and again in 2004, the majority of Palestinian civil society organizations signed statements rejecting this certification as a condition of funding, thereby setting up confrontations with USAID at grant renewal time (PNGO 2003 and 2004).

Palestinians pointed out that the language in the certification is unclear and vague, to the extent that a significant majority of NGO activities could be labeled as terrorism. Indeed, the designation criteria under Executive Order 13224 include

- foreign individuals or entities that ... have committed, or pose a significant risk of committing, acts of terrorism that threaten the security of U.S. nationals or the national security, foreign policy, or economy of the U.S.
- assist in, sponsor, or provide financial, material, or technological support for, or financial or other services to or in support of, acts of terrorism or individuals or entities designated in or under the Order; or
- [are] otherwise associated with certain individuals or entities designated in or under the Order (Office of the Coordinator for Counter-Terrorism, n.d., p. 2).

The second and third of these points, in particular, can clearly be quite broadly construed.

Palestinian organizations provide services without regard to the political affiliation of their clients, but this certification would require them to do so.

Organizations also feared that the interpretation of this language could go as far as "preventing Palestinians who want to take part in international events to give presentations about the situation from a Palestinian perspective" (PNGO, 2004, p. 1). Indeed, as Eid-Alldredge notes, "most NGOs in Palestine are politicized; they have a strong advocacy component" (PNGO, 2003, p. 18). While advocacy and political activism should be core elements of democratic reform, they are threatened by broad interpretations of EO 13224. The core issue is the definition of terrorism, and of "attempts to portray the struggle of the Palestinian people for freedom and independence as 'violent and terrorist acts' " (PNGO, 2003, p. 1). As the joint NGO statement of 2003 notes, "the root problem in Palestine remains the continued illegal Israeli military occupation of Palestinian lands, not the work of Palestinian NGOs and their constituencies" (PNGO, 2003, p. 1).

Indeed, many NGOs argued that signing this certification would violate Chapter 7, Article 32 of the Palestinian NGO Law, which allows only unconditional funding for Palestinian NGOs (PNGO, 1999). As USAID was a significant supporter of this law, it is particularly ironic that it requires organizations to violate it. It is also counterproductive: limiting the range of organizations that are encouraged to participate in the political process of reform only increases the likelihood of violent efforts by those not invited to take part. Already suspect as an effort of the American government, USAID's whole program of civil society assistance is undermined by this certification requirement.

Tamkeen (2004d) was unable to meet its grant targets in 2003 as a result of organizations refusing to sign the certificate. However, as grant funding neared cutoff for a number of organizations in 2004, they did sign the certificate, even while "expressing their extreme dissatisfaction" (p. 12). Tamkeen's granting process also targeted groups in 2004 that the initiative felt might be more willing to sign, with a resulting increase in grants. However, "many other [organizations], including influential ones and previous Tamkeen partners, have refused to sign the certificate" (Tamkeen, 2004e, p. 8). Indeed, "the introduction of a revised version of the certificate has had little impact on increasing [NGO] willingness to sign it," (p. 8) perhaps because the revisions do not reflect the substantive concerns of the Palestinian NGO community.[7]

The certificate has also affected Tamkeen's ability to implement its own planned activities. Particularly negative effects are likely for sustainability and project impact over time. Planned capacity building for use of the PONAT (Participatory Organizational Needs Assessment Tool) has been postponed, as Tamkeen (2005) was "unable to locate a qualified Palestinian service provider willing to sign a contract containing the USAID-mandated anti-terrorism language" (Tamkeen, 2005, pp. 20–

21). The planned comprehensive evaluation of civic education activities under the program has also been indefinitely delayed, because Tamkeen has been "unable to locate a suitable a suitable firm ...to carry out the study at a high standard ... due to the unwillingness of institutes attached to Palestinian universities [the most qualified potential partners] to sign" those same contracts (p. 27). Clearly, the certificate is undermining the program's ability not only to reach a broad range of PNGOs but also its effect on those it reaches.

RESOLVING THE CONFLICTS

Overall, USAID and other donors' civic education assistance to Palestinian civil society has had mixed results. On the one hand, as the USAID evaluation shows, knowledge about democracy and governance has increased and some related practices have appeared. On the other hand, this aid has created many skeptics, who argue that the values represented in programs are not practiced by donors, that the organizations selected to provide civic education programming are elitist and not representative, and that the political constraints on Palestinians do not support the development of a sustainable civil society and a healthy democracy. USAID's terrorism certification is a particularly clear example of why this skepticism exists.

Aid to Palestinian civil society can be improved in a number of ways. First, the priority of donors on "safeguarding Israel" (Brouwer, 2000, p. 44) has to change. This priority leads to undemocratic practices in Palestine and donor support for bad government and internal oppression. Many donors supporting Palestinian civil society appear hypocritical about their political goals, favoring stability rather than actually supporting the development of a vigorous civil society.

Following from this, civil society development in Palestine needs to be more inclusive, as argued broadly for the field in Carothers and Ottway (2000). Opposition to the Oslo accords should not be construed as opposition to peace, but rather skepticism about whether that particular mechanism would bring peace or support Palestinian rights (and in fact, it has not). Donor support should not be tied to particular political positions by recipients, but rather support the development of a range of organizations and a strong public debate about issues that matter to Palestinians. As Brouwer (2000) notes, many organizations that opposed Oslo (in particular, those with "a moderate Islamic outlook or with nationalist ideologies" [p. 45]) have significant grassroots connections, and involving them in civil society development will make the sector more strong and diverse. In fact, as Candland (2000) observes, "NGOS that are rooted in religiously articulated programs for social reform can be particularly effective at community development and building social capital" (p. 145). Including people who are marginalized more actively in the development of civil society will also help meet this goal, rather than just focusing on training the elites to run the country.

Third, civil society assistance needs to respect Palestinians' ability to think and act for themselves. Brouwer (2000) argues that "donors should not show up with the blueprint of what a partner organization looks like; instead, they should be guided by local individuals and organizations" (p. 45). Indeed, as one respondent to the Tamkeen evaluation put it, "[h]istory has shown that in the Palestinian context, civil society is not built by telling people how to practice democracy; rather, it is built by empowering people to practice democracy" (Dajani, 2003, p. 41). Donors need to avoid "turn[ing] so-called civil society organizations into mirror images of their donors, rather than distinctive organizations that focus directly on their countries' particular problems" (Ottaway, 2001, p. 2). Donors need to support, and try less to shape, local institutions. They also need to hold government accountable and let Palestinians make their own development decisions, not ask them to act primarily in the interests of the donors.

Within such a framework, civic education can be an important tool for building Palestinian democracy. Such democracy is an important goal, because it can contribute to sustainable human development in Palestine (in the sense of greater justice: improved use of resources in the interest of all and a more equitable social system). The questions are how to make Palestinian civic education more relevant and how to improve its outcomes in terms not only of knowledge but of practice. How can civic education help Palestinians internalize the norms that support strong democracy, and act to transform their society in that direction?

For programs to be truly effective, donors should include and encourage more participatory methods of instruction and concentrate on issues that are more meaningful and have direct links to Palestinians' daily lives. Such programs should also give opportunities for learners to use their skills in engagement with systems of power, and operate in environments that reflect the ideals of democracy that civic education is trying to promote.

In order to contribute to a vision of development that "create[s], in a world of chronic inequality and disequilibrium, new civilizations of solidarity" (Goulet, 1996, p. 9), Palestinian democracy must be participatory for all Palestinians, not just those who agree with donor positions, or even with the narrowly defined "peace process." A wide range of civil society organizations should be supported in the process of democratization; these should include not only the "modern" NGOs that have developed in the last 30 years, but also Islamic and leftist organizations. Civic education should not be based on a minimalist conception of democracy and its related focus on behavior such as voting, but should foster skills for analysis and problem solving, and provide people with experience in political action for change. Conditions that reflect the interests of donors more than the interests of the Palestinian people should not be placed on funding for these programs—Palestinian interests should be served first. Such an approach would enable civic education to support Palestinians not only in their efforts, as Goulet (1996) puts it, at "having more," but at "being and becoming more," as well.

NOTES

1. I use this term to refer broadly to the policies of trade and investment liberalization, privatization/deregulation, and fiscal discipline commonly promoted by donors as keys to macroeconomic development since the 1980s.
2. The sensitivity of the Israeli-Palestinian conflict among many donor constituencies, the indeterminate status of the Palestinian territory, and the tendency by observers to describe the conflict in religious rather than political terms significantly complicate donor-Palestinian interactions, as I will discuss below.
3. For most donors, the term "Palestine" typically refers to only the territory of the West Bank (including East Jerusalem) and the Gaza Strip. As I am describing donor programs in this paper, I use "Palestine" here in that sense.
4. This liberalism, which guaranteed notable autonomy and discretion to PNGOs, was threatened by a proposed amendment to the law in 2005, which would centralize authorization for NGO establishment in a special government committee, and prohibit political activity by any NGO.
5. While comparable governmental figures for 1990 are not available (budgeting authority transfer from Israel to the PNA did not begin until 1994), the PNA's budget for 1996 was nearly $800 million, and GDP was $3.6 billion (Palestinian Central Bureau of Statistics, n/d).
6. Indeed, USAID significantly cut funding to the initiative in the final year, hampering operational activities including quality assurance and sustainability promotion (Tamkeen, 2005).
7. It should be noted that Tamkeen staff have expressed their concern about the certificate's negative impact on democracy development in Palestine to USAID in public reports (see, e.g., Tamkeen, 2004d, 2004g, and 2005). However, those staff have no control over policy design and implementation in this arena.

REFERENCES

Boggs, D. L. (1992). Civic education: An adult education imperative. *Adult Education Quarterly 42*(1), 46–55.

Brouwer, I. (2000). Weak democracy and civil society promotion: The cases of Egypt and Palestine. In M. Ottaway & T. Carothers (Eds.), *Funding virtue: Civil society aid and democracy promotion* (pp. 21–48). Washington, DC: Carnegie Endowment for International Peace.

Brynen, R. (2000). *A very political economy: Peacebuilding and foreign aid in the Palestine.* Washington, DC: U.S. Institute of Peace.

Candland, C. (2000). Faith as social capital: Religion and community development in South Asia. *Policy Sciences 33,* 355–374.

Carothers, T., & Ottaway, M. (2000). The burgeoning world of civil society aid. In M. Ottaway & T. Carothers (Eds.), *Funding virtue: Civil society aid and democracy promotion* (pp. 3–17). Washington, DC: Carnegie Endowment for International Peace.

Christina, R. (2004). Contingency, complexity, possibility: Palestinian NGOs and the negotiation of local control in educational development. In M. Sutton & R. Arnove (Eds.), *State-NGO relations in educational policy formulation and appropriation: Case studies from the field* (pp. 133–158). Norwood, NJ: Ablex.

Dajani, S. (2003). *Impact assessment of Tamkeen Service delivery grants.* Retrieved from September 1, 2005, from http://www.tamkeen.org/tamkeen1/tn/files/Tamkeen_Impact_Assessment--Service_Delivery.pdf

Eid-Alldredge, E. (2003). *Assessment of the Tamkeen impact on the disability sector: Democracy in action.* Retrieved September 1, 2005, from http://www.tamkeen.org/tamkeen1/tn/files/Tamkeen_Impact_Assessment--Disability.pdf

European Council. (2003). *A secure Europe in a better world: European Security strategy.* Retrieved April 1, 2008, from http://ue.eu.int/ueDocs/cms_data/docs/pressdata/en/reports/76255.pdf

Finkel, S. (2003). Can democracy be taught? Adult civic education, civil society, and the development of democratic political culture. *Journal of Democracy, 14,* 137–151.

Friederich-Ebert-Stiftung. (2003). *Introduction.* Retrieved September 1, 2003, from http://www.fes.de/intro-en.html

Galston, W. (2003). Civic education and political participation. *Phi Delta Kappan, 85*(1), 29–34.

Golub, S. (2000). Democracy as development: A case for civil society assistance in Asia. In M. Ottaway & T. Carothers (Eds.), *Funding virtue: Civil Society aid and democracy promotion* (pp. 135–158). Washington, DC: Carnegie Endowment for International Peace.

Goulet, D. (1996). *A new discipline: Development ethics.* Kellogg Institute Working Papers No. 231. Retrieved September 1, 2005, from http://www.nd.edu/%7Ekellogg/WPS/231.pdf

Hammami, R. (2000, Spring). Palestinian NGOs since Oslo: From NGO politics to social movements? *Middle East Report,* 19–19, 27.

Himal, J. (1999). *NGOs and state in Palestine: Negotiating boundaries.* Retrieved from, http://www.ids.ac.uk/ids/civsoc/final/palestine/pal1.doc

Institute for Development Studies. (1999). *Civil society and governance: A concept paper.* Retrieved September 1, 2005, from http://www.ids.ac.uk/ids/civsoc/public.doc

Mabe, A. (1993). Moral and practical foundations for civic education. *Social Studies, 84*(4), 153–158.

McGowan, L. (1997). *Democracy undermined, economic justice denied: Structural adjustment and the aid juggernaut in Haiti. The development group for alternative policies.* Retrieved September 1, 2005, from http://www.developmentgap.org/haiti97.html

O'Brien, J. (2004). *Good governance efforts by donor agencies. Speech to the International Consortium on Governmental Financial Management.* Retrieved September 1, 2005, from http://www.ethics.org/resources/article_detail.cfm?ID=455

Office of the Coordinator for Counter-terrorism. (n/d). *Fact Sheet on Executive Order 13224. U.S. Department of State.* Retrieved September 1, 2005, from http://www.state.gov/s/ct/ rls/fs/2002/16181.htm

Ottaway, M. (2001, June). Strengthening civil society in other countries. *Chronicle of Higher Education,* 14.

Palestinian Non-governmental Organizations Network. (1996). *Legislation regulating Palestinian non-governmental organizations.* Ramallah, Palestine: Author.

Palestinian Non-governmental Organizations Network. (1999). *Legislative update.* Ramallah, Palestine: Author.

Palestinian Non-governmental Organizations Network. (2003). *Position statement calling for the halting of conditional support.* Retrieved September 1, 2005, from http://www.pngo.net/activities/cond_funding/12-07-2003.htm

Palestinian Non-governmental Organizations Network. (2004). *PNGO reiterates its call for halting conditional support.* Retrieved September 1, 2005, from http://www.pngo.net/activities/cond_funding/05-01-2004.htm

Patrick, J. (1997). *Global trends in civic education for democracy.* Retrieved April 1, 2008, from http://www.indiana.edu/nssdc/glotrdig.htm

Patrick, J. (2002). *Improving civic education in schools.* (Report Number?) Bloomington, IN: ERIC Clearinghouse for Social Studies/Social Science Education (ERIC Document Reproduction Service No. ED 470039)

Sabatini, C. (2001, August). *Whom do international donors support in the name of civil society?* Paper presented at the 97th American Political Science Association Conference, San Francisco.

Sen, A. (1999). *Development as freedom.* New York: Anchor Books.

Sida. (2001). Human rights and democracy. Retrieved September 1, 2005, from http://www.sida.se/Sida/road/ Classic/article/0/jsp/PrintRender.jsp?a=9175&d=514

Sullivan, D. (1996). NGOs in Palestine: Agents of development and the foundation of civil society. *Journal of Palestine Studies, 25*(3), 93–100.

Tamkeen. (2004a). *About Tamkeen.* RetrievedSeptember 1, 2005, from http://www.tamkeen.org/ tamkeen1/about_tamkeen/index.asp

Tamkeen. (2004b). Empowering Civil Society Organizations in the West Bank and Gaza Strip. Retrieved September 1, 2005, from http://www.tamkeen.org/tamkeen1/Uploaded _Files/Tamkeen.pdf

Tamkeen. (2004c). *Partners/Grantees*. Retrieved September 1, 2005, from http://www.tamkeen.org/tamkeen1/grants/Grantees/ Tamkeen_Partners.asp

Tamkeen. (2004d). *Quarterly Progress Report, First Quarter 2004*. Retrieved September 1, 2005, from http://pdf.usaid.gov/pdf_docs/PDACA529.pdf

Tamkeen. (2004e). *Quarterly Progress Report, Fourth Quarter 2004*. Retrieved September 1, 2005, from http://www.dec.org/pdf_docs/PDACD485.pdf

Tamkeen. (2004f). *Success stories*. Retrieved September 1, 2005, from http://www.tamkeen.org/tamkeen1/successes/index.asp

Tamkeen. (2004g). *Work Plan for 2004*. Retrieved September 1, 2005, from http://www.tamkeen.org/tamkeen1/includes/Tamkeen%20%20Work%20Plan-%202004.pdf

Tamkeen. (2005). *Quarterly Progress Report, First Quarter 2005*. Retrieved April 1, 2008, from http://pdf.dec.org/pdf_docs/PDACD835.pdf

Thomas-Slater, B. (2003). *Southern exposure*. West Hartford, CT: Kumarian.

Tyack, D. (1997, February). Civic education: What roles for citizens? *Educational Leadership*, 22–24.

United States Agency for International Development. (2002). *Acquisition and Assistance Policy Directive 02-19, Implementation of E.O. 13224—Certification regarding terrorist financing*. Washington, DC: USAID Office of Procurement.

United States Agency for International Development. (2004a). *Budget for Palestine programs*. Retrieved September 1, 2005, from http://www.usaid.gov/wbg/budget.htm

United States Agency for International Development. (2004b). *West Bank democracy and governance programs*. Retrieved September 1, 2005, from http://www.usaid.gov/wbg/program_democracy.htm

World Bank. (2004). *Governance*. Retrieved September 1, 2004, from http://www.worldbank.org/wbi/ governance/about.html#approach

Youngs, R. (2004). *Europe's uncertain pursuit of Middle East reform*. Carnegie Endowment for International Peace, Working Papers of the Democracy and Rule of Law Project. Carnegie Paper No. 45. Washington, DC: Carnegie Endowment for International Peace.

CHAPTER 5

FOREIGN INFLUENCE AND ECONOMIC INSECURITY IN INTERNATIONAL PARTNERSHIPS FOR CIVIC EDUCATION

The Case of Post-Soviet Estonia

Doyle Stevick

INTRODUCTION: "TRAINING OF THE DONORS"

The Berlin wall fell in November, 1989, and not long after the Baltic states—annexed by the Soviet Union during World War II—declared independence. Within months, Gorbachev officially dissolved the Soviet Union, instigating a flood of aid and triumphalism from the West. Well-meaning donors and experts arrived in lands whose histories, languages and cultures they mostly did not know, ready to provide the right answers for countries that were expected to make a smooth transition to democratic

Advancing Democracy Through Education? U.S. Influence Abroad and Domestic Practices, pp. 97–127

governance and market economies. Education reform—particularly the removal of propaganda and the development of appropriate materials to fill the void—was perceived to be critical to ensuring the long-term sustainability of the recent political and economic changes. American and European programs were developed to support the development of democratic citizenship education across Central and Eastern European Europe. Very little, however, was known about the effectiveness or influence of foreign programs for civic education.

There was cause for concern about the effectiveness of international partnerships. In the Baltic states in particular, and across Central Europe in general, the experts or consultants brought in by foreign-funded programs were seldom experts in the region or fluent in the countries' languages. Persuasion is difficult when the audience's views are neither known nor understood. Technical experts without a strong understanding of the local context could not be much help in shaping the adaptation of ideas or programs for local contexts. Tolerance programs from the United States that targeted racism, for example, could be only tangentially relevant in Estonia, where relations between minority ethnic Russians and majority ethnic Estonians were fractured over history, religion, culture, and language, but not skin color. Foreign programs that had been developed in particular contexts for specific local goals were promoted as if they would apply anywhere. Labeling culturally specific and situated programs as "best practices" was often sufficient to lay claim to universal applicability.

Of paramount concern was the possibility that donors' and recipients' divergent ideological positions would subvert the considered adaptation of those ideas or practices that could be meaningful in transitional contexts, where people were casting about for foreign models to replace the inherited Soviet ones. Obstacles could arise between donors and recipients through ignorance and insensitivity on either side, through misunderstandings, or through explicit promotion of unwelcome views. Ignorance of cultural differences could be quite significant. One American partner explained to me that the Estonian language is deficient and undeveloped, suggesting both that it would fade away in the natural order of things and that efforts to preserve it were inappropriate and would ultimately fail. The Estonian language is the core element of Estonia's national and civic identity; partners with such a deficit model of the language are unlikely to be sensitive to the complex role the Estonian language plays in domestic questions of citizenship.

While ideological differences between donors and recipients were a mix of fits and misfits—Americans' tradition of skepticism about government, for example, resonated quite well in countries that endured Soviet hegemony—economic ideology seemed likely to be a stumbling block. Americans frequently evoked Milton Friedman's name, but I speculated that the implications of his ideas might not sit well with Estonian teachers. While some of Estonia's macroeconomic indicators were moving in a positive direction by the end of the twentieth century, the economic transition had been stressful and individuals in countries like Estonia felt a great deal of anxiety, not least about the loss of social guarantees. American partners' opposition to a welfare state, I hypothesized, might alienate teachers who worried about the dismantling of government-supported services and experienced a decline in economic security and purchasing power. Would high levels of economic stress make teachers unreceptive to foreign programs, or even nostalgic for Soviet-era guarantees, and hence undermine the reform of civic education practice? This issue seemed particularly important since Estonia often associated itself with the Scandinavian countries, and the Swedish model of social democracy, with its strong social guarantees, might be more amenable to teachers.

Understanding the influence of these foreign partnerships and the obstacles to their success required more than simply studying student outcomes. The full range of the process is relevant, from global influences down to classroom practice. This research, therefore, concerned not just the teaching of civic education, but the policy context within which it took shape, including the role of global actors and their ideologies. It draws upon a multi-sited ethnographic study of the policy and practice of civic education in postcommunist (and pre-European Union) Estonia. The research was conducted between September, 2001, and December, 2004 and spanned nine countries, including all three Baltic states. It involved people at international levels (including, for example, officials from the European Union and Council of Europe), national actors (in curriculum, teacher-training, etc.), teachers and students, and particularly, the sites in which they interacted: international conferences, teacher-training events, and hundreds of hours of classroom observation.

Ideology did play a role, but not primarily through attempts to transmit ideals directly to others. Rather, ideology manifested itself through an emphasis on civil society and in the selection of participants in teacher-training sessions. Economic issues were critical, too, but primarily through the pressures they inflicted on people working in the nonprofit sector (that foreign ideology had helped to foster in the first place). And although teachers faced considerable economic stress, few ever expressed any reservations about the changes that took place in society. Instead, the donors, the recipients, and the relationships between them emerged as the most important issues in understanding international support for civic education. This chapter focuses on the complexity of these partnerships and such aid generally, with particular attention to the myriad factors that complicate these efforts.

Both the structure of the aid and the nature of the partnerships often created perverse incentives that pitted domestic partners' self-interest against donor goals. This problem was particularly acute in contexts of high economic stress and uncertainty, where individuals may feel particular compulsion to make decisions according to their perceived economic insecurity before other considerations. A greater awareness of the dynamics of these programs within the recipient countries, and the impact and meanings that such programs have there, can lead to improvements in the design and effectiveness of foreign aid in civic education. Less emphasis should be placed on the promotion of certain ideals and the advancement of the donors' interests, and a democratic ethos should pervade the entire process. While such an ethos is often sincerely intended—and even perceived—by the donors and foreign experts, they are not often privy to the circumstances that impinge upon their partners and that undermine a true democratic dialogue.

Such a dialogue is perhaps unattainable, but here I refer to an ideal of a dialogue unencumbered by power imbalances and resembling the ideal speech situation elaborated by Habermas. In one formulation,

> Dialogue … refers to *engaged, inclusive* and *respectful* communications among … stakeholders about their respective stances and values, perspectives and experiences, hopes and dreams, and interpretations of gathered data relevant to what is being evaluated. (Abma et al., 2001, pp. 168–169)

This dialogue is difficult to achieve in contexts of high economic insecurity in which one partner has access to the resources the other needs or wants, particularly when these economic circumstances are often hidden from view. Knowledge of how "stakeholder interactions [are] governed by role and status differences and protected through self-interests" is critical for addressing the way those factors influence the dynamics of the partnership and can help move towards a more democratic process in which "interactions [are] guided by reciprocity, appreciation for the worldviews and interests of others and a willingness to make space for their concerns and agendas" (Abma et al., 2001, p. 169).

The disparity in economic resources often subverted an open dialogue between recipients and donors. Janine Wedel, an anthropologist who studied civil society assistance, particularly to Poland and Russia, wrote in her 2001 book, *Collision and Collusion: The Strange Case of Western Aid to Eastern Europe,* that "the funding of almost any group affected internal politics, the intricacies of which outsiders usually did not comprehend" (p. 122). For this reason, a Polish diplomat who was "too gracious and well bred to be overtly critical of" a lavish U.S. Department of Treasury banquet for officials from former Eastern bloc countries in February, 1991, "meekly suggested" to Wedel "that some 'training of the donors' might be helpful" (p. 1).

This chapter is organized into three primary sections. The first section discusses some aspects of donor ideology and funding practices and how they shaped the selection of foreign presenters for civic education events. It argues that donor agencies are not neutral, but advance specific ideologies or philosophies either explicitly or through their approach to partnerships. The lack of neutrality means that donors typically have a "transmission orientation." The second section addresses the dynamics between donors and recipients, the influence that outside groups have, and the problem of selecting appropriate domestic partners. It argues that donors are in a poor position both to select appropriate recipients and to evaluate how effectively their resources are spent. The great imbalances between donors and recipients mean that foreigners are less successful at promoting certain ideas, but do have the power to drive the agenda and to influence the shape that civil society takes. The third section provides a typology of nongovernmental organization (NGOs) according to the level of economic security that they provide for their participants and discusses the internal dynamics of civil society in recipient countries, including the criteria that shape the selection of seminar participants. These dynamics include a number of unintended results of foreign influence that are largely hidden from the view of outsiders.

Donors: Ideology and Civil Society

While political ideologies come in many variations, one core strand of American conservative ideas seemed to me to be pronounced within the American networks for civic education that I encountered prior to beginning my research in 2001. Generally, this cluster of ideas included not simply representative democracy and other broadly held tenets of a free society, but also a strong emphasis on small government, free markets, civil society, and opposition both to group rights and to a welfare state. Although American and European aid for democracy shared broad common goals, these particular elements were not typically common to both sides of the Atlantic. The importance of civil society was the exception.

As Sutton and Arnove (2004) explain, the American emphasis on civil society is part of a neoliberal agenda that,

> calls for a diminished role of the state, which is often seen as inefficient and corrupt, combined with an expanded role for civil society. The argument is made that NGOs can be more responsive to local needs and more efficient

in the delivery of basic social services than governmental agencies. By encouraging local participation in important decision-making processes and strengthening grassroots advocacy organizations, NGOs contribute to the building of social capital ... and to greater levels of democracy. (p. viii)

In much of postcommunist Europe, the state was discredited and the nonprofit sector was untainted by association with government, making these societies receptive to such views.

Robert Putnam's book, *Making Democracy Work*, published soon after the collapse of the Soviet bloc, became quite influential and his emphasis upon social capital was closely linked to civil society. Civil society advocates often behaved as though the creation of civil society was not only a key goal, but one that could be accomplished by providing large infusions of foreign money and expertise. Such an approach disregarded the forces that lead to the development of civil society institutions in the first place.

The U.S.'s strong preference for civil society organizations meant that that money was channeled both through American NGOs, as distributors of funds and as providers of technical assistance, and into postcommunist countries' NGOs, as recipients and providers of services, among other functions. Both American and postcommunist organizations lobbied and competed for access to this substantial new stream of revenue. "By the end of 1999, the U.S. had obligated $379 million to promote political party development, independent media, governance, and recipient NGOs" (Wedel, 2001, p. 86). The European Union (EU) did not lag far behind in its civil society investments, providing through its PHARE program approximately $194 million for civil society by early 1998 (p. 87).[1] In any case, "Americans tended to talk the loudest about establishing civil societies in the region" (p. 86).

The European-American discrepancy in funding for civil society must be understood in the context of education reform in the region. Two important differences are at work here. First, the EU worked directly with governments and thus had both better access to pursue influence and, through the promise of membership in the EU, much greater leverage. Their civil society support is just one small aspect of their overall work in education and democratization. Second, as a Council of Europe official explained, "While Europe must be concerned with the whole education system, the U.S. can concentrate its resources on the ideological aspects" (personal communication, June 2002).

Civil society was an ideological aspect both as an "end"—an emphasis within and goal of civic education, for example—and a "means"—their chosen avenue for promoting reform. The Americans' choice to work primarily through civil society, however, sometimes undermined their own potential influence. Some institutions, including USAID (United States

Agency for International Development), "have preferred to circumvent national governments to promote programs through NGOs, which they view as more efficient and accountable than the state" (Sutton & Arnove, 2004, p. viii). Without the participation of government personnel, there was little chance that important policy changes would be made.

The ideological emphasis upon civil society is just one example of how donor organizations in civic education partnerships are not neutral. First, those using public funds must serve the national interest and face public pressure. Second, some are transparently ideological or explicitly advocate certain ideas or positions. Third, and perhaps most common, "aid agencies tend to promise neutral technical solutions, [but] they nonetheless reflect political ideologies that have important unanticipated consequences for the recipients" (Wedel, 2001, p. 10).

American civics partners worked primarily with U.S. government funding, which was often channeled through USAID. Groups such as USAID, writes Samoff (1999),

> were created to serve national interests, including the provision of financial and technical assistance overseas. Even those that most energetically assert their role in providing development aid must defend their programs and budgets in terms of their contribution to the national economy and polity. (p. 63)

The obligation organizations have to advance national interests is illustrated by the mission statement of the Swedish Institute (SI, n.d), which promptly after the Soviet collapse hosted for 6 months Sulev Valdmaa, who became a prominent figure in civic education in Estonia through his work at an Estonian nongovernmental organization, the Jaan Tōnisson Institute. (This sponsorship likely contributed to Estonias subsequent adoption of the Swedish framework for its first post-Soviet civic education curricula.) The SI's goals are specific (and have an explicit economic component):

> The SI is a public agency entrusted with disseminating knowledge abroad about Sweden and organising exchanges with other countries in the spheres of culture, education, research and public life in general. In doing so, it seeks to promote Swedish interests and contribute to economic growth. (Swedish Institute, n.d., para. 1)

Similarly, within the specific realm of foreign aid for civic education, Quigley and Hoar (1997) lay out explicitly the national interest in the goals of Civitas International, the U.S. funded collaboration with postcommunist countries. The first stated goal of the program was "to acquaint educators from EEN/NIS [Eastern European nations/Newly

Independent States] with exemplary curricular and teacher-training programs in civic education *developed in the United States*" [my italics] (p. 13).

Public funding of such organizations also invites public scrutiny and political pressure. Such pressure constrains what the organizations are able to do and say and requires time and energy to defend their practices and to justify their funding. The Center for Civic Education (CCE), the leading organization for international programs in civic education in the United States, for example, provides a good example of the political pressure such organizations face. Particularly since 1995, when it spearheaded the formation of Civitas International, CCE has played a leading role in the promotion of civic education programs in Central and Eastern Europe and beyond. Although CCE has something of a conservative and traditional reputation, it has faced political pressure that apparently threatened its existence from conservative organizations in the United States. The presence of well-known conservatives including Representative Henry Hyde and Senator Orrin Hatch on its board has not diverted this pressure, although it may have helped to protect its government funding from elimination. Some conservatives feel that CCE programs such as *Res Publica: An International Framework for Education in Democracy* (2001) is propaganda for one-world government and that *We The People: The Citizen and the Constitution* constitutes an attempt to impose a standard curriculum on the entire country and thus to trample on states' rights (Schlafly, 2002; Turner, 2002).

Despite the constraints imposed by public funding, such organizations are, through a Byzantine set of relationships, able to advance politically untenable ends by funneling money through affiliates. This task is not difficult because, as Samoff (1999) writes, "the grid of internationally active education organizations and their affiliates is dense, many with overlapping memberships" (p. 63), and that was certainly true with civic education. A review of early civics partnership programs found in Estonia's Pedagogical Archive Museum show that the International Federation for Election Systems (now just IFES) and the National Endowment for Democracy (NED) were important early partners for civic education in Estonia, and an exploration of the overlapping memberships—what the anthropology of policy refers to as "social network analysis" (Wedel & Feldman, 2005, p. 2)—reveals deep connections with other conservative American organizations, such as the Heritage Foundation and the Cato Institute. NED, which has cooperated with the CIA, has used CIA funds, and was established by Ronald Reagan in 1983, channels money from Congress to the International Republican Institute (IRI) and the National Democratic Institute for International Affairs (NDI)—which are institutions of the two dominant political parties in the United States— as well as to The Center for International Private Enterprise (CIPE) and the American Council on

International Labor Solidarity (ACILS, which has merged with the AFL-CIO's Free Trade Union Institute, or FTUI).

> Those organizations, deliberately chosen to convey a sense of balance between left and right, labor and big business, then determine which groups abroad receive grants for their activities to further democracy. The remaining 30 percent of available grant money is designated "discretionary" funding to be distributed directly by NED. (Conry, 1993, Section: "NED's Quasi-Private Status," para. 2)

Established as a private corporation so that it would not be restricted in the same ways that USAID is, NED's structure of double-funneling the money, first from the government into NED and then through these groups, removes it considerably from public control (Conry, 1993).[3] Nation journalist David Corn has described NED as "a porkbarrel for a small circle of Republican and Democratic party activists, conservative trade unionists and free marketeers who use the endowment money to run their own mini-State Departments" (Conry, 1993, "NED as Political Pork," para. 4).

The third factor that defies the conception of donor neutrality, after the influence of public funding and donor advocacy, is the way ostensibly neutral organizations reflect broader ideologies. Guntars Catlaks (2006) provides crucial background for understanding how these different political ideologies are reflected in practice. He discusses how the different American and European philosophies are manifested in civic education programs and thereby sheds light into the different goals that each pursued through civil society:

> American model Civics programs favor more individual liberty and responsibility, while European programs emphasize the social network and sense of belonging to various social groups, from family to neighborhood, and from native town to country and nation.... In the American Civics model, the focus dominantly centers on Law and Constitution, or more precisely, Fundamental principles of constitutionalism, as a base of democratic politics.... The society here is basically the playground of the responsible individual, who knows the Law and is able to interpret it according to the Fundamental principles. The interpretation of Law (Constitution on highest level) and ability to defend one's own rights (and interests) accordingly are crucial skills in American Civics.... This is why court cases analysis, mock trials, and discussions on Constitutional amendments and the issues behind them occupy a very significant place in American Civics courses.
>
> European curriculums endorse Lawfulness but in a different way. The Laws in general are more perceived as given value and sphere of specific knowledge and expertise (tradition of Roman law). On the other hand they are products of Parliament and tools of government, which are constantly

changing. They represent the changing tasks of new policies implemented by changing governments, according the popular vote. In a way, the perception of Laws in the concept of democracy in European Civics is more diverse and complex: traditionally inherited as part of heritage and treated as Medieval architecture, but also flexible and subject to short term social agreements through political processes, rather than surfaces of underlying Constitutional concepts or fundamental principles as in U.S. (Catlaks, 2006, Section: "Individual Liberty versus Collective Responsibility?" Para. 1–6)

In light of these often implicit ideological differences, the mission statement of IFES—an organization with early involvement in Estonia shows its clear American (and nonneutral) aspects: "if democracy is to take root and thrive, a society must possess free and fair elections, an informed, engaged civil society, the rule of law, and ethical public officials who are accountable to the citizens they serve" (IFES, n.d.). While unobjectionable, its emphases upon the rule of law, accountability, and individual ethics are characteristic of American partners. Nowhere in this statement, for example, is there mention of cultural pluralism or minority rights, which are central concerns for European organizations.

Delivering the Experts: Ideology and the Selection of Participants

IFES provides a good example of the way that funneling public funds permits the advancement of a narrower political agenda. This pattern is evident in the selection of participants for seminars in Estonia. I gathered the records from early postcommunist civic education training from Estonia's Pedagogical Archive Museum and investigated the participants, their affiliations and relationships. Archival and internet research revealed that these participants were connected through conservative American think-tanks. The interrelationships of these individuals and the institutions with which they were involved are, in fact, complex. The interlaced political networks seem to have facilitated the selection of like-minded people for participation in projects in Estonia.

An overview of civic education activities in 1993–94 by an Estonian NGO noted that, "Mr. Peter W. Shramm [sic] and Mr. Christopher Siddell [sic], from the International Foundation of Electoral Systems proposed a series of seminars for youth and teachers in Estonia" and brought in foreigners, including Americans, to provide lectures for the teachers in Estonia (Jaan Tõnisson Institute, 1995b). Peter W. Schramm and Christopher Siddall have strong connections with the American Republican Party and conservative institutions. Schramm now heads the conservative Ashbrook Center at Ohios Ashland University.[5] Christopher Siddall has a lower profile, but was singled out for thanks in recognition of his volunteering efforts on its behalf by the 2004 annual report of the International Republican Institute. IFES is also listed in that document as a contributor to IRI.[6] Schramm's and Siddall's affiliations coincide with that of the contemporary IFES director, Richard W. Soudriette. Although IFES has a board of prominent corporate officials and lawyers as well as important Republican and Democratic politicians, Soudriette himself served as chief of staff to Republican Senator James Inhofe of Oklahoma.[7]

Mr. Schramm's background, which included growing up in Budapest and witnessing the 1956 Revolution, make him a compelling choice for such programs. The story he tells of his life experience captures very powerfully the symbolism that the United States and its flag held for many people who were living under communist regimes (Schramm, 2006). The documents show that he was a featured speaker during at least 5- or 6-day seminars for youth leaders and civics teachers during 1993–94 alone (Jaan Tõnisson Institute, 1995a, pp. 3–8). Juliana Geran Pilon, a Romanian who speaks Hungarian, had lived as an adult under an oppressive communist regime and in the United States. Her conservative credentials include 8 years as a policy analyst at the Heritage Foundation (Pilon, n.d.). NED would later fund the publication of one of her books, *Ironic Points of Light*, in Estonian and Russian. Of the two other Americans who participated, one scholar with a conservative reputation was recruited by Dr. Pilon. The other, a lawyer and one-time participant, resided in Bucharest and may well have been known to Dr. Pilon for this reason; he is the only foreign participant without a clear, publicly-accessible set of political affiliations.

The last foreign participant was an intriguing choice for the IFES seminars in Estonia: a Swede, Mr. Peter Stein, Managing Director and Chairman of Stein Brothers AB, a private Swedish consulting firm and think tank (Jaan Tõnisson Institute, 1995b, p. 7). If a neoliberal economic agenda and free-market perspective were to be promoted at these conferences, the third way of Sweden was certainly its antithesis, or at least a glaring counterexample. Sweden is well-regarded in Estonia, which likes to think of itself as a Nordic country. Mr. Steins message, however, seems clear from the title of his talk: "Why the Model of the Swedish Welfare State Does Not Work" (Jaan Tõnisson Institute, 1995, p. 7). Like other participants in the IFES seminars, Mr. Stein was known in the circles of American conservative foundations and think-tanks. He may well have come to the attention of the IFES coordinators on the basis of his recent publication for the Cato Institute, "Sweden: From Capitalist Success to Welfare-State Sclerosis" (Stein, 1991).

Both through networking and through funneling resources, American public funds could be used to advance a relatively narrow economic and political doctrine. Foreign partners were as much advocates of particular viewpoints as they were technical experts helping their local partners advance locally-developed goals. In part as a result of this advocacy, a transmission orientation exists: foreign experts speak, lecture, answer, and provide, but much less frequently ask in-depth questions or engage in a real dialogue.

Unequal Partners: Economic Security, Language, and Influence

The individuals who work for donor and recipient organizations have drastically different levels of resources, educational attainment, expertise, local knowledge, experience under oppressive and free governments, language ability and economic security. "[R]hetoric of collaboration and partnership notwithstanding" (Samoff, 1999, p. 60), many partnerships "employed the language of collaboration and joint effort as they created an institutional apparatus for the leading role of international organizations" (p. 62). Control of the purse-strings and the ability to dictate the agenda went hand in hand with the transmission orientation discussed earlier. The mission-statement of IFES is representative of this paradoxical dynamic between democratic rhetoric and unequal relationships:

> Our staff is truly global, with 150 professionals from 25 countries leading technical assistance projects for international and bilateral donor organizations such as USAID, the UN, DFID, the OSCE and others ... IFES' international professionals ensure that democracy solutions are home grown. Every IFES project team partners with local organizations, and every project is staffed by local personnel ... IFES professionals work closely with local networks to deliver expertise that fits the needs of the country or client ... IFES professionals provide technical assistance across many areas of democracy development. We have developed service lines and regional representation around the world that allow our professionals to deliver democracy solutions rapidly—with the innovation, experience and results that only an organization with almost 20 years of dedicated democracy work can do.[10]

IFES's statement of philosophy clearly articulates the value of local knowledge and involvement in democratization, and yet, despite the emphasis upon "home-grown solutions" (which are "ensured" by their professionals—the language all implies transmission: solutions are "delivered" by professionals who "provide technical assistance." That all projects are staffed by local personnel hints at the power imbalance involved. The American leader of another partnership was more blunt about the balance of power in his relationship: when one of his Baltic partners followed the money and engaged in project work with Americans who had managed to procure this partner's usual source of funding, he noted that, "I didn't punish him for cooperating with our competitors."

These imbalances result in unequal relationships and complicate the possibility of the participants engaging in free and open discussion. These problems are particularly acute among partners who are largely dependent on foreign funding for their own economic security, an issue that is explored in the next section. Domestic partners may be less than forthcoming about their own views and problems if they want to cultivate their donors' good will by agreeing with their positions or by making them feel important or needed. Wedel called this tendency the

> *ritual of listening to foreigners,* in which the naïve but self-assured Westerner would encounter the shrewd Pole, who deftly charmed his guest while revealing nothing of what he truly thought.... Many Poles had mastered the sophisticated art of impressing Westerners while maneuvering to get what they wanted. (emphasis in original, Wedel, 2001, p. 3)

Foreigners, however, are in a poor position to see beyond what they are told and have no obvious grounds to by suspicious of what they are told. Many foreigners come in—or are brought in—as experts or consultants only for brief visits, and are profoundly ill equipped to understand the local context, culture or language. They make their best guesses about what may be of interest, but have little information on which to base their decisions. The results can be condescending: a teacher whom I observed regularly told me after one such international seminar that, "They treat us like children" (personal communication, November 2003). One speaker at a civic education event in the Baltic states, who was flown in to give a lecture by his embassy, expressed concern at a coffee break to a domestic colleague that his talk might not have been useful or relevant for the audience. His colleague—who, unbeknownst to him, had arrived as the break began and had not actually been present for the talk—nevertheless reassured him that, "Oh no, I think that was exactly what our teachers needed to hear."

Among foreign donors or partners who have extended relationships with domestic colleagues, the situation can be better. Some had taken the time to develop a detailed knowledge of local history. In this particular case, Wedel's (2001) scathing account of her own experience was not necessarily representative of civic education partnerships:

> Deficient in cultural and historical sensibilities, consultants and aid representatives often made social fools of themselves, failing to realize that their chief source of attractiveness was in their own pocketbooks or their perceived access to others' pockets. (p. 92)

The crucial issue of economic incentives will be explored in more depth in the final section. This section focuses upon the issue of cultural and historical knowledge and language ability.

Even foreign experts or donors with good historical knowledge and cultural sensitivity cannot transcend a language barrier. The time required to develop the necessary language skills may be prohibitive for most foreign partners—especially those working in areas with more than one language—which meant that the vast majority of contact with local teachers and other significant figures was mediated by their domestic partners, who do not need to let foreign partners know anything they don't want them to know. Unfortunately, these networks did not actively seek out scholars or even immigrants who were fluent in local languages and who could communicate effectively without translators. With the numbers of highly-education refugees and immigrants from these societies who prospered in the United States, they would not have been difficult to locate. Even though the Russian language is contentious in many Soviet-occupied countries, it nevertheless is a medium to communicate directly and effectively with people throughout the region. Further, there are many Russian-speaking scholars available, and virtually all are clearly anticommunist and would not be strongly associated with the occupation. Further, these scholars could have direct contact with large Russian-speaking minorities in the Baltic states. The importance of such unmediated contact was emphasized by an Estonian who fled during the Second World War but returned to write a civic education textbook. He explained that,

> I found it psychologically impossible to write the Estonian text while being in [the U.S.]—if you want to write about the number of ministries and blah-blah-blah, but if you want to change attitudes, you have to be in the surroundings where the counterproductive aspects of interpersonal relations hit you literally everyday. (personal communication, July 2003)

Without an understanding of what people truly thought, foreigners' ability to persuade anyone was greatly compromised. When the recipient partners indicated to their visitors that they agreed about something—during the "ritual of listening to foreigners"—the speaker would not feel a need to make a compelling case for that specific idea or position because it was apparently already embraced by the listener; as a result, differences in their partners' positions or understandings were hidden from view and could not be probed or explored. Foreign experts or donors are likely to hear the same response from people who agree with them deeply in principle and from people who are eager to obtain their economic support, regardless of the issue at hand.[11]

The gap in language skills and the incentive to conceal differences made the pursuit of appropriate partners problematic,

> Foreign financing in the form of grants meant that choices had to be made about who the appropriate grantees were. Donors were profoundly ill equipped to make these choices. They were easily outdone by Central and Eastern Europeans skilled in the necessary arts of self-preservation through their experiences under communism. (Wedel, 2001, p. 87)

In extreme cases, suppressed disagreements and the inability to judge the merit of potential partners would lead to the selection of people who were fundamentally opposed to the premise of the project. In two separate cases, for example, Holocaust education networks selected a partner who either: (1) believed that the Holocaust should be taught only in conjunction with the human rights abuses suffered by Estonians generally and not as a unique and important event that deserved specific independent study, or (2) was singled out in a book on racist extremism for writing a textbook that attributed Estonians' participation in the Holocaust to revenge on Jews for the Bolshevik revolution (Stevick, 2007). When even the domestic partners do not embrace the aims of a project, they are unlikely to be compelling ambassadors for the viewpoint themselves. For these reasons, I found little evidence that the specific interests, ideas or philosophies advocated by foreign partners ever had much of an impact in Estonia.

While foreign partners did not have a great deal of success advancing specific views, they did have a significant influence, however inadvertently, in three areas: in privileging English-speakers, in shaping the forms that civil society would take, and in setting the agenda. English language ability was not widespread among adults in the former Soviet Union, so projects or partnerships that required English-language ability as a criterion immediately eliminated a great number of worthy—perhaps the most worthy—partners. Those who already had some knowledge of English often constituted a (relatively) privileged group. Bruno observed this pattern in Russia itself, "presumably involuntarily, donor agencies are offering, through development projects, new sources for reinforcing the elitist, feudal-type system of social-stratification" (as cited in Wedel, 2001, p. 114). This kind of reinforcement of elites occurs in part because, as Chris Hann explains, "the focus [on NGOs] has tended to restrict funding to fairly narrow groups, typically intellectual elites concentrated in capital cities" (as cited Wedel, 2001, p 114.) These elites, in turn, are those most likely to have English language skills, although that criterion is no guarantee that an appropriate partner will be found, as Jay Austin points out:

Elevating a class of English-speaking people who can absorb enough
buzzwords from an RFP [Request for Proposals] in order to put together
something that looks like a Western budget may or may not be the kind of
people that we'd like to most encourage in the environmental sector. (as
cited in Wedel, 2001, p. 120)

English language skills are, however, pronounced among civic
education specialists. The six Estonian individuals who do the most work
with international networks related to civic education speak English quite
well. The individual involved with civic education at the Curriculum
Development Center was fluent in English, as was his replacement. The
person who oversees the approval of new materials and textbooks in civic
education is fluent in English. The leading researcher into civic education
speaks English fluently. Two additional people who have been involved in
textbook writing or national exam preparation were chosen to participate
in different international civics programs without an interpreter. In the
cases of the international networks and at least one government-funded
position, English language was a clear criterion for selection. The
concentration of English-speakers among civics experts comes into play
below in the discussion of the translation of American civics standards into
Estonian.

In addition to privileging English speakers, foreign organizations—
and particularly their money—were very influential in shaping civil
society. IFES, for example, emphasizes in its mission statement that,
"[w]hile IFES can provide support and expertise to officials and citizens,
the impetus for change lies with citizens and with their governments"
(IFES, n.d.). Archival documents, however, show clearly who was the
source of initiative in the IFES-Estonia case and who had the authority
to set the agenda. After IFES representatives monitored the first free
post-Soviet Estonian elections,

They came to the conclusion that among all the population groups the
youth were the least active at the elections. As a result they proposed to the
Jaan Tõnisson Institute to start a joint programme for organizing civic education seminars for the youth organizations [sic] leaders and the teachers of
the particular subject at high schools. (Jaan Tõnisson Institute, 1995b, p. 2)

These seminars provided a model that could be marketed out to other
funders. Funding was obtained from Soros Open Society Institute and the
National Endowment for Democracy. Once the opportunity to pursue
foreign support became clear, the JTI's Civic Education Center opened, an
example of the process described by the Carnegie Endowment report by
which, local groups proliferated often around issues that Western donors
found important, but rarely around issues that locals confronted on a daily

basis (as cited in Wedel, 2001, p. 110). Through these seminars and the selection process discussed above, an Indiana University representative got involved in Estonia and became a key partner, as a later document indicates: The Jaan Tõnisson Institute [Center] for Civic Education [was] created in cooperation with Indiana University (Valdmaa, 2002, p. 76). As a Carnegie Endowment report indicated, Western NGOs have played a large and important role in the *design* and *building* of institutions associated with democratic states" (italics in original; as cited in Wedel, 2001, p. 110). Democratic rhetoric aside, much of the initiative was coming from abroad.

Foreign priorities would continue to have a very large role in the activities undertaken by NGOs. A review of the projects undertaken by JTI's Civic Education division with American or European partners reveals a consistent emphasis on the priorities of the foreign partners (which were discussed above by Catlaks [2006]). Indeed, the American projects included Street Law, Inc., which supported the development of a law textbook and teacher education seminars; the translation of American national civics standards into Estonian; and the preparation of materials to help students prepare for the national examination in civics. The materials supported by European organizations, on the other hand, were strongly oriented towards multiculturalism, tolerance, human rights, and ethnic pluralism. At least nine of these European-funded projects were connected to these themes.[13]

The discrepancy between those projects carried out with foreign partners and those done with domestic funding reveal a different set of priorities and concerns. Notably, one of these seminars dealt explicitly with religion, a topic not broached by foreign partners. According to the description of the event,

> In 1997 was arranged a seminar on the issues of religion. The teachers, who now, after the collapse of communism have to teach among other new content areas about the religious topics, also, poorly know that particular area. The two-days [sic] seminar offered to the participant's [sic] lectures about the essence of Protestantism, church history under the Soviet era, about religious music and arts, held by Lutheran church priests and art specialists.[14]

It is worth noting that the interest in Protestantism and Lutheranism is another dimension along which ethnic Estonians are distinct from ethnic Russians (who are mostly Russian Orthodox.) The exclusion of Russian Orthodox Christianity in this context therefore implies that this project was not a general study of the most important religions of Estonia, but one that framed the religion of Estonians as one that was suppressed under the Soviets (hence Russians). The domestic initiative in this case did not involve a special effort to be inclusive of the country's largest minority, something that would be almost unthinkable from a Western European partner (but not an American partner.)

The second particularly noteworthy event addressed a subject that foreign organizations have neglected badly: supporting NGOs' engagement in the policy processes that are necessary to implement good new programs on a wider basis. It is telling, therefore, that another of the early self-financed projects was a conference related to education policy. The conference,

> aimed to raise into the focus of society's interest the current processes in the development of education in Estonia. Among the 40 participants there were Members of Riigikogu [the unicameral legislature of 100 people], representatives of 5 political parties, representatives of the Ministry of Education, school headmasters etc. During the conference several issues of public interest and expectations towards the education were touched. The conference earned lots of interest in the media—in the newspapers, radio and TV.[15] (para. 5)

The extent to which projects were driven by the foreign donors reinforces Wedel's point: "with the outside donor[s] as chief constituent[s], local NGOs are sometimes more firmly rooted in transnational networks than in their own societies" (Wedel, 2001, p. 114). As these examples suggest and the Carnegie Endowment report notes about assistance, it "often forces them to be more responsive to outside donors than to their internal constituencies" (as cited in Wedel, 2001, p. 114). But as Samoff (1999) makes clear, the responsiveness of NGOs to foreign partners and donors is not an isolated dynamic; it is consistent with the relationships between the small countries of Central and Eastern Europe and the EU, NATO, and other great powers (pp. 66–67). Indeed, under pressure from NATO and the EU, Estonia officially adopted a policy of Holocaust Day for schools, despite widespread opposition from the population (Stevick, 2007). Whether involving NGOs or governments, these are not democratic relations between equals, but "heavy-handed and top-down approach[es that] involved, on the recipient side, elites who knew English and had quickly learned how to write grant proposals" (Wedel, 2001, p. 117).

"The Necessary Arts of Self-Preservation"—Economic Insecurity and Appropriation

Recipient organizations manage to function in competitive markets and under the constraints of donors while simultaneously taking over projects for their own ends and purposes. The language barrier only enhances their ability to act independently of foreign constraints. Bruno characterizes this process in Russia quite well:

Russians have accepted the "given" of international aid and co-operation projects (whether wanted or not) and are weaving them into the complex system of patronage, social relations and survival strategies which are taking shape in postsocialist Russian reality. (as cited in Wedel, 2001, p. 114)

In their discussion of policy implementation, Levinson and Sutton label the process through which policy—or in this case, foreign aid—is adapted, "appropriation." They characterize appropriation as

an active process of cultural production through borrowing, recontextualiz-ing, remolding, and thereby resignifying cultural forms.... [It] emphasizes the agency of local actors in interpreting and adapting [resources] to the sit-uated logic in their contexts of everyday practice. (Levinson & Sutton, 2001, p. 17)

Perhaps the most important factor contributing to the forms of appropriation that diverge from donor goals is economic insecurity. Since civil society often flourishes in tandem with a prosperous economy that can support NGOs, and such a robust economy was manifestly absent in postcommunist countries in the years immediately following the Soviet collapse, civil society organizations had to look elsewhere for support. As Sutton and Arnove (2004, p. ix) point out, "what all NGOs have in common is their unique status as (usually) nonprofit, private sector actors located between the state and market institutions involved in the provision of educational [and other] services." Although NGOs (and governments) may be distinct from markets, they, and the people who work within them, are nevertheless subject to market forces. Sometimes, the uncertainty and pressure of the market are used to motivate their activity. Such an approach can be effective at spurring initiative and responsibility for oneself; it can also produce a set of incentives that pit individuals' self-interest against the public's best interest and the common good.

This typology of nongovernmental is organized according to the nature of their activities and the level of economic security they provided to the people who work for them. They are termed Letterhead, Endowed, and Revenue-Dependent NGOs (see Table 5.1).

Letterhead NGOs do not have full-time staff. When they lack funding, a Letterhead NGO may be little more than a post-box address, Web site, or some pamphlets. They do not need to maintain an office or other infrastructure, which helps to keep their expenses low. When money is obtained from foundations or other sources, they carry out projects. These NGOs are usually part-time commitments for people who have some security in their regular jobs (often university professorships). Foun-dation grants therefore provide supplemental, but not survival, income

Table 5.1.   Typology of NGOs

Type of NGO	Full-Time Employees?	Responsible for Generating Own Funding?	Need Funds to Maintain Infrastructure?	Role of Pay/ Income From NGO to Individual	Level of Exposure to Economic Stress
Letterhead	No	Yes	No	Supplemental to Primary Income	Low/Average
Endowed	Yes	No	Yes	Primary Source of Income	Low/Average
Revenue-Dependent	Yes	Yes	Yes	Primary Source of Income	High

for those involved. They may be selective and opportunistic because they are not under the same levels of pressure to procure funding.

Endowed NGOs have a secure and often substantial source of funds that provides job security for their employees. People in these organizations do not need to spend their time pursuing new revenue streams, and are therefore free from external constraints and the pressure to cultivate donors. They can concentrate on activities that they deem important and thus have more flexibility to address directly the problems they perceive. There is not a structural conflict between self-interest and principles and there is no need to propagate problems, avoid real solutions or manufacture crises. Their time can be committed to policy work and program implementation.

Revenue-Dependent NGOs offer little or no job security. They are subject to market forces: they either obtain funds for themselves or they fail. As Sutton and Arnove note (2004, p. xi), "Some [NGOs] are very dependent upon binational, philanthropic and international agencies for their own funding." Funds can be obtained through markets by competing to provide educational services (e.g., in service teacher-training) or, usually, by competing for foreign financing. They are uniquely vulnerable to foreign agendas. Their need for funds puts them in an inferior or dependent relationship with foreign partners. They must justify or articulate their projects in terms that are acceptable to the donors. They may lack the means to conduct those activities that they would endorse independently but that lack foreign support. As a result, they have an incentive to engage in projects about which they are ambivalent at best. Their success in cultivating foreign donors, on the other hand, can free them from the concerns of domestic constituents and enable them to avoid cooperation with domestic rivals. Foreign income can actually encourage them to exempt themselves from the domestic policy process. Such organizations can be tremendously productive and hard-working without accomplishing wider goals of program implementation. They have no financial incentive to do so. In fact, the need to sustain outside support may turn their attention first to finding new revenue streams, to cultivate a wide range of external funding sources, and to pile up projects that fragment their time and energies. Worst of all, their ability to procure funding is linked directly with urgent problems in the national system; the more flawed the system, the easier it is to justify projects and hence to support themselves.

In Estonia, the wide range of new materials to be covered in postcommunist civics courses, and, more recently, the creation of a national exam in the subject, combined with the absence of formal university teacher-training in the subject to create a need and demand for in-service teacher-training in civic education. Since teachers are free to choose the provider of their teacher-training (subject to approval from their school director), there is significant competition among public universities, nongovernmental organizations and private training firms in civic education (Toots, 1997, p. 3).[16] The need to attract these teachers generated a mixed set of market effects. On the one hand, teachers who may need to grapple with difficult issues like the integration of the Russian-minority are free to avoid sessions whose subjects they do not like. Thus, important, difficult issues were often avoided. I was unable to identify a single teacher-training event of this sort that brought together ethnic Estonian and Russian teachers, for example. On the other hand, the fact that Russian teachers had these resources available created an incentive for teacher-trainers who otherwise might not have been interested in interacting with them to provide services for them anyway.

This market pressure is seen by some as a means to instill personal responsibility and initiative, despite the stress is can impose. A good example is Mart Laar (1997, 2004), a former school teacher, historian, two-time prime minister, leader of a nationalist party, founder of the Jaan Tõnisson Institute, and winner of the Cato Institutes Milton Friedman Prize. Toots (1997) wrote that,

> The most basic and vital change of all, however, had to take place in the hearts and minds of Estonia's people. Without a major readjustment of attitudes, the postcommunist predicament would become a trap, and the nation would never move forward to become a "normal" country with free government and free markets under law. In the era of Soviet-imposed socialism, most people withdrew into a kind of private quietism; associations seldom extended beyond small circles of relatives and close friends, and the public realm was dominated by the Communist Party-state and its enforced

conformities. People were not used to thinking for themselves, taking the initiative, or assuming risks. Many had to be shaken out of the illusion—common in postcommunist countries—that somehow, somebody else was going to come along and solve their problems for them. It was necessary to energize people, to get them moving, to force them to make decisions and take responsibility for themselves. (p. 98)

One representative from a Revenue-Dependent NGO explained how this way of thinking was implemented in his/her organzation: people there were quite passive and did nothing beyond what they were told to do; lacking direction, they would simply sit at their deks. Once the organization made employees responsible for generating their own revenue, the institution was transformed. "They were so lazy before" (personal communication, October 2003).

The insecurity was nevertheless a source of great stress. One Baltic NGO official who was involved in civic education was asked in an exercise, "What is the worst thing that could happen?" He responded, "Saturday, my neighbor hung himself. It is hard. I worry all the time, what if my organization collapsed, God forbid?"

The need for Revenue-Dependent NGOs to pursue funding could result in exclusionary, competitive practices, patronage, a lack of candor (as discussed above), and perfunctory work. One civics expert (in a secure government job) gave an example of how poor work was connected to economic pressure:

Once we organized this Council of Europe conference about civics—it was 1996 ... I invited [one Baltic NGO] to introduce themselves and what they are doing. They made a movie about multiculturalism and they traveled six countries—it was very expensive—and they just had interviews during the two hours, interviews only with important persons. We said that, "This isn't multiculturalism at all." The person from the Council of Europe said that, "I believe, as a representative of the Council of Europe, that they only want to make money; they are an NGO, and their main interest is to have supporters, and their work is probably not very much focused on school." (personal communication, November 2003)

In a competitive education market, expertise in civic education, knowledge about the national exams, and unique access to the practices and materials coming from high-status countries like the United States all become commodities that have clear economic value. Control over the distribution of a commodity becomes a source of considerable power. For people whose income is dependent upon these commodities, access to and control of these assets need to be protected. These assets are not simply resources to be disseminated as widely as possible, as donors would hope and expect, but valuable commodities that can be used for patronage and to earn favors as well as to generate income. This account of the early civic education seminars carried out in Estonia shows why these assets could be so valuable:

> The first in-service training seminars, lasting from three to five days, were popular among the teachers, who were invited to participate and to become acquainted with the new ideas and teaching methods.... Working together with people [people from the West] was a new and exciting experience for teachers coming from the atmosphere of the closed Soviet society, where there had been no freedom of expression or thought.... The seminars were completely free [of cost] for the participants and were particularly popular because of that fact. (Valdmaa, 2002, p. 73)

The selection of participants for programs emerged as one of the most important issues in these partnerships. These opportunities were not always distributed according to merit. "Central and Eastern European NGOs often distributed Western perks to themselves and their peers on the basis of favoritism rather than merit" (Wedel, 2001, p. 113). Indeed, across the region, people selected for such events had strong connections to those with the person with the authority to select them. As Bruno writes,

> Individuals in postsocialist societies still tend to privilege those social relations determined exclusively through personal connections.... These frameworks of social relations usually escape Westerners' sensibilities, unless they are project workers with extensive knowledge of local cultures. (as cited in Wedel, 2001, pp. 113–14)

Indeed, foreign experts in civic education often gave their partners complete freedom to select participants of their choice, and this practice was one of the greatest obstacles to broad dissemination of donors' materials and ideas. Foreign donors and experts who are aware of this problem could structure aid so that opportunities and resources are more likely to be distributed on the basis of need or merit, rather than through social networks and patronage. As Chris Hann explains,

> Those who succeed in establishing good relations with a western organization manoeuvre to retain the tremendous advantage this gives them ... [in these hierarchies] where everything depends on patronage and personal connections. (as cited in Wedel, 2001, p. 114)

These practices both served to avoid competition and to exclude rivals. Wedel (2001) observed that, "The promise of Western money and access often inspired secrecy, suspicion and competition among groups" (p. 93). Bruno further observed that, "It can be counterproductive to bring together previously unacquainted recipients ... other recipients are seen as undesirable competition and the dominant attitude is one of suspicion" (as cited in Wedel, 2001, pp. 113–114). In addition, "Central and Eastern European groups often were unwilling to share information or otherwise cooperate with anyone who had not reached the status of personal friend" (Wedel, 2001, p. 113). In Estonia, one of the country's leading figures indicated that s/he had never been invited to the sessions sponsored by another organization. A review of training documents revealed just one such invitation, dating from 1996. When I explained these dynamics to an American partner who had encountered him/her at conferences, he exclaimed "So that's why [that person] avoids me at conferences!" (personal communication, July 2003). Without an awareness of these dynamics, foreign partners cannot address this typical problem: "In the absence of sophisticated, well-conceived incentives on the part of donors to help build bridges among groups, funding frequently inspired competition among groups, rather than cooperation" (Wedel, 2001, p. 114).

To protect themselves, however, recipients do not want their foreign partners to be aware of these dynamics. Steven Sampson noted that "individuals [who] serve as brokers in the unequal relationship between the west and east.... Like brokers everywhere ... manipulate resources and thrive off the maintenance of barriers. The forum for such activity is the world of projects, and civil society development is part of this world" (as cited in Wedel, 2001, p. 88). Foremost among these was the language barrier, and it was maintained in part by bringing participants who were not capable in the relevant language. With remarkable regularity in conferences that I attended with participants from across the Baltic States, those who were leading delegations would bring participants who had little ostensible connection to the subject area and who did not speak the language of the conference. Even for multiday conferences, participants would sit in long English-language sessions with no understanding of what was being said, because often no translation was provided. Foreign partners, who generally socialize with the leaders, were relatively oblivious to this fact. One speaker pleaded repeatedly for the audience to quiet down so that s/he could be heard despite being hoarse, to no avail and mounting frustration. They were unable to understand her pleas, and s/he was unaware that they could not understand her. Being compelled to sit for hours on end in sessions that one cannot understand can be a numbing experience. It is unsurprising that such participants sometimes whisper to each other to enliven the experience. When I pointed out this problem to a group of Americans at another conference, one listener later stopped me to express thanks because s/he had simply assumed that the Baltic participants would understand English and had concluded that they were extremely rude to be talking through the presentations, when in fact they were (likely) just trying to get something out of it.

One of the teachers whom I regularly observed was selected for a very expensive, 3-week trip to the United States. We had developed a friendly relationship, and I was excited for him/her to have the opportunity, but in fact, his/her lack of English-language ability meant that most of the resources spent on this person's trip were squandered. For weeks, this teacher expressed stress over the need to give a short presentation in English as part of the trip. The teacher's spouse, who spoke English, composed it, and the teacher spent a good deal of time practicing it, afterwards recounting how s/he had read it word for word from the printed copy. While this person was a useful contact to cultivate, and served in a national capacity, the professional benefits of participation in the trip was minimal. Despite the large investments in such exchanges and seminars, no procedures were in place to insure that participants' language abilities met a minimal threshold for participation.

Many of these dynamics are illustrated by a defensible project, but one of questionable value: the translation of American standards for civics into Estonian. Having the standards that were drawn up for the United States translated into local languages could provide a valuable resource for any country that is working to prepare civic education standards. But was it necessary? We documented above that virtually every significant figure in civic education already spoke English. So for whom was a translation really needed? The recipients of the finished product were mixed about the translation's real and potential value.

The account addresses the quality of the document, the perceived need for it and its possible contribution, and continues to suggest that the problem-solving narrative built up around the project breaks down at the level of implementing the solution.

> American civics standards were translated into Estonian—but I am not sure that the translation is good, because government has different meanings in English. I thought it was an interesting idea, to use the standards as an example, and to try to reevaluate the curricular outcomes because they're too general at the different levels. He wanted to go deeper with that, which is a fine idea, and I said, "Just speak with the responsible person from the Curriculum Development Center [which has the official responsibility for the curriculum] and work together; don't do illegal work outside the proper channels with one subject." Probably it is good to talk in general about all the social studies outcomes. But he wanted to start with a project to open outcomes in civics … but I just thought it has to be legal work and done together with people who are officially responsible. (personal communication, November 2003)

This suggestion entailed cooperation with a rival, and was not followed. Another recipient was more skeptical, complaining the translation was of low quality and pointing out that the translators were the grant-writer, as well as one of the grant-writer's offspring. The grant money was not acquired to hire professional translators to carry out the task, but directly benefited the family of the person who articulated the task. This critic believed that the grant-applicant's priorities concerning civic education were not entirely rooted in a principled commitment to the selfless promotion of democratic development: "fundraising is maybe the first master" (personal communication, October 2003).

Such projects are a natural by-product of the nature of partnerships and the structure of aid. The funding organization is obliged to promote certain ideas and interests, including materials developed in its own country. The applicant articulates a project that fits the needs of the funder and implies that their help is important and influential. The donor has no independent access to assess whether the project is really needed at all. The income provides, however temporarily, some income for the party in question, and further legitimizes that person as an expert with unique access to important foreigners. The interests of both parties are met.

Restructuring Aid and Partnerships

A number of steps can be taken to reduce the pressures that contribute to these problems and to improve the nature of foreign aid in such partnerships. The selection of partners and participants is problematic throughout the process. Teachers expressed the least satisfaction with the one-day events that bring in experts or consultants with no knowledge of the context for talks or lectures, although this remains a popular technique. Donor organizations' initial selection of partners should be done with independent people who are fluent in the local language and not simply on the basis of English-language fluency. Increased use of immigrants or refugees from the country who were able to cross the language and cultural barriers would have been a great asset as well. Particularly for contexts like Estonia where German and Russian language skills are widespread, it should be very easy to find experts who can interact with people unmediated by national "brokers." People able to cross the language barrier can overcome the transmission-orientation and are better able to engage in dialogue with their partners and the teachers in a given context.

Once partners are selected, donors should be aware of what resources they have to distribute. In cases in which they are distributing valuable opportunities like those discussed above, clear procedures should be in place that increase the likelihood that decisions will be based on merit rather than favoritism. Such criteria could include the diversity of the participants, their geographic distribution, and so forth. Notices of opportunities should be distributed widely through public channels. In cases that require foreign language ability (like English), independent language evaluators should be employed, and brief final interviews could be conducted over the phone. Although these procedures are appropriate and justifiable, they do risk the possibility of transferring even more power to the foreign donor. On occasion it may be appropriate to reserve a slot or two for the partner to distribute according to his/her discretion. Such a "set-aside" may increase the odds that the procedures will be followed as described.

Another crucial step could be taken to ensure the partner's financial stability. If the many overlapping, cooperating and competing donors, networks, foundations and other organizations would join forces to give some approximation of economic security to an appropriate specialist, that person or persons could then draw upon the variety of resources and expertise as needed. The needs assessment research done in South Africa provides an excellent model for generating the knowledge needed to address problems as people in the field perceive them. Assistance with conducting appropriate research would be very valuable, and the results must be published (since such knowledge can be used in proprietary fashion and not for the common good.)

This economic stability should not be a long-term appointment, however. Some level of rotation can be very beneficial, particularly as individuals' own biases and weaknesses can leave important issues unaddressed. Partnerships can calcify, and the concentration of resources in certain hands for too long can inhibit broader dissemination of ideas, opportunities, and resources. A rough estimate would be offering a position for four and a half years, at 150% of the annual salary of the country, so that the job is attractive enough to bring in someone well-qualified for the job. The final 6 months would be spent overlapping with the next person, who would ideally build on what has been accomplished and start new initiatives as well. The person moving into a new position, would, with his or her accrued experience and expertise, ideally would remain involved in the field. It would be beneficial to move out beyond the capital or large cities and to work directly with members of minority groups.

CONCLUSION

Foreign influence on civic education, though shaped by ideological goals, was nevertheless not characterized by the direct transmission of ideological views from foreign experts through nationally prominent civics experts to teachers and students. Instead, foreign resources and donors were often used instrumentally by domestic actors for their own purposes. One clear purpose was the acquisition of foreign funds, which was too often the end—rather than the means to some other end—of the partnerships for those under economic stress. Ironically, perhaps, the free-market ideology that pervaded the push for civil society development ultimately subverted the message, as those under economic pressure took on projects whose values they did not endorse and ceased advocating for further policy or implementation of those projects once the funding ran out. Foreign resources, donors and experts were often more empowering of partners' local goals than they were effective advocates for the positions they espoused. These dynamics are best understood in the context of power and resource imbalances between partners, the perverse incentives that pit recipient self-interest against project goals, and the lack of donor knowledge of local languages and cultures. These various dynamics and contextual factors were manifested within the selection of participants in civic education partnerships: who gets the floor, which domestic partners are selected, and how they select those to be trained.

NOTES

1. PHARE originally stood for the Poland and Hungary: Assistance for Restructuring their Economies.
2. As Conry (1993), writing for the Cato Institute, indicates, critics from the left and right disagree about the ideological balance of its spending:

    > although the four core grantees appear to represent diverse constituencies, Corn and other liberal critics accuse NED of leaning too far to the right, because the Republican party, business (represented by the Chamber of Commerce group), and organized labor all generally adopt a conservative stance when it comes to foreign policy. That leaves only the National Democratic Institute to represent more liberal views. At the same time, conservative critics bring up the issue of proportion among the four main recipients: the AFL CIO receives approximately 40 percent of available funding, while each of the other groups receives around 10 percent. (Conry, 1993)

    > By 2006, NED, which is also criticized for its links to neoconservative thinkers including Francis Fukuyama, had received considerable negative publicity for channeling close to one million dollars to the coup leaders who attempted to overthrow Hugo Chavez in Venezuela, as well as for controversial activities in Cuba and Haiti. A well-connected former Republican congressman, and "superlobbyist" Vin Weber, was chairman of the board at the time.

3. The Ashbrook Center was founded when long-serving Representative John M. Ashbrook died in April of 1982 during a race for the U.S. Senate. Schramm also "served in the Reagan Administration as the Director of the Center for International Education in the United States Department of Education" (retrieved July 3, 2006 from, http://www.ashbrook.org/columns/

schramm/). In his columns on the Ashbrook Center Web site and the weblog *No Left Turns*, he identifies himself as a long-standing conservative who was an active supporter of Barry Goldwater and the Vietnam War and continues to be outspoken about conservative causes. Speaking of Vietnam War protestors, he writes, "No matter what they were saying, when left-wing groups would get together and chant, it always sounded like 'Sieg Heil!' to us" (retrieved July 3, 2006 from, http://www.ashbrook.org/publicat/onprin/special/schramm.html). Although he was leading talks in Estonia during the early Clinton administration for an IFES that was partly supported by government funding, he apparently was no fan of the pair in the White House. As he wrote in 2003, "I don't dislike the Clintons because I have policy disagreements with them, I dislike them for what they are. I still think both Clintons have tyrannic souls, Hillary more like Lady Macbeth (dark souled woman), Bill more like Richard III (a very amusing tyrant, easy to like). But both are tyrants: there is nothing above them, nothing but them, and only them; their own interests and their own passions; they press, always press, to satisfy their desires. They are users. And, as the Poet says, it is time to fear when tyrants seem to kiss." Last retrieved July 3, 2006 from http://noleftturns.ashbrook.org/comment.asp?blogID=1940.

4. Last retrieved July 3. 2006, from http://www.iri.org/pdfs/AR2004.pdf. Chaired by John McCain and prominently featuring President Bush next to a quote from his 2005 inaugural address, the document is a who's who of Republican power-brokers.

5. Senator Inhofe has recently attracted attention for a civics-related proposal for the United States: requiring immigrants to be quizzed on the Federalist Papers—on which, coincidentally, Indiana University scholar John Patrick has published extensively—presumably in English, which Inhofe wants to be legally established as the national language of the United States (Rich, 2006). Such nationalist views towards minorities and immigrants resonate well with a number of Estonians, as we will see below, and raise the possibility of ideological convergence in international collaborations, the idea that people who come together philosophically through common practices or emphases will share common ground on other key issues, even if they are never discussed explicitly.

6. Last retrieved July 3, 2006, from http://www.ifes.org/about.html. Data since removed from Web site.

7. The amount of money available from foreign assistance seemed to be substantially more than what was available by trying to start a small business that provided goods or services to people who were struggling economically. The difference was enough to make me wonder both how much of a country's entrepreneurial energies were directed out of the private sector and into the pursuit of unsustainable (but highly lucrative in the short term) foreign project funding, and how civil society could have developed differently if those who were in fact deeply committed had not been displaced by entrepreneurs who were more adept at managing foreign donors.

8. A list of these partnerships can be found here: http://www.jti.ee/en/civic/projects.shtml

9. http://www.jti.ee/en/civic/pro_holybible.shtml
10. http://www.jti.ee/en/civic/pro_educindemoc.shtml
11. This competition involves fairly substantial revenue: when I enrolled in a weekend teacher-training seminar, which spanned Friday evening until Sunday morning, the cost was over $100, which at the time was equivalent to about a third of the average monthly income in the country.

REFERENCES

Abma, T., Greene, J. C., Karlsson, O., Ryan, K., Schwandt, T., & Widdershoven, G. (2001). Dialogue on dialogue. *Evaluation 7*(2), 164–180.

Catlaks, G. (2006). European and American approaches to citizenship education in the context of European Union Enlargement. *Civitas International.* Retrieved May 7, 2008, from http://www.civnet.org/contenidos.php?id_secciones=OA==&ACTION=TW9zdHJhclVuQ29udGGV uaWRv&id_contenido=NTM=

Conry, B. (1993). *Loose cannon: The National Endowment for Democracy.* Retrieved July 3, 2006, from http://www.cato.org/pubs/fpbriefs/fpb-027.html

IFES. (n.d.). *About.* Retrieved July 3, 2006, from http://www.ifes.org/about.html

Jaan Tõnisson Institute. (1995a). *Civic education programs for the years 1993–1994.* Tallinn, Estonia: Jaan Tõnisson Institute. Pedagoogika Arhiivmuuseum Fond R32389.

Jaan Tõnisson Institute. (1995b, May 17-19). *Rahvusvaheline nõupidamine: Balti koostöö kodanikuõpetuses.* Tallinn, Estonia: Jaan Tõnisson Institute & Avatud Eesti Fond. Pedagoogika Arhiivmuuseum Fond R32393.

Kutsar D. (1995). Social change and stress in Estonia. *Scandinavian Journal of Social Welfare, 4,* 94–107.

Laar, M. (1997). Estonia's success story. *Journal of Democracy, 7*(1), 96–101.

Laar, M. (2004, August 20). When will Russia say sorry? *Wall Street Journal (Eastern edition),* p. A12.

Levinson, B. A. U., & Sutton, M. (2001). Introduction: Policy as/in practice—A sociocultural approach to the study of educational policy. In M. Sutton & B. A. U. Levinson (Eds.), *Policy as practice: Toward a comparative sociocultural analysis of educational policy* (pp. 1–22). Westport, CT: Ablex.

Pilon, J. G. (n.d.). *Juliana Geron Pilon.* Retrieved July 3, 2006, from http://www.iwp.edu/docLib/20060606_JGPresume.pdf

Putnam, R. D., Leonardi, R., & Nanetti, R. Y. (1994). *Making Democracy work: Civic traditions in modern Italy.* Princeton, NJ: Princeton University Press.

Quigley, C. N. & J. N. Hoar. (1997). Civitas: An international civic education exchange program. *International Journal of Social Education, 12*(2), 11–26.

Rich, F. (2006, June 11). How hispanics became the new gays. *The New York Times,* p. C1.

Samoff, J. (1999). Institutionalizing international influence. In R. F. Arnove & C. A. Torres (Eds.), *Comparative education: The dialectic of the global and the local* (pp. 51–89). Lanham, MD: Rowman & Littlefield.

Schlafly, P. (2002, April). How did we get a federal curriculum? *Torch*, 9(2). Retrieved July 3, 2006, from http://texaseagle.org/torch/04-02.html

Schramm, P. W. (2006, April). *Born American, but in the wrong place. On principle.* Retrieved Retrieved July 3, 2006 from http://www.ashbrook.org/publicat/onprin/special/schramm.html

Stein, P. (1991, September 10). Sweden: From capitalist success to welfare-state sclerosis. *Cato Policy Analysis No. 160.* Retrieved July 3, 2006, from http://www.cato.org/pubs/pas/pa-160.html

Stevick, E. D. (2007). The politics of the Holocaust in Estonia: Historical memory and social division in estonian education. In E. D. Stevick & B. A. U. Levinson (Eds.), *Reimagining civic education: How diverse societies form democratic citizens* (pp. 217–244). New York: Rowman & Littlefield.

Sutton, M., & Arnove, R. (2004). Introduction: Civil society or shadow state? State/NGO relations in education. In M. Sutton & R. Arnove (Eds.), *Civil society or shadow state? State/NGO relations in education* (pp. vii–xviii). Greenwich, CT: Information Age.

Sutton, M., & Levinson, B. A. U. (Eds.). (2001). *Policy as practice: Toward a comparative sociocultural analysis of educational policy.* Westport, CT: Ablex.

Swedish Institute. (n.d.). *About us.* Last retrieved May 7, 2008, from http://www.sweden.se/templates/cs/CommonPage____5105.aspx

Toots, A. (1997). *Abbreviated phase I case study (Estonia). Document prepared For Estonia's acceptance as a participant in the IEA Civic Education study.* Unpublished manuscript.

Turner, S. (2002, April). No Child Left Behind encompasses global education. *Torch*, 9(2). Retrieved July 3, 2006, from http://texaseagle.org/torch/04-02.html

Valdmaa, S. (2002). Developing civic education in Estonia. In S. Tawil (Ed.), *Curriculum change and social inclusion: Perspectives from the Baltic and Scandinavian countries: Final report of the Regional Seminar Held in Vilnius, Lithuania 5–8 December, 2001* (pp. 71–79). Vilnius, Lithuania: Open Society Foundation.

Wedel, J. (2001). *Collision and collusion. The strange case of Western aid to Eastern Europe.* New York: Palgrave.

Wedel, J., & G. Feldman. (2005). Why an anthropology of public policy? *Anthropology Today, 21*(1), 1–2.

CHAPTER 6

CIVIC EDUCATION REFORM FOR DEMOCRACY

U.S. Models in Mexico and Indonesia

Bradley A. U. Levinson and Margaret Sutton

Although the meanings of democratic citizenship are as varied and complex as the corresponding mechanisms of democratic governance, we still know relatively little about how such meanings are negotiated in the global context of power politics, where dominant models of democratic citizenship are made available to, if not imposed upon, emerging democracies. Civic and citizenship education programs that are being developed in newly democratizing countries constitute one important arena of negotiated meaning; in this arena, globally circulating conceptions of political citizenship, and citizenship education, encounter local cultural and institutional norms. What results in practice from this encounter can only be dimly foretold.

In order to reveal contrasts and commonalities across two national cases, in this chapter we compare new programs in democratic citizenship education for Mexico's and Indonesia's secondary schools. We show that globally circulating conceptions of democratic citizenship, typically

Advancing Democracy Through Education? U.S. Influence Abroad and
Domestic Practices, pp. 129–157
Copyright © 2008 by Information Age Publishing

originating in the constitutional democracies of the North, become uniquely appropriated by national education ministries in the development of policy and curriculum reform for civic education. The forms that such appropriation take are strongly conditioned by three dynamics. First is the nature of the interaction between national and global actors charged with developing educational programs for democratic citizenship. Second are both the historical and contemporary political dynamics of the national contexts in which reform takes place. Third are the institutional dynamics of national education ministries, in relation to other educational agencies, as the primary policy making bodies. We follow a historical-institutionalist perspective that takes seriously the possibility that there can be "modernization without Westernization" (Hayhoe, 1999; Mazrui, 1975, 2001). Specifically, countries that are modernizing and democratizing their political structures can recover and elaborate democratic traditions from within, and thereby define democratic citizenship in terms uniquely inflected by local cultural contexts.

Our work here is informed in part by long-term study of these national education systems. As anthropologists, each of us has studied various aspects of the Mexican and Indonesian education systems, respectively, for 15 or 20 years (e.g., Levinson, 2001). More specifically, we report here on recent ethnographic forays into the respective worlds of Mexican and Indonesian policy formation for civic education. In 2001 and 2003, Levinson spent more than 6 weeks in Mexico interviewing key policymakers, administrators, and teachers, collecting documents, and observing the teaching of civic education in a range of local secondary schools (Levinson, 2004, 2005a, 2005b). Since then, he has continued to track the development of civic education reform in Mexico, primarily through interviews and document analysis. Margaret Sutton first conducted research in Indonesia in 1988; beginning in 2000, she engaged in a 5-year collaboration with teacher educators in West Sumatra, Indonesia, to reform the education of future civic educators at the Universitas Negeri, Padang; and currently she is working with colleagues at two other U.S. universities to establish a consortium of U.S. and Indonesian teacher education universities. In Spring, 2005, Sutton spent 2 months in Indonesia observing teacher education classes and conducting interviews to determine how democratic civic education is being defined and practiced by teacher educators in Sumatra.

This paper, then, reports primarily on national efforts at creating new programs and curriculum for democratic citizenship education. Yet we hope that our attempts here to disentangle the meanings of citizenship involved in national reforms of civic education may serve as an initial breaking of the ground for more complete, multilevel studies of civic teaching and learning in school, as well as other local spaces where meanings and identities are produced. Ideally, the study of national reform should open out to the complexity of both international borrowing, on the one hand, and subnational processes of policy appropriation on the other (Sutton & Levinson, 2001).

SETTING THE STAGE FOR EDUCATION REFORM: POLITICAL CONTEXTS AND STRUCTURAL CHANGES

Mexico and Indonesia provide an interesting comparison of "democratization" processes and their accompanying reforms of civic education. Both are emerging from long periods of authoritarian rule—70 years of single-party dominance after a revolution in Mexico, and 30 years of single-party rule (and 50 of an authoritarian presidency) in Indonesia. Both have significant colonial and postcolonial histories, in which European ideas and institutions have become deeply entwined with the development of postindependence forms of governance. Each has a relatively long history of independence (although Mexico, as with most Latin American countries, achieved independence in the early 1800s, while Indonesia did not become independent until 1949); each is a growing, highly populous country that plays a large role in regional geopolitics. Finally, each has a historically centralized education system that is charged with creating national identity and citizenship. As we show below, recent civic education reforms cannot be understood without contextualizing them in each country's political history.

A major difference between the two is in the governmental powers of the military in Indonesia, and the legal separation of powers in Mexico. As we shall see, there is also a significant difference between them in the conditions of religious expression. Both are nominally pluralist societies nevertheless dominated historically by a single religion: Mexico is mainly Roman Catholic, while Indonesia is home to the largest national population of Muslims in the world. In Mexico, there has long been a firm tradition of church-state separation. In Indonesia, much like in the United States, the confessional neutrality of the government is often in tension with deep religiosity in civil society.

Mexico

The Mexican Constitution of 1917—an updated version of the original Liberal Constitution of 1857 forged during the years of the revolution against the dictatorship of Porfirio Díaz—still remains the law in Mexico. Although the Constitution stipulates a progressive federal regime with a bicameral congress, considerable state and municipal autonomy, and a separation of executive, judicial, and legislative powers, the reality in postrevolutionary Mexico has rarely matched Constitutional ideals. Deeply rooted in the habits of colonial and dictatorial rule, Mexico quickly turned into what many have called a presidentialist regime. The concentration of power in the president's office led to a subordinate judiciary and a rubber-stamp legislature. By 1929, the president had formed the political party that eventually came to be known as the Partido Revolucionario Institucional (PRI). Drawing together different sectors of society (skilled labor, the peasantry, business groups, etc.), the PRI developed a disciplined corporatist machine that helped identify the party with the state and thereby perpetuate single-party rule. Importantly, the national teachers' union (SNTE) effectively came to serve as one of the bastions of PRI support. Although a nominally democratic nation, for over 70 years the PRI ruled Mexico with an iron hand, using a combination of carrot and stick, and sometimes outright electoral fraud, to keep itself in power. In addition to holding a constant majority in the Congress and controlling all major ministry appointments, the PRI controlled most mayoralties and virtually all of the 31 state governorships.

It was not until the late 1970s that significant electoral reforms began to open the possibility for meaningful opposition politics in Mexico. The democratic student movements of the 1960s and early 1970s, repressed by the PRI, began to bear fruit as its former participants moved into decision-making positions. Then, the economic crisis of the 1980s, followed by a series of neoliberal reforms, further reduced the legitimacy of the single-party state, which had long used the profits from oil sales to finance a populist agenda. Several important mayoralties and governorships fell to opposition parties over the 1980s, and in 1988 the PRI resorted to massive electoral fraud in order to reclaim the presidency from the renegade candidate Cuauhtémoc Cárdenas. The PRI attempted to recover legitimacy throughout the 1990s by agreeing to further electoral reforms and conducting more transparent business, yet certain democratic gains were irreversible. The economic crisis deepened, and so too did the presence of new democratic actors who were determined to force the peaceful resolution of social problems, through civil disobedience if necessary. Chief among these nongovernmental organizations (NGOs) were those devoted to human rights, women's rights, indigenous peoples, economic justice, and the environment (Preston & Dillon, 2004).

Throughout these changes, the national ministry of public education, called the Secretaría de Educación Pública, or simply SEP, has played an important role. An ideological child of the revolution, the SEP was created in 1921 to advance the integrative and developmentalist agenda of the nascent state. Modeled on the French system, and highly centralized in

Mexico City, the huge bureaucracy of the SEP controls most of the formal educational enterprise in Mexico. Through the control of teacher education, the hiring of all teachers, and the production of common textbooks for all of basic education, the SEP has historically been a key instrument of state formation and the creation of national identity (Ornelas, 1995; Vaughan, 1997). The "basic agreement on educational modernization" of 1992, followed by constitutional reforms of 1993, have both augmented and curtailed the power of the SEP. For instance, administrative decentralization has put the states in charge of budgeting and teacher hiring; yet so-called "middle basic education," or *secundaria* (Grades 7–9, roughly ages 12–15), has now been made compulsory. Meanwhile, matters of curriculum and educational planning, especially, are still highly concentrated in the SEP.

The reform of Mexican civic education began in the early 1990s, when the PRI still held federal power. For nearly 20 years, civic education at the secondary level had been folded into the general area of "social sciences." The modernization reforms of 1992–93 led to the return of a distinct course of civics (*civismo*) and the introduction of a new course called "educational orientation." Then, during the last PRI presidential administration (1994–2000), the secretary of education gave an internal team the charge to create an ambitious new program in "civic and ethical formation" (FCE) for all 3 years of *secundaria*. Blessed by the PRI President Ernesto Zedillo, the FCE program attempted to respond to a number of social and political concerns. Different sectors of society across the political spectrum had begun to agitate for a stronger education in "values" in order to offset the palpable effects of what was generally called "social disintegration": the breakdown of the nuclear family, youth's challenge to adult authority, rampant crime and street-level violence, an aggressive consumerism, and so forth. Meanwhile, many advocates of the ongoing democratic opening saw in the schools a chance to build a new political culture from the ground up. For them, values of democratic participation, equity, and tolerance were paramount.

Thus, while the reform of Mexican civic education began in the early 1990s, what gave it renewed impetus, and special interest, was its convergence in 2000 with the end of PRI hegemony. Long-standing single-party rule was effectively ended in Mexico with the election of the opposition candidate, Vicente Fox, and with the achievement of an opposition-majority in the bicameral Congress. From 2001–2006 Fox's party, *Partido de Acción Nacional* (PAN), controlled all major ministries, and Fox made significant new appointments within the education ministry. While most Mexicans hailed these new developments as important steps on the road to full democracy, many worried that the rightist PAN, historically allied with the Catholic Church, would use its power to erode the strong separation of church and State that has characterized public education perhaps since the Liberal constitution of 1857, and certainly since the revolution ended, in 1921. The FCE program, because it centrally addresses questions of ethics, morality, and citizenship, was thought to be one area where the PAN might seek to introduce religion back into the schools. Yet most policymakers and curriculum experts in the education ministry maintained non-PAN political sympathies and, like the vast majority of schoolteachers themselves, strongly upheld the principle of "*laicidad*" (secularism) in schools.

The new course for civic and ethical education in Mexican secondary schools is ambitious and complex. Most strikingly, it has been mandated for all *secundarias* throughout the country. For three hours a week, all 3 years of *secundaria*, the new program not only covers the traditional themes of civic education (Constitution, structure of government, laws, electoral processes, etc.), but includes a variety of "ethical" considerations, including sex education, gender relations, environmental awareness, prevention of drug addiction and gang membership, and multicultural awareness and tolerance. These issues are interspersed throughout all 3 years, and heavy emphasis is placed on active, participatory, student-centered learning.

Indonesia

Civic education reform began much more abruptly in Indonesia than in Mexico, in the context of profound political change that is still ongoing. On May 22, 1998, Indonesia's second president, Suharto, resigned after 32 years in power. The Asian economic crisis, bringing an end to years of economic growth and expansion of the Indonesian middle class, provided the context for President Suharto's resignation; the murder by Indonesian security forces of four demonstrating university students on May 12, 1998, was the proximate cause. In the wake of Suharto's resignation, the structure of government and the political culture of Indonesia have been profoundly altered. The parliamentary elections of 1999 marked only the second free elections in the history of the Republic, the first having been held 6 years after independence, in 1955, during the presidency of Sukarno. In response to public pressure, the parliament elected in 1999 enacted massive decentralization of government functions—most, including education, to the district and city level—effective in 2001. In 2002, parliament divested itself of the authority to select the nation's president. In 2004, Indonesia held its first direct presidential election; President Susilo Bambang Yudhyono took office in October, 2004 This era, known in Indonesia as *Reformasi*, provides an historically novel opportunity for all Indonesians to express their interests and to develop their visions of a just society. Civic education, formerly a venue for reinforcing state ideology and obedience to national authority, is now called upon to create the new democratic Indonesian citizen. Who this citizen is, what values he or she holds, and what behaviors are expected of him or her, are topics that are widely debated in the Indonesian press.

Indonesia is an enormous and diverse nation, comprising some 250 million souls living on 6,000 of its 17,000 islands and speaking around 250 languages, though united linguistically by the national language, *bahasa Indonesia*. Throughout its modern history, the central government has responded with military force to recidivist movements and other forms of dissent, as well as to conflict between contiguous ethnic and religious groups. In the process, the military became strongly entrenched as a political entity. It is difficult to appreciate fully the place of the military in Indonesian society, and indeed, some of the fundamental challenges of defining democracy in Indonesia today, without an understanding of the events that transpired in 1965 and 1966 and led to President Suharto's assumption of executive power. On September 30, 1965, seven generals in the Indonesian army were murdered, an event known in Indonesia as GESTAPU (Gerakan September Tiga-Puluh, or the September 30th Movement). According to analysts outside of Indonesia, the murders were likely committed by a faction of the armed forces themselves (Aveling, 1980). However, the official story of the New Order, consistently and persistently repeated in textbooks and speeches, is that the murders were undertaken by the *Parti Kommuniste Indonesia*, or PKI. The first communist party established outside of Europe and the largest in a noncommunist state, the PKI and the Indonesian military were uneasy partners in the latter years of the Old Order (Hindley, 1966). GESTAPU occasioned an outbreak of civil strife, defined as a purge of communists, which left between 500,000 and 1 million dead. The horrors of that year, and its lingering effects in the form of imprisonment of social critics, are the subject of an outpouring of literature in this period of *Reformasi.*

Throughout the "Old Order" of President Sukarno (1949–1965) and the "New Order" of President Suharto (1966–1998), constitutional amendments and executive orders granted the military ever-growing powers, including authority over its own affairs, internal security, and foreign affairs; designated seats in national and regional governing bodies; ownership of profit-making enterprises; and administrative appointments at all levels of government. The latter privilege reflects the philosophy of *dwifungsi,* or the "dual functions" of the military, to ensure stability and to foster development. An ideology first promoted during the Old Order, *dwifungsi* was legally enshrined through Law No. 20/1982, which defines the Indonesian military as

> a social force that acts as a dynamizer and stabilizer, in line with other social forces, [which] will perform its duties and guarantee the success of the national struggle in development and raising the people's standard of living. (*International IDEA*, 2000, p. 91)

One concrete manifestation of *dwifungsi* is the 4,000 military personnel who held civil service appointments in 1999 (p. 99). In 7 years of *Reformasi*, numerous steps have been taken to disentangle the Indonesian military from government, and to create civilian control over it. In 1999, the police force was separated from the military, and the number of reserved national parliamentary seats was reduced from 75 to 38; in the 2004 elections, there were no seats designated for the military. In 2004, all holders of administrative positions were required to resign either from the military or from their civilian post. As a consequence of these changes, the Indonesian military is much more directly under civilian control today than in 1998. In the aftermath of the December, 2004 tsunami, a peace accord ended nearly 30 years of violence between Acehnese rebels and the Indonesian military. However, as noted recently by *Human Rights Watch*,[1] the Indonesian military still commands private finance through a massive network of military-owned businesses. All military ownership of profit-making entities is slated to end in 2009; until that time, the military will not be entirely under civilian rule.

Human rights, both in the negative sense of freedom from abuse and in the positive sense of freedom to live in dignity, have been strongly enshrined in Indonesian laws of the *Reformasi* era. In 1999, the president signed an extensive new law enforcing human rights in Indonesia. In 2002, a major amendment to the 1945 constitution provided Indonesian citizens and residents with one the most extensive constitutional guarantees of human rights in the world. Indeed, the 2002 amendments ensure virtually the entire Universal Declaration of Human Rights as basic citizenship rights of Indonesian citizens. These amendments further explicitly ban gender and ethnic-based discrimination, and guarantee government support to children, the elderly, and the infirm. While the more generous social rights are far from realized in practice, their existence as law is well known among Indonesians, and provides a platform for advocating for their realization.

The process of demilitarization of government and the outpouring of free speech are clear signals of a process of democratization that is reflected in the new civic education curriculum. Yet the sociocultural practices shaped through authoritarian rule may take longer to change. The "big three" of these—corruption, collusion and nepotism—have earned an acronym in Indonesia, KKN (*Korupsi, Kolusi, Nepotisme*). In 2003, the watchdog group *Transparency International* designated Indonesia as the world's seventh-most corrupt country, a slight improvement from its fifth-place standing the previous year. Within Indonesia, newly formed (or newly legalized) NGOs have been both whistle-blowers on, and practitioners of, corruption. In December of 2002, a Jakarta-based education NGO accused the city government of over-paying for textbooks, to fictitious publishing houses (Harsanto, 2002). Ironically, an NGO ostensibly devoted to reforming civic education, the Institute for Civic Education in Jakarta, was accused in April 2002 of misappropriation of funds intended for flood victims (*JakartaPost.com* 8/28/02). Even with the strict press censorship of the Old Order, ordinary Indonesians were well aware of KKN, which touched their daily lives. Not surprisingly, one researcher found a high degree of cynicism among youth towards the lessons conveyed in the old civic education curriculum (Moeis, 2000).

In the spirit of *Reformasi*, both military rule and corruption are widely viewed in Indonesia as problems standing in the way of realizing a just society. A much more complex element in the realization of democracy centers around the role of religion in law and political culture. Indonesia is a secular state encompassing the world's largest Islamic population, with 87% of Indonesians professing Islam. Although religious pluralism is enshrined in law, the state ideology, *Panca Sila*, places "belief in God" among the five (*panca*) principles (*sila*) of Indonesian civic identity. That is, freedom of conscience is ensured in religious matters, but that freedom must encompass a religious identity. This stance in itself suggests a major point of difference between Indonesian democracy, however defined, and liberal democratic traditions originating in the West. Throughout modern Indonesian history, sporadic violence framed by religion has problematized the status of religious pluralism. And, while the 2002 and 2005 bombings in Bali and Sulawesi drew world attention to the presence of al-Qaeda associates and sympathizers within the country, Indonesia also hosts institutions that actively promote reformist Islam. In particular, the Islamic institutions of higher education in Indonesia have a vigorous program devoted to the development of democratic civic education based on Islamic thought and practice (see Tim ICCE, 2003).

POLICY PROCESSES AND THE PRODUCTION OF NEW CURRICULUM FOR CIVIC EDUCATION

The policy processes of civic education reform, like the overall processes of democratization in Mexico and Indonesia, provide interesting points of

contrast. Decentralization of national government authority over education is a recent phenomenon in both countries, preceding civic education
reform in Mexico and accompanying it in Indonesia. The interaction
between national reforms and global models of civic education is evident
in both countries, though in different forms.

The Policy Process and Curriculum Reform in Mexico

The policy process for the reform of civic education in Mexico received
a strong impulse, according to many, from then President Ernesto Zedillo
(1994–2000), who had actually served as secretary of education for much
of the prior presidential administration, from 1988–1993. Zedillo had
been the primary architect of the modernization reforms of 1992 and
1993, which among other things enshrined new language in the Federal
Education Law that made participatory and "pertinent" education a cor-
nerstone of national development. Such emphases were reiterated in the
national Program for Educational Development 1995–2000 under
Zedillo's presidency, which highlighted the goals of achieving educational
"equity, quality, and relevance."

There is good evidence that Ernesto Zedillo was reading and channeling
a variety of social concerns that had been brewing for over a decade. Based
on previous fieldwork (Levinson, 2001), a reading of popular and scholarly
literatures, and ongoing trips to Mexico, Levinson has identified at least
three powerful societal discourses that formed and expanded throughout
the 1980s and 1990s. Each one of these discourses expressed certain
understandings of democracy, and each one would arguably impact the
eventual formation of a new program for citizenship education. Such
discourses emerged out of rather different social sectors and movements,
but each one articulated a set of existential concerns that cut across broad
sectors of Mexican society. Each one also highlighted a different set of
"values" that needed to be recovered or constructed. Finally, if there is one
theme that cuts across all the discourses it is the concern with human rights
and the creation of a culture of "tolerance." Fed up with political violence
and economic misery, and disgusted by the impunity accorded to most
perpetrators, many Mexicans by the 1990s had seized upon human rights
as a crucial value. The notion of human rights, in turn, was often vitally
linked to the attainment of democracy. However, human rights could also
become a kind of Rorschach of cultural projection: the place of human
rights, and the route to achieving a regime respectful of such rights, would
vary by discourse and social sector.

One discourse, which Levinson calls "lost values" (*valores perdidos*), drew
attention to the signs of what many observers call "social disintegration,"

such as increased violence, corruption, divorce, and disregard for adult authority. The assumption made by this discourse was that traditional values of respect, honesty, and obedience had once effectively ordered society, but had since fallen into disuse. There was a strong sense of proper social hierarchy having become challenged and turned upside-down. Most strongly articulated through conservative Catholic organizations such as the national Parents' Union (UNPF), the discourse on lost values nevertheless resonated with a much broader public. The often explicit solution proposed by the very same discourse was the recovery of values that had been "lost" in recent years—typically through religious education or other kinds of catechistic instruction, and the reassertion of paternal control.

Another discourse, which Levinson calls the active and "critical citizen" (*el ciudadano crítico*), highlighted the importance of creating deeper democratic habits and a political culture that would support a democratic transition over the longer term. Most strongly articulated by a generation of left-leaning Mexican intellectuals and leaders who had come of age in the political opposition to the PRI-dominated state, the discourse of the "critical citizen" called for a new participatory sensibility amongst citizens, most of whom were seen as having grown complacent, fatalistic, or too accustomed to state largesse. This form of participation presupposed an ethos of respectful dialogue but also critical questioning, in which existing social hierarchies and received norms would be subject to constant critique. Through deliberation, the new citizen would actively consider different social and political options through, and arrive at independent stances. The discourse of the critical citizen implicitly valued equality over hierarchy—gender equity was often prominently touted as a goal. Although it originated in the more highly schooled sectors of society, this discourse, too, found resonance across broad sectors of society that had been irrevocably changed by experiences of immigration and/or consumption of cultural media such as television, movies, popular music, and the Internet.

The third discourse, which Levinson calls "accountability" (*rendición de cuentas*), virtually created a new phrase in Mexican Spanish overnight, since there had been no adequate predecessor to this cultural import. The discourse on accountability called for greater transparency in public management, and more valid and neutral forms of evaluation in assessing educational "quality." One of the important assumptions of this discourse was that the goals of transparency and quality called for both institutional and personal transformations. On the one hand, new kinds of institutional arrangements, such as the creation of a quasi-independent National Institute for Educational Evaluation, or the implementation of a merit-based assessment of teacher performance, would leverage higher quality and greater public accountability. On the other hand, the discourse called for the cultivation of a new subjectivity which placed responsibility for public outcomes—such as students' learning—on individuals as well as institutions. In this sense, the new democratic citizen had to learn to become more responsible—that is, accountable—for his/her actions.

The growth of these societal discourses clearly put the need for some kind of citizenship education on the national agenda. Time and time again, people who were involved in some way with the creation of the FCE program alluded to aspects of these societal discourses and the social pressures that accompanied them. Usually the pressures were characterized in rather general terms, with reference to "values," above all. As the main author of the FCE program put it, for instance, "There was an urgent social demand, expressed in many different venues, that values be taught, that there was a lack of values [in the current generation]." Such social pressures, of course, would have to be channeled and mediated in concrete ways through the bureaucracy of the SEP. Indeed, the final impetus for development of a program like FCE would come from the personal initiative of key actors—the president, the secretary of education, and perhaps most decisively and remarkably, the secretary's wife.

Miguel Limón, Secretary of Education, who took over shortly after the beginning of the Zedillo administration, is a professor of constitutional law with a long trajectory of civil service. After having served as dean of social sciences at the Autonomous Metropolitan University in Mexico City and academic secretary at the National Pedagogical University, Limón went on to serve for a number of years as director of the national Institute for Indigenous Affairs, subsecretary of the interior (*Gobernación*) in charge of issues of corruption and extortion, and finally as attorney general for environmental protection. This list of positions covers a remarkable range of issues and concerns that were eventually encompassed by the FCE program; indeed, the former secretary himself pointed out that each of these positions had a strong "ethical" dimension (*contenido ético*), and that he saw his appointment as secretary a grand opportunity to bring this ethical dimension to public education.

The societal discourses already discussed created impetus and formed an important backdrop for the work of the FCE team. In effect, such discourses provided a critical "problem diagnosis" for policy reform. Public concerns about values were often expressed through the media, or directly to the President's office, and then channeled to Limón and his team. Such discourses also established a set of parameters within which the FCE team would have to conduct its work. Still, as discussed in the next section, the personal goals of the secretary and the secretary's wife, and the international experiences of the FCE team members, were more proximately determining of the way that global ideas of democratic citizenship were appropriated in the creation of the FCE.

Legitimated by public discourse, supported by the president, and bolstered by the general goals of the Plan for Educational Development 1995–2000, by 1995 Secretary Limón felt a clear mandate to begin the reform of civic education to include a stronger component of "values formation" as well as participatory pedagogy. Ordinarily, proposals for curricular reform within the SEP would have been routed through the appropriate content "team" in the General Directorate Of Educational Methods And Materials, under the subsecretary of basic education. But Limón took the unprecedented step of convening a separate team to draft the new program in civic education. The team was literally housed in Limón's private offices and figuratively taken under his wing. His wife, a professional educator, would come to form the symbolic heart of the team, and a Harvard-trained educational philosopher was selected to head it up. Then two more male members were added—one a classical musician and music professor of broad reputation, another a writer of fiction and social commentary.

This team went about seeking additional input from a variety of organizations and government agencies that had rarely been consulted in the past. Clearly, this was going to be a new, more collaborative process for curriculum and program design. Among the organizations that were invited to submit proposals for content, and to vet the early drafts of the program, were: the Catholic Church, the National Autonomous University of Mexico, the National Pedagogical University, the National Youth Institute, the Human Rights Commission of the Federal District, the Institute of Health, and the Council on Addictions. Particularly important was a burgeoning collaboration with the Federal Electoral Institute (IFE), which had its own parallel program in citizenship education for a democratic political culture.[2] In the end, the four-member FCE team delivered a comprehensive 3-year program to the civic education team in the General Directorate of Educational Methods and Materials. It had been made clear to this team, with all due discretion, that their expert input would be valued, but that all final decisions belonged to the FCE team and the secretary for whom they directly worked. The civic education team was in accord with the basic orientation of the program and its pedagogical focus.

With regard to conceptions of democratic citizenship, there are several implications of the novel way in which the FCE program was created. First, the decision was made to combine the traditional goals of civic education with the multifaceted aim of "ethical" values formation. This brought together under the discourse of "democracy" a set of core attitudes and competencies that had not been articulated in quite the same fashion before. Education for democratic citizenship became inextricably linked with the clarification of values and, as we shall see, the "prevention" of undesirable attitudes and activities. Moreover, the influences on the program were rather heterogeneous, and this allowed for a new amalgam of citizenship discourse that juxtaposed theretofore separate or even contradictory principles.

Policy Processes and Curricular Reform in Indonesia

The policy process surrounding civic education reform in Indonesia has been complex, uncertain, and embedded in two over-arching reforms: general decentralization of the national government, accompanied by transformation of the curricular role of the Ministry of National Education (MONE). Specifically, MONE has moved from detailed scope-and-sequence curricula, to curriculum frameworks that are meant on the one hand to provide for "outcomes based" education and, on the other, to allow for local autonomy in the development of specific curricular material. These structural changes are occurring simultaneously with substantive ideological changes in the content and processes of civic education.

Both decentralization and the move to curriculum defined by standards were looming prior to *Reformasi*. The International Monetary Fund and World Bank had been promoting decentralization of government, with little success, for the last decade of the New Order. The more technocratic factions of the MONE (then the MOEC, or Ministry of Education and Culture), in conjunction with education specialists from major donor agencies such as the World Bank, had been lobbying for "outcomes based" education for the last few years of the Old Order. As noted above, decentralization of government was approved early in the first *Reformasi* parliament, in large part as a measure to co-opt recidivist movements that simmered throughout the archipelago in the context of economic decline and political turmoil.

The process of divesting the Indonesian military of its civilian authority underlies one of the first changes made to civic education in the spirit of *Reformasi*. Prior to 1999, civic education was conveyed in two mandatory courses: *Panca Sila* Moral Education (character education and education in the state ideology) and PSPB, the History of the National Struggle. The latter course looks at 300 years of national history as a continuous struggle of the state against enemies—first, externally, the Dutch colonizers, and then, internally, the communists and regional separatists (van Klinken, 2002). This course was discontinued in early 1999. In the same year, the MONE published revisions to the 1994 civic education curriculum that has been mandatory since national public schooling was established in 1950, at all grade levels from first through twelfth as well as for 1 year in college. This first set of revisions included the elimination of some clearly ideological lessons, such as those considered to be promoting militaristic and unthinking actions, for example, the topics of *ketaatan* (obedience) and *rela berkorban* (willingness to sacrifice).

All of the major issues raised by *Reformasi* were reflected in the process of developing the new civic education curriculum, piloted in 2001 and introduced nation wide in the 2002 school year. There was debate around the title of the course. Certainly, it would continue to include *Panca Sila;* this is the defining ideology of Indonesian nationhood and has survived three distinctly different regimes. Early in the process, there was still talk of including "security" or "military" studies in the title, a position which faded as successive steps were taken to remove the military from government. The character education aspect, *budi pekerti*, was also subject to debate. Should it stand alone as a separate course? If so, at all grades from 1–12, as is the case for *Panca Sila*? Ultimately, elements of *budi pekerti* have been incorporated into health, physical education, and social studies.

Even before the introduction of the new curriculum, decentralization provided a platform for innovation and experimentation, at least among those educators who were so inclined. Some high school civic education teachers have actively sought out opportunities for pedagogical development, such as those who have participated in workshops on active and democratic pedagogy at the Universitas Negeri Padang and other teacher education institutions. Others, perhaps the majority, fall back on familiar didactic techniques to convey the revised curriculum. Decentralization offers not only more autonomy in instruction but also in school regulations. One interesting manifestation of this was the decision by the educational leadership of Padang, a West Sumatran town with a reputation for promulgating moderate Islamic knowledge, to require all secondary school girls to wear the head-scarf to school—including Christians and ethnic Chinese. One can foresee a long and unpredictable dialogue between newly-valorized local norms and those of the nation-state.

The New Mexican Curriculum for Civic Education

Our exposition of the new programs in Mexico and Indonesia will pay particular attention to content, pedagogical innovations, and embedded conceptions of citizenship. An analysis of two key documents—the Annotated Program of Studies (SEP, 1999), and the Teachers' Guide (SEP, 2000)—provides us with the major organizing themes and principles of the new Mexican secondary course in "civic and ethical formation" (FCE).

After affirming the special importance of citizenship education (*formación ciudadana*), the opening pages of the Annotated Program of Studies (SEP, 1999, pp. 12–13) go on to emphasize that the new subject adopts a focus that is "formative, secular, democratizing, nationalist, universalist, preventive, and communicative" (*La asignatura ... adopta un enfoque ... formativo; laico; democratizador; nacionalista; universal; preventivo; comunicativo*.). Each of these terms, of course, encompasses a broad domain of meanings, yet they can be fairly glossed as follows.

The first term, *formativo*, points to the widest educative intent of Mexican schooling: to mold the habits, values, and attitudes of future citizens. In the Mexican lexicon, *educación* has always had a broader meaning than mere *instrucción*, and *formación* has meant something even more than *educación*. While instruction, and even education, can refer to the transmission and acquisition of facts and knowledge through mental processes, formation points to habit and affect, with the intention of shaping forms of perception and conduct in everyday life. The Mexican *secundaria* has always presumed to be *formativo* and *integral* (holistic), thus the new FCE program does not so much propose a new focus as recover and reinforce one of the *secundaria's* perennial goals.

The next four terms point to foundational concepts of the Mexican Constitution. Rooted in the Liberal Constitution of 1857, but reformulated during the revolution (1917), the current Mexican Constitution gives the federal state a broad tutelary role through public education. Because of the historical struggle against the power of the Catholic Church, the Constitution stipulates that public education will be secular (*laica*), and shall not be used to propagate the beliefs of specific religions. The Constitution also provides the foundation for a democratic form of governance, so civic education should contribute to the formation of democratic habits.

An emphasis on both nationalism and universalism might seem a contradiction to some, but throughout its modern history Mexico has tried to couple a strong sense of national identity with gestures of international solidarity for peace and justice. Because of its troubled history with the U.S. colossus to the north, and because of its own regional, class, and ethnic diversity, Mexican basic education has always attempted to form strong allegiance to the nation. Civic ceremonies and the celebration of national holidays and heroes figure prominently in the lives of all Mexican schoolchildren. Yet for all this nationalist pride, Mexican schools have also tried to inculcate in their children an appreciation for world history and the contributions of different cultures.

The new FCE subject establishes a "preventive" focus in relation to certain growing problems in Mexican society, such as drug addiction, early, unwed pregnancy, and organized crime. Students learn about the causes and consequences of such problems in order to "prevent" their own involvement. Finally, and very importantly, FCE highlights a "communicative" rationale. Instead of merely digesting received opinion and fact, students in FCE are to learn to dialogue and question received wisdom, expressing their doubts and opinions openly. In this way, knowledge and value can be constructed through communication, not imposition.

This latter point seems especially important when one glances over the remainder of the Annotated Program of Studies and Teachers' Guide. Throughout the text, the authors of these documents place emphasis on a communicative pedagogical stance, and a new role for the teacher as facilitator rather than provider of information. Such communication is intimately linked to the urgent need for students to take control of their learning and to begin practicing democratic virtues:

> [The program] seeks to strengthen the student's capacity for critical analysis, for group work and participation in both individual and collective decision-making processes based on the values of a democratic life. (SEP, 1999, p. 14)

> It will be necessary to create a learning community, understood as a space of dialogue and joint construction between teachers and students, in which knowledge is sustained by information, experience, and reflection. The students will learn equally from their classmates and their teachers, manifesting in this way the importance of a dialogical and horizontal educational process. (SEP, 1999, pp. 21–22)

The documents go on to criticize the heavy emphasis on information in the previous curriculum, saying, for instance, that

> in [the old civics] the contents were dominated by detailed description of our public institutions and the recital of human rights, to the detriment of a more systematic development of abilities and attitudes that might lead to greater civic participation. Even though important concepts and information were presented, because they showed no clear relation to their lives such concepts could not be easily experienced by the students as a "priority" in their education (*prioritarios para su formación*). In the new subject (FCE), we seek to make the connections between civics and students' lives more apparent. (SEP, 2000, p. 3)

Correspondingly, the new plan establishes a number of "pedagogical and didactic guidelines" for teachers. Such guidelines include, among other things, clear directions to:

- relate themes to students' lives

- foment ... attitudes of respect and acceptance that encourage freedom of expression for all, taking special care to promote gender
  equity
- practice abilities of communication, dialogue, expression, and critical judgment
- encourage the practice of values, attitudes, and habits related to
  democratic life, to group work and collective organization

Clearly, these new guidelines create a significant break with the older,
teacher-centered approach to civics instruction.

While civics has a long and illustrious history in Mexican schools, the
term "ethical" is less familiar to most Mexicans. It also raises more
eyebrows. This is because of its possible connection to specific moral values
derived from the dominant religion of Catholicism. Steeped in the
tradition of "lay" education, schoolteachers are especially vigilant about
the introduction of religion to the public classroom. However, a close
analysis of the new FCE program reveals strict adherence to a secular
conception of ethical values, one that allows, but does not promote, the
adoption of specific moralities.

What exactly is the difference between "civic" and "ethical" education,
and how do they mesh? The Teachers' Guide explains it this way:

> *Formación cívica* can be defined as a process of personal development
> through which individuals articulate values and form conceptions ... that
> lead them to conceive of themselves as members of a political and social
> community, and to thereby exercise ... the qualities of citizenship that the
> Constitution grants them.
>
> *Formación ética* can be defined as a process of human development in
> which the individual acquires and forms a set of abilities, attitudes, values,
> and knowledge that enables her to know herself and to recognize others as
> equal in dignity and rights. (SEP, 2000, p. 9) (Note: Levinson's translation
> provides the female pronoun)

Each of these formative goals, in turn, is linked to the overarching
concept and goal of democracy. Civic education can make students aware
of their rights and responsibilities as democratic citizens, the Guide seems
to say, but only ethical education can deepen the attitudes that make
respectful participation possible. Importantly, the "individual" and her
"personal development" are placed at the heart of civic education, but it
is a development oriented toward "political and social community" and
the "recognition of others."

The 3 years of *secundaria* study have been organized around three main
themes that run throughout the FCE program. The first theme, focused
on ethics, consists of "reflection about human nature and human values."

The first year course of study opens with a broad exploration; students consider the evolution of culture and the characteristics of homo sapiens as a species. Before long, the course centers on the perennial issue of gender relations, and has students discussing what it means to "be a woman and be a man." This is just one of many points where gender becomes salient. Even here, at this early stage in the program, students are encouraged to explicitly reflect on the goals of equity, the economic and educational disadvantages women typically face, and so on (SEP, 1999, p. 39).

The second theme, unusually reflexive with regard to their life stage, considers both "problems and possibilities for adolescents and youth." A major section of the first year, called "youth and goals" (*juventud y proyectos*), opens an explicit reflection about the promises of adolescence. Students are encouraged to project their aspirations into the future, to imagine their possibilities. There is a good deal of language here seemingly borrowed from humanistic psychology: "personal realization," "life cycle and life goals," and "human potential." There is also the first opening toward vocational orientation, as students are encouraged to "identify tastes, aspirations, and goals during the stage of adolescence" (SEP, 1999, p. 46). Finally, the first year ends with 40 hours of instructional time spent exploring how to "live in society." Concepts include interdependence, communication, emotional connection (*afectividad*), enjoyment (*gozo*), solidarity, and reciprocity, as well as the "spirit of service, creativity, and work." Activities direct students to pose examples of such concepts in everyday life (SEP, 1999, p. 50).

The second year of the program picks up at the same point but gives a different twist to "living in society." Under the rubric of democracy now, students learn about the "values of living together" (*valores de la convivencia*), as well as the more specific "civic values and citizenship formation." What are considered the key values of democracy are imparted to students: liberty, equality, equity, justice, respect, tolerance, solidarity, and responsibility (SEP, 1999, p. 55).

As if to give concrete and immediate meaning to these values, the second year moves on to consider students' relation to the *secundaria* itself. In an interesting example of institutional self-reflection, students are encouraged to explore their "reasons for attending the secundaria," and to ask themselves, "How do I take advantage of what the secundaria has to offer?" The goal here is to urge students to "acquire the elements for actively participating in society," by taking the *secundaria* as a microcosm of the broader society (SEP, 1999, p. 79).[3] From the *secundaria*, teachers and students make the leap to the nation, exploring concepts such as "nationalism, love of country, and national pride," as well as "unity and cultural pluralism." Students are even asked to examine the "possibility of participating in, and influencing, matters of national interest" (SEP, 1999,

p. 85). Finally, the second year ends with a further opening out to the study of "humanity." It is here, for the first (and perhaps only) time, that students explicitly consider their "relationship to the environment" (SEP, 1999, p. 89). This relationship is framed not only by a national interest, but with reference to worldwide environmental issues and problems. Here is one of the few moments where the curriculum opens explicitly to consider a global perspective.

The third and final theme centers on traditional civics concepts, "social organization, democracy, citizenship participation, and forms of government in Mexico," in other words, the Constitution, the political structure (elections, parties, etc.), the governance structure (federal, state, and municipal agencies), and the separation of powers (executive, legislative, and judicial). Yet toward the middle of the year, the program of study returns to refocus some themes that have already been introduced in previous years. These themes are considered now under the rubric of "responsibility and individual decision-making." References to gender inequality are sprinkled throughout the consideration of sexuality, addiction prevention, and "study, work, and personal realization" (SEP, 1999, p. 97).

The program in civic and ethical formation ends with an ambitious final project meant to foster "responsibility, collective decision-making, and participation." Either in small groups, or as a whole class, students must

> demonstrate that they are capable of making change in some aspect of their school or immediate environment. For this the youth must identify an improvable aspect of one of the broad fields that they've studied throughout the course: education, work, health, environment, and free time.

Through this project, students should learn how to arrive at decisions through consensus; how to conduct an empirical investigation and divide the work fairly among themselves; and how to present the results of an investigation to authorities and peers in order to effect positive change. The program description ends with a final observation of the anticipated "formative" benefits of this group project:

> [This project will serve], above all, for the students to evaluate themselves, so that they can see in their practice how much the three years of being in the course has benefited them; [it's assumed that] upon completing the elaboration of their project the students will discover that they're capable of cooperating, joining a team, finding a problem and proposing viable solutions, coming to an agreement, respecting one another, and researching. (SEP, 1999, pp. 103–104)

Clearly, the Mexican FCE program places primary emphasis on the enactment and embodiment of democratic values in everyday classroom practice. A constructivist and dialogical pedagogy postulates that through classroom process and explicit content, students will practice and learn democratic habits of participation, tolerance, dialogue, and cooperation. Not surprisingly given Mexico's history, the values and dispositions of democracy include a strong emphasis on group work, solidarity, and the collective good. This is one of the key aspects of Mexican education for democratic citizenship that would seem to distinguish it from those strictly liberal models sponsored by the countries of the North, which tend to place higher emphasis on the rights of possessive individualism. It might be said that, historically, Mexico's strong collective traditions and identities have served authoritarianism well, and that a democratic education must now balance the forces of collectivism with a focus on individual conscience. Yet in the articulation of this balance, the FCE still clearly highlights the importance of collective life and responsibilities.

The New Indonesian Curriculum

The 1999 curriculum, which eliminated the study of the national struggle and specific lessons from *Panca Sila*, served as a stop-gap measure while the MONE developed a fully fledged new curriculum that was introduced in 2004, a process described in the last section. The new civic education course is titled "Citizenship and Social Knowledge" (*Kewarganegaraan dan Pengetahuan Sosial*) at the elementary and junior secondary levels, with citizenship as a stand-alone course in upper secondary. In the sixth grade, competency standards include understanding human rights; this understanding is elaborated in the competency standards for subsequent years. This content marks a significant departure in the content of civic education in the new Indonesia. A large portion of early *Reformasi*-era USAID (United States Agency for International Development) funding for civic education went to support the work of the Center for Civic Education, which has focused on translating its service-learning curriculum, Project Citizen, into Indonesian, and training master trainers and teachers in its use. In 2001, Project Citizen was designated by the MONE as a model extracurricular component of the new civic education curriculum. In June of 2003, a national competition showcased the accomplishments of several teams of secondary students who had analyzed local social issues according to the Project Citizen format. By 2004, however, Project Citizen had lost most of its USAID funding and was set aside as an approach to civic education. However, the service-learning element and exploration of local policy issues have been incorporated into the pedagogy of many Indonesian teachers who were exposed to the project. Other USAID funds have supported community-based civic education, while both USAID and the Department of State have funded projects in leading Islamic universities to develop democratic forms of civic education based in Islamic thought.

One obvious "missing link" in the reform of Indonesian civic education is sustained attention to pedagogy. It is obvious to most who reflect upon the fact, whether teachers, students, or educational leaders, that the promotion of values that have long been suppressed in Indonesia, such as universal human rights and multiculturalism, requires as much change in delivery as in content. After all, religious and ethnic diversity were quite literally forbidden topics for public discourse in the New Order. How will teachers, and students, develop the discursive practices necessary to engage vigorously but peacefully in debate over pluralism, a matter that too often has been life and death in Indonesia? The new curricular regime of "Competency based Curriculum," while still the source of much confusion among Indonesian teachers, has the virtue of promoting attention to active teaching and learning processes.

THE GLOBAL AND THE LOCAL: INTERSECTING FORCES IN DEFINING THE NEW DEMOCRATIC CITIZEN

To this point, we have traced the broad outlines of the policy processes through which the new Mexican and Indonesian civic education programs, respectively, took shape. We have also provided the main themes, concepts, and pedagogical stances of these programs. In each case, substantive meanings of democracy and democratic citizenship get negotiated through the policy process to eventually find their places embedded in the curricula and teachers' guides. To be sure, the civic education programs themselves do not exhaust the possible range of meanings of democratic citizenship present and circulating in each society; yet they do crystallize prominent themes of democratic citizenship for the educational arena. We are now in a position to reflect more explicitly on how global and local forces intersect to structure ideas in this arena. Given the nature of democracy as a highly visible and contested concept on the global stage, it is only natural that democratic citizenship in any given nation should be subject to a range of global influences. Some of these influences are rather direct, in the form of institutional linkages and contracts; others are less direct, and are exercised through a more diffuse kind of cultural contact. At the same time, local cultural influences, along with religious identities and practices, are also powerful features of local dialogue concerning democracy. A brief look at such influences across Mexico and Indonesia reveals a good deal about how and why civic education takes different form in each place.

Mexico

In Mexico, direct global institutional influences on the process of civic education reform are hard to find. Perhaps because of its own submerged democratic tradition, and perhaps because of its strong sense of national autonomy fostered during years of U.S. hegemony, Mexico has preferred to develop its own programs. International organizations have rarely been invited to Mexico to work directly with the education ministry. The U.S.-based and government funded Center for Civic Education, which provides consultation and technical support for civic education reform around the world, had, as of 2001, collaborated only with the IFE in adapting extracurricular programs for citizenship formation.[4]

It is at the state and local level in Mexico where openness to institutional global influence is greatest. The new secondary program for civic education leaves quite some latitude for local states and schools to supplement the national curriculum with other resources. In some states, technical supervisors and principals have been especially active in seeking such resources, and they are usually to be found in NGOs with global reach. The Mexican section of Amnesty International, for instance, has developed a parallel set of materials for the professional development of civic education teachers, and such materials contain novel ideas for classroom exercises and activities around themes of human rights. Other global organizations that concentrate on issues of gender equity, the environment, indigenous rights, "interculturalism," or "moral values" have also begun to make their presence felt in Mexican schools, often through locally-based branches or sister organizations.

Cultural influences of a global nature are easier to discern in Mexico. Such influences are manifest principally in the biographies of the principal actors charged with formulating the FCE program. The convener of the FCE team, the secretary of education's wife, Maestra Campillo, placed strong emphasis on the multiplicity of perspectives and materials that shaped the program. As she traveled with her husband to numerous international meetings, she took advantage of each site to gather materials on civic education. Among the sites she mentioned most prominently were Switzerland (for UNESCO [United Nations Educational, Scientific and Cultural Organization]), France (where her husband had studied many years before), Spain, England, the United States, various countries of South America, and perhaps most intriguingly, Japan. As she put it in response to Levinson's question about whether foreign influences had shaped FCE:

> I had the advantage that my husband was speaking regularly with the ministers, the policymakers, so the obligatory question on my part was always, "Please, ask them what they're doing in this area [of civic education]" .... There's no influence from a single place but we are certainly, and necessarily, influenced by the materials that we have read.

Maestra Campillo went on to describe the involvement of prominent curriculum experts in civic education from Spain and Argentina, who were invited at different times to share their experiences and review the emerging Mexican program.

One other measure of global cultural influence also can be inferred from patterns of citation and reference in program documents and supporting literature. The chief author for the program, a Harvard PhD in educational philosophy, had incorporated certain ideas from the American tradition of democratic education, and was a frequent international conference participant during the years in which the program was being elaborated. And in support of ideas about participatory democracy and student-centered pedagogy, one finds frequent reference to John Dewey, Michael Apple, and others in the U.S. critical tradition. Yet even more frequently, one finds substantive citations of Spanish, French, and Italian educators, philosophers, and political theorists. The affinity for Spain is perhaps obvious because of the common language, yet also because of the long struggle against military dictatorship that formed the Spanish twentieth century. The celebrated Spanish philosopher Fernando Savater is often cited. In the case of France and Italy, it is not uncommon to find support for certain conceptions of democratic citizenship in the writings of well-known liberal philosophers and political theorists like Alain Touraine, Norberto Bobbio, or Giovani Sartori.

The Roman Catholic Church is obviously an institution with global reach, and the Mexican branch of the church has exercised strong influence on social policy, despite a long legacy of church-state separation. Not surprisingly, the Church in Mexico, along with its allies in the educational arena, such as the UNPF, had been pushing for a stronger values-based education for some time. Especially alarmed at growing rates of unwed pregnancy, the flaunting of adult authority, and the hemorrhage of church faithful, the Catholic Church, constitutionally banished from public education, had been advocating a stronger foundation in moral values. Although Church doctrine and structure would seem to support a rather more authoritarian conception of citizenship, Catholic actors and organizations articulated democratic citizenship most strongly in terms of lawfulness and transparency. The Church has also been a strong presence in human rights activism throughout Mexico.

Finally, while business interests in Mexico wield important power over economic policy through direct contacts and a set of coordinating associations, business has been surprisingly absent from the reform of most education policy in Mexico. While leftist critics feared the incursion into citizenship education of "business values," such as punctuality, obedience, and conformity, such appears not to have been the case. The corporate textbook publishers' lobby, to be sure, sought to exercise influence over the direction of the FCE program. However, because of the absence of mechanisms for direct policy influence in the creation of the FCE, even such influence was highly diffuse.

Indonesia

Global institutional influences in Indonesia are far more obvious than those in Mexico. Since the mid-1980s, Indonesia has been among the largest borrowers from the World Bank, in the field of education as well as for infrastructure and industry. USAID has a long history (and large "mission") in Indonesia, though by the mid-1990s, very little of its activity was in the field of education. With near-universal primary education (a result of the oil boom of the late 1970s) and relative gender parity in basic education, Indonesia did not fit the profile of USAID's priorities in education. During the 1990s, large World Bank and Asian Development Bank projects aimed at expanding lower secondary education constituted the bulk of external efforts directed at Indonesian education. This situation changed with Suharto's resignation. Both the Department of State and USAID began to support aspects of civic education reform soon after *Reformasi* began. The Dutch and German governments are also supporting both school and community based civic education programs.

The events of September 11, 2001, and the 2002 and 2005 bombings in Bali, have amplified U.S. interests in Indonesian education generally and civic education in particular. Shortly after the 2002 bombings, during a meeting with Indonesian President Megawati Sukarno, President Bush announced a major new USAID investment in Indonesian basic education, totaling U.S.$150 million. The U.S. administration overtly presents this support, like similar educational aid efforts that it is promoting in the Middle East, as a means of combating terrorism associated with radical Islam. Misgivings are already evident in Indonesia, particularly against plans to invest some of these funds in the Islamic schools known as *pesantren* in Indonesia. *Pesentran*, both public (sponsored by the Ministry of Religious Affairs) and private (sponsored by a variety of

Islamic organizations), account for about one-tenth of the children enrolled in basic education, and they disproportionately serve the rural and urban poor. Simultaneously, they serve families who opt for an Islamic rather than secular education. Hasyim Muzadi, chairman of Nahdlatul Ulama, one of the largest Islamic groups in Indonesia and an intended beneficiary of these funds, lauded the infusion of funds, but warned the U.S. Ambassador that the U.S. should not "interfere" with the curriculum of the *pesentran* (Nugroho, 2003). When the U.S. embassy attempted to introduce a set of Indonesian language textbooks on U.S. history and culture to the Islamic schools, they were refused by Islamic educators.

The dialogues on Islam, citizenship, democracy, and civil society that are taking place in Indonesia today represent the most powerful set of local forces contributing to the development of a uniquely Indonesian perspective on citizenship. Indeed, the common Indonesian language translation of the concept of civil society, as "*masyarakat Madani,*" derives from Islamic teaching. "Madani" is the Indonesian language form of "Medina," the town in which the Prophet Mohammed settled after being forced from Mecca. While residing in Medina, the prophet promulgated concepts of peaceful social existence in a pluralistic society whose members represent a diversity of ethnicities and faith communities. Couching the discourse on civil society "*masyarkat Madani*" thus turns the focus squarely onto issues of diversity and pluralism, which have often been pushed to the side in the Western European discourse on civil society. In Indonesia today there is an explosion of thought concerning multiculturalism, framed both in terms of secular democracy (see Tilaar, 2004), and liberal and modernist Islam (see Firmansyah 2003; Tim ICCE, 2003).

CONCLUSIONS

In this paper, we have concentrated our analysis on the national level of education reform in Mexico and Indonesia, and we have sketched an answer to the central questions involved in how the global meets the local: What are the primary influences on civic education reform, how are those influences negotiated institutionally to produce a final curricular product, and what varied conceptions of democratic citizenship are reflected in this final product? We have tried to show that despite their rather different political histories and cultural configurations, Mexico and Indonesia share some important structural features for policy reform and implementation. Most strikingly, they maintain highly centralized education ministries, where programs and decisions of national import are still concentrated, yet they have also embarked on decentralization efforts with varied emphases and consequences. Such decentralization measures have differed in the degree to which local autonomy and decision-making have been effectively enhanced. Then there are the sharp differences that emerge upon comparing the process by which both countries have undertaken the reform of civic education. Indonesia has actively sought international assistance for the development of new civic education programs; in turn, it has been actively courted by international agencies, especially U.S.-based, because of its strategic role as a "moderate" Islamic country. Mexico, meanwhile, has remained much more firmly independent in its development of national programs, while selectively incorporating models and insights from Spain, France, and Italy, as well as the U.S. and Japan. Religion in Indonesia remains a central feature of the debate on what a good and just society means. It is also the "marker" of Indonesia in the eyes of the West. Indonesians are all too aware of the current U.S. social vision of Islam as a renegade religion—a social understanding that will complicate Western/Indonesian, and especially, U.S/Indonesian integration around civic education.

NOTES

1. See the report, "Too High a Price The Human Rights Cost of the Indonesian Military's Economic Activities." Human Rights Watch, June 2006. http://hrw.org/reports/2006/indonesia0606/

2. The IFE is a government-funded yet independent agency created in the late 1980s mainly to administer fair and clean elections. However, a significant part of its work also includes fomenting civic education and the creation of a new democratic political culture. Through its Department of Electoral Certification, Civic Education, and Citizenship Participation, the IFE has run several educational programs that complement the school-based FCE curriculum: these include the Jornadas Cívicas Infantiles y Juveniles, day-long programs of activity that range from mock elections to drawing and role-playing; "Project-Citizen," a program adapted from the U.S.-based Center for Civic Education that fosters community involvement and problem solving among adolescents; and the elementary program, "Rights and Values for Mexican Children" (see Salazar Ugarte, 2001).

3. Part of this section includes a reflection on the local institution of "Student Council" (*Sociedad de Alumnos*), in which virtually every *secundaria* student body elects officers and representatives. While this tradition had fallen into disuse in some schools, by 2001 the IFE, an independent government body charged with conducting elections, was collaborating with the secretariat of education to revive and strengthen student elections in *secundarias*.

4. See Levinson (2005a) for an account of a more recent program for citizenship education, "Education for a Culture of Lawfulness," introduced after 2001 by the new PAN-dominated education ministry. This newer program originated in the pedagogical experiments of a U.S. professor of government and security expert.

REFERENCES

Aveling, H. (1980). *The development of Indonesian society: From the coming of Islam to the present day*. New York: St. Martin's Press.

Firmansyah, J. (2003). *Islam liberal: Versi anak muda*. Jakarta, Indonesia: Anas Urbaningrum.

Harsanto, D. (2002, December 19). NGO alleges corruption of education fund. *The Jakarta Post*. Retrieved April 6, 2008, from www.thejakartapost.com

Hayhoe, R. (1999). Modernization without Westernization: Assessing the Chinese educational experience. In R. Arnove & C. Torres (Eds.), *Comparative education: The dialectic of the global and the local*. (pp. 75–92) Lanham, MD: Rowman & Littlefield.

Hindley, D. (1966). *The Communist Party of Indonesia, 1951–1963*. Berkeley: University of California Press.

International IDEA (Institute for Democracy and Electoral Assistance). (2000). *Democratization in Indonesia: An Assessment*. Stockholm: International IDEA Publications.

Levinson, B. A. U. (2001). *We are all equal: Student culture and identity at a Mexican secondary school, 1988–1998*. Durham, NC: Duke University Press.

Levinson, B. A. U. (2004). Hopes and challenges for the new civic education in Mexico: Toward a democratic citizen without adjectives. *International Journal of Educational Development, 24*(3), 269–282.

Levinson, B. A. U. (2005a). Programs for democratic citizenship education in Mexico's Ministry of Education: Local appropriations of global cultural flows. *Indiana Journal of Global Legal Studies, 12*(1), 251–284.

Levinson, B. A. U. (2005b). Citizenship, identity, democracy: Engaging the political in the anthropology of education. *Anthropology and Education Quarterly, 36*(4), 329–340.

Mazrui, A. A. (1975). The African university as a multinational corporation: Problems of penetration and dependency. *Harvard Education Review, 45*(2), 191–210.

Mazrui, A. A. (2001). Pretender to universalism: Western culture in a globalizing age. *Journal of Muslim Minority Affairs, 21*(1), 11–24.

Moeis, I. (2000, March). *Pendidikan Kewarganegaraan sekarang dan akan datang: Sebuah review kritis atas sikap politik siswa di kota Padang* [Civic education: Now and future. A critical review of political attitudes of students in Padang]. Paper presented at International Conference on Civic Education, Bandung, Indonesia.

Nugroho, I.D. (2003, November 11). Hasyim tells U.S. not to intervene in "pesantren." *The Jakarta Post.* Retrieved April 6, 2008, from www.thejakartapost.com

Ornelas, C. (1995). *El sistema educativo Mexicano* [The Mexican educational system]. Mexico City: Secretaría de Educación Pública.

Preston, J., & Dillon, S. (2004). *Opening Mexico: The making of a democracy.* New York: Farrar, Strauss, and Giroux.

Salazar Ugarte, S. (2001). El IFE ante la educación cívica [The Federal Electoral Institute takes on civic education]. *Educación 2001, 1*(7), 43–46.

Secretaría de Educación Pública. (1999). *Formación Cívica y Etica, Educación Secundaria: Programas de estudio comentados* [Civic and ethical education, secondary education: Annotated program of studies]. Mexico City, Mexico: Author.

Secretaría de Educación Pública. (2000). *Formación Cívica y Etica, Educación Secundaria: Libro para el maestro* [Civic and ethical education, secondary education: Teachers' guide]. Mexico City, Mexico: Author.

Sutton, M., & Levinson, B. A. U. (Eds.). (2001). *Policy as practice: Toward a comparative sociocultural analysis of education policy.* Stamford, CT: Ablex.

Tilaar, H. A. R. (2004). *Multikulturalisme: Tantangan-tantangan global masa depan dalam transformasi pendidikan nasional.* Jakarta, Indonesia: Grasindo.

Tim ICCE UIN. (2003). *Demokrasi, Hak asasi manusia dan masyarakat madani.* Jakarta, Indonesia: Prenada Media.

van Klinken, G. (2002). The battle for history after Suharto: Beyond sacred dates, great men, and legal milestones. *Critical Asian Studies, 33*(3), 323–350.

Vaughan, M. K. (1997). *Cultural politics in revolution: Teachers, peasants, and schools in Mexico, 1930–1940.* Tucson: University of Arizona Press.

CHAPTER 7

DEVELOPING CITIZENSHIP EDUCATION CURRICULUM CROSS-CULTURALLY

A Democratic Approach With South African and Kenyan Educators

Patricia K. Kubow

INTRODUCTION

School curricula in democracies of sub-Saharan Africa have been more heavily influenced by Western educational reforms rather than by the knowledge of educators in African contexts or the direction they consider appropriate for formal democratic instruction in their respective countries. This situation is the result of historical conditions such as colonialism, contemporary influences such as globalization, and even international "collaboration" whereby Western (read: United States) democracy and culture are imparted to educators in other nations through "civic" education projects. The term *democracy* itself has become a slogan, and U.S. civic educators who seek to spread democracy globally have considered an

Advancing Democracy Through Education? U.S. Influence Abroad and Domestic Practices, pp. 159–178
Copyright © 2008 by Information Age Publishing

159

American model of democracy as appropriate. In general, therefore, there is a need to examine American funded projects for the kinds of assumptions about democracy that underlie such projects, as well as the procedures American educators have used with international participants as they engage in democratic education efforts. Democratic citizenship education constitutes not only an important area of study for the field of comparative education, but also provides an opportunity for comparative educators to emphasize the role that culture plays in shaping democracy in different contexts. Moreover, attention should be given to using democratic-oriented research methodologies in the conduct of citizenship education projects.

Comparative research is an appropriate analytic approach for these tasks because it provides new assessments of the seemingly familiar in terms of the less familiar (Kubow & Fossum, 2007). In other words, examining democracy in a country different from one's own enables new insights on a seemingly familiar concept and practice. A research approach that starts from the viewpoints of democracy held by citizens themselves, positioned within their own unique cultural and social contexts, represents a methodological *shift from* social educators using American democratic principles and imparting those values through workshops and civic projects, *to* educators providing dialogic space for international participants to share their own knowledge about democracy, developed from lived experiences and shaped by global and local influences, and then using that knowledge to develop democratic classroom curriculum. Life-world, a concept from the phenomenological tradition advanced by Alfred Schutz (1995) and further developed by Jurgen Habermas (1996), implies that people's lived experiences shape their hopes, goals, ideals, and practices. Attention to the life-worlds of project participants represents an important methodological shift. It rejects the traditional approach whereby social educators use their own life-world as the basis for conducting international democratic citizenship education projects. Instead, social educators provide space for dialogue in which the interests, goals, and views of the international participants are sought and used as the basis for democratic project work.

South Africa and Kenya are two democratic countries that largely have been on the receiving end of American aid and partnerships and, therefore, are illustrative cases for helping social educators understand perspectives on democracy from some teachers working in sub-Saharan African contexts. Although democratic forms of political governance and established democratic constitutions exist in each country, little is known about the ways in which *schoolteachers* (i.e., those responsible for formal instruction in citizenship education) in each country view democracy, or how historical-political, sociocultural, and economic factors, intertwined at local and global levels, impact the educational content and practices that are considered essential for students' citizenship development. The term *democratic citizenship education*, as opposed to civic education, is purposefully chosen because it is more holistic in perspective and application. Whereas *civic education*, especially in the United States, is often relegated to history and social studies, and often focused on a society's formal political governance and economic structures, democratic citizenship education addresses the social, cultural, historical, economic, and political spheres, and recognizes that the development of democratic citizens is the responsibility of all of society's members. If democratic education is to have a lasting impact, then an interdisciplinary, multifaceted approach to citizenship education must be implemented in formal schooling.

Recently, I led a project in which an international team composed of Kenyan and South African educators developed classroom lessons for use in their respective schools. The lessons created by the international teacher team were developed from the findings that emerged from the focus group research that I helped conduct. Focus group participants were selected with help from South African and Kenyan in-country coordinators who had connections to schools and teachers. An analysis of the focus group findings revealed five democratic themes: *human and individual rights, values/traits of citizens, gender equality, tensions between cultural practices and democracy*, and *building community*.

In this chapter, I briefly describe the methodology and procedures used to facilitate a democratic approach for use in cross-national, citizenship education work. A sampling of lessons developed for use in upper primary and junior secondary schools in South Africa and Kenya are discussed. The lessons speak to the complex intersection of democracy and culture, which led me to consider some of the general functions of culture and the application of those aspects to the development of democratic culture. The development of a temporal consciousness—attention to the past, present, and future—is advocated as important in cross-cultural projects in the area of democracy and education. As Nelson Mandela (as cited in Crwys-Williams, 1997) cautions, "What is important is not only to attain victory for democracy, it is to retain democracy." The conceptualization of democracy that emerges from this American-funded project, as demonstrated in the classroom lessons created by the South African-Kenyan curriculum team, identifies a direction for further curriculum work in the area of democratic citizenship education in each country. The project provided a comparative experience not only for the American project codirectors, but also for the Kenyan and South African schoolteachers who came to see the familiar (i.e., democracy) in a new light as a result of interaction with their counterparts from each African country.

DEMOCRACY'S CULTURAL CONNECTION

Democracy is enlarged and constrained by both global and local influences. Economic interdependence and the "convergence of formal institutions within and across nations toward similar goals and operating structures" (Astiz, Wiseman, & Baker, 2002, p. 67) are but two examples of globalization's intensifying effects. This convergence of ideas and practices in education is manifested in the national curricula in South Africa and Kenya, as elsewhere, which have been fashioned to help prepare learners for global competition and to foster national development. To compete successfully on the world's stage, governments and educational policy makers in democratic countries want students who can think, make decisions, and solve personal and social problems (see Collinson & Ono, 2001; Gutek, 1993; Hahn, 1998; and Karsten, Kubow, Matrai, & Pitiyanuwat, 2000). Despite a global movement toward democracy and some emerging consensus across countries regarding the kinds of values and skills necessary for democratic citizenship, tensions around self-identification are also rising between and within nations in relation to cultural, ethnic, linguistic, and religious difference. The oppositions and challenges within democracies worldwide serve as stark reminders of the limits of these political systems to "democratise societies as entities" (von Lieres, 2005, p. 24).

Thus, democratic education projects must attend to what von Lieres (2005) describes as the marginalization that exists within liberal democracies. In South Africa, the conditions for democracy are not simply inclusion in nominally democratic processes, such as voting or resource distribution, but rather a concern for citizens on the margins and the ways people have created different forms of associated life through culture, ethnicity, and religion (Robins, 2005). The values underlying South Africa's postapartheid educational curriculum, for instance, have included democratic principles such as equal treatment across races, equal educational opportunity, and equity to redress past inequalities and oppression (Fiske & Ladd, 2004). In reference to African countries in general, South African President Thabo Mbeki (1999) explains that there is not a single democratic model to be copied; rather, Africans themselves must consider "the specific conditions in our countries to find the organizational forms which, while addressing those specific conditions, still live up to the perspective that the people shall govern" (p. xv). Democracy in African countries, therefore, is being shaped by the experiences of people within local communities and in response to what citizens perceive as barriers to democratic life, such as poverty, disease, and various forms of violence. The challenge for all democratic societies is for democracy to expand from "the enjoyment of civil and political rights" to one where citizens are protected from disease, hunger, and crime (Manganyi, 2004, p. 7).

People's conceptions of their lived experiences reveal the implicit assumptions and particular rules that govern a society (McGovern, 1999). These are aspects of a society's culture, which also involves "the particular ways in which a social group lives out and makes sense of its 'given' circumstances and conditions of life" (McLaren, 2003, p. 74). According to Makgoba, Shope, and Mazwai (1999), the task for citizens in African countries is "to define who we are and where we are going in the global community, and to formulate practical strategies and solutions for future action that would benefit the African masses" (p. i). A one-size-fits-all or homogenous brand of democracy, therefore, is untenable because the relationship of the individual to his/her society is conceptualized from different cultural assumptions within and between different democratic countries. The research methodologies and attendant procedures employed in citizenship education efforts at home and abroad, therefore, must seek to provide a forum in which people speak from their own knowledge bases and lived experiences within democracies.

A DEMOCRATIC METHODOLOGY FOR CROSS-CULTURAL STUDY

To ascertain how people in different nations conceptualize democracy, a democratic methodology for cross-cultural study was fashioned during the international project. The methodology, called *democratic concept development* or DCD (Kubow, 2005; Kubow & Fischer, 2004b; Kubow & Fischer, 2006), consists of six major steps, each of which generated data and analysis at each of these research stages:

1. conduct focus groups with participants in each country to ascertain their views of democracy;
2. identify both unique and shared conceptions of democracy from focus group data;
3. construct a graphic that reveals the shared democratic themes, while also depicting the different ways in which the country participants spoke of democracy;
4. assemble an international curriculum team composed of a small number of the original focus group participants to draft classroom lessons on the democratic themes;
5. teach the classroom lessons in each country to determine their effectiveness with learners; and,

6. finalize the lessons based on feedback from pilot teaching.

The DCD methodology helped to facilitate a process of revisiting, defining, and evaluating democracy, and for participants to discuss who they are and where they are going as citizens of African nations. The methodology is based on several assumptions. Because people are constructors of knowledge, the project participants already possess knowledge about democracy as a result of their own lived experiences within democratic countries. Their knowledge is informed by local and global discourse because their countries and respective cultural communities exist within a global network. Because many South Africans and Kenyans speak English as a result of their colonial pasts and globalizing factors, English was used throughout the research process and lesson construction. Fluency in English, both spoken and written, guided participant recruitment and selection. However, translation was available during the focus groups and subsequent curriculum team meetings.

Focus groups, which enable the documentation of participants' viewpoints about democracy in relatively short periods of time, provide dialogic forums for participants to think aloud about democracy, discovering for themselves and with others their views on democracy. Ascertaining knowledge about democracy from citizens at the grassroots level is paramount because these are the individuals responsible for any systemic changes desired by governments and educational policymakers. In the international citizenship education project, a gender-balanced group of 26 secondary and primary educators (13 from KwaZulu-Natal, South Africa and 13 from Nyanza, Central, and Nairobi Provinces in Kenya) took part in focus groups facilitated by two American project directors. Three major questions centered on the participants' understandings of democracy, the values and skills they considered important for democratic citizenship, and the ways that formal schooling could develop the knowledge, skills, and values/dispositions they viewed as essential to democratic citizenship. The participants used the focus groups as an opportunity to engage in a critical assessment of their nation's democratic progress, and to describe the ways that culture promotes and hinders democracy's advancement in their respective countries.

Eleven (5 South Africans, 6 Kenyans) of the 26 focus group participants constituted the international curriculum development team. The curriculum team, composed of 5 women and 6 men, engaged in in-depth discussions on the democratic themes that emerged from the focus group data. The team also created 32 classroom lessons in English on the democratic themes during a curriculum-writing seminar in Durban, South Africa. The lessons were then pilot tested in over 100 Kenyan and South

African classrooms by the curriculum team members, other focus group participants, and some of their colleagues. Each teacher completed a reflection sheet (developed by the curriculum team) after the teaching of a lesson, which provided an assessment of the lesson's effectiveness with students, as well as guidance to the international curriculum team in their final lesson editing sessions held at Bowling Green State University in the United States. The curriculum writing process generated data (e.g., the identification and summaries of key democratic concepts and social concerns), which was the substance of classroom lessons. Ten of the 32 lessons are examined in the next section.

CULTURAL CONSTRUCTIONS OF DEMOCRACY

The meanings the participants ascribe to democracy are captured in the particular themes that emerged from the focus group data. These include: *human and individual rights, values/traits of citizens, gender equality, tensions between cultural practices and democracy,* and *building community.* Of the 32 lessons developed by the curriculum team for use in upper primary and junior secondary schools, 10 lessons feature the method of storytelling to facilitate student interest, and thinking, through small and large group discussions where learners are asked to provide justifications for their perspectives on each of the stories. Table 7.1 displays the title and content focus of each of the democratic lessons that employ storytelling—a feature of rich oral traditions—as the primary teaching method for use with students ranging from 10–15 years of age.

Human and Individual Rights

The work with the Kenyan and South African teachers reveals that, for these participants, human and individual rights are the foundation of a democratic society. Through classroom lessons on this theme, students learn the importance of social contribution, examine issues (e.g., violence, corruption, and inequitable resource distribution) that pose threats to democratic existence, and consider the kinds of activities that either build or threaten a safe, democratic environment where all community members can thrive and prosper. Students are challenged to name the injustices they see, to use their freedom of expression to confront social issues that are difficult to talk about, and to share and exchange ideas about how to safeguard their political, social, and economic rights. For example, in the lesson *Accessible Education*, a story of a headmaster, parent, and student is told in which the student is expelled from school

Table 7.1. Democratic Lessons With Storytelling as Teaching Method

Lesson Title	Content Focus
Human and Individual Rights	
Accessible Education	Student expulsion, unable to pay school fees
Children's Rights	Female circumcision and genital mutilation
Freedom to Choose Dress Style	Female rape
Values/Traits of Citizens	
Discrimination	Male child with special needs ridiculed by peer
Respect	Family conflict due to envy of material goods
Gender Equality	
Equality vs. Equity	Equality of opportunity or equitable impact
Tensions Between Cultural Practices and Democracy	
Rituals	Opposition to performing burial rites
Initiation from Childhood to Adulthood	Circumcision as qualification for adulthood
Building Community	
Participation in the Community	Importance of community participation
Empowerment	Dependent vs. independent development

due to a lack of money to pay school fees. Although the student is aware of his/her right to education, the learner is caught in the middle when the headmaster compels the parent to remove the child from school. The discussion of the story serves as a platform for further exploration on the right to education in the constitutions of South Africa and Kenya, and reinforces the notion that formal education is a primary means of individual and social development, with the potential to change a person's life circumstances.

In the lesson *Children's Rights*, learners explore the difficult decisions youth face within their cultural communities. A story is told of a girl who chooses to run away from genital mutilation through female circumcision, which she views to be a negative social norm because the procedure is sometimes done without sterilized equipment. Students are challenged to consider how youth might face their concerns and fight for the protection of their rights, as opposed to running away from their problems. The lesson concludes with a discussion on children's rights and how cultural communities can protect an individual's right to challenge tradition. This is best captured in the lesson summary developed by the South African-Kenyan teacher curriculum team:

Every human right has a corresponding duty and responsibility that includes respect, recognition, protection, and fulfillment. The learners should know that they are entitled to these rights and that they have responsibility to study and respect these rights (e.g., the right to equal medical care and the responsibility to care for themselves, … the right to get the special care for special needs and the responsibility to be the best people they can [be]. (as cited in Kubow & Fischer, 2004a)

In the lesson *Freedom to Choose Dress Style*, students debate issues of freedom and responsibility in a scenario involving rape. Students are presented with a story of a girl who wearing a short skirt and walking down a city street at night is gang-raped in an isolated sports field by two young men. Community members blame the rape on the victim for her choice of dress, stating that she was asking for trouble. The class is then asked to consider the issue of responsibility as well as violations to personal safety and security. Students learn that despite dress choice, no one has a right to rape another person.

Values/Traits of Citizens

The traits deemed vital to maintaining democracy include trust, honesty, loyalty, faithfulness, and hard work. People become democratic when they consider socially desirable ways to act. Character formation—how to behave and relate to others in society—is crucial to developing participatory, healthy communities. Honesty, for example, is not only an individual attribute, but also serves a social function, for it provides a benchmark from which to identify social ills and to work to alleviate their negative effects on people. In the lesson *Discrimination*, defined by the teachers as "not allowing someone to do what they are negatively inclined to do toward others" (as cited in Kubow & Fischer, 2004a, p. 82), learners identify discrimination's various forms and consequences. The following story by the curriculum team illustrates the emotions involved in discriminatory acts and provides a context for discussion and learning.

Mkhuhumeli was a grade 10 learner in Durban. He was shy, but very clever at his school-work. Teachers always praised him. They always said he would be a scientist one day. When other children were playing soccer, he would sit under the tree and cheer the other children playing soccer. He really loved sports, but he could not play because polio affected both of his legs. He used crutches to walk. One day he arrived late at school. The teacher had already started with the lesson. He got into the class, apologized to the teacher for being late and proceeded to his desk. On his desk there was a folded piece of paper. He sat down, took the paper and read it. He cried, took the crutches and went out of class. One learner was heard laughing. On the piece of paper was written, "Go get another set of legs so that you come to school on time." (Scenario constructed by curriculum team, as cited in Kubow & Fischer, 2004a)

Respect is a value that plays a major role in organizing social relations in African communities in relation to deference to elders and the building of self-esteem in learners. In the lesson *Respect*, students are told the story, written by Catherine W. Gichuba, of a boy named John who envies the material goods of others and who makes demands on his poor father to provide the items he desires. Learners explore the behavioral responses that cause social conflict, and envy is contrasted with the value of respect. Because cultural norms affirm that children and youth are to respect parents, the elderly, and those in positions of authority, students are asked to consider how they might communicate more effectively and in a respectful manner with adults in their homes and communities.

Gender Equality

Gender relations play an important role in divisions of power, leadership, labor, and social roles. Tradition—understood as the rules by which the community is bound—can support or pose a barrier to gender equality. Through lessons in this thematic category, students examine their positive rights (freedom to such things as speech and physical movement) and negative rights (freedom from such things as pain, suffering, and threats to safety) as enshrined in their respective national constitutions. Learners discuss the different experiences that males and females encounter in relation to access to legal protection and resources, and how traditional cultural practices sometimes disadvantage females. A person's identity is influenced by culture; therefore, it is important for learners to consider how the identities and abilities of every citizen can be used to improve community life. For example, in the lesson *Equality vs. Equity*, students examine the issue of gender equality in terms of tasks and responsibilities, and explore concepts such as equal pay for equal work and women's rights to own property. Through the following story, students learn that more equitable social relations can be developed, and they consider the specific actions they might take to realize social change.

A fox and a stork may be given equal opportunity to eat from a dish. Who gets the most depends on whether the dish is wide and shallow to suit the fox, or deep and narrow to suit the stork. For equitable impact each would have to eat a share of the food from its own dish. In development, do we seek equality of opportunity or equity of impact? (Scenario constructed by curriculum team, as cited in Kubow & Fischer, 2004a)

Tensions Between Cultural Practices and Democracy

This democratic theme explores how practices within cultural communities can enhance or conflict with individual choice, autonomy, and human rights. The lessons on tensions between cultural practices and democracy ask learners to consider the ways in which citizens' voices are restricted or enlarged in the decisions that affect their personal well being. In the lesson *Rituals*, a story is told of a person forced by the community to perform burial rites, which refer to certain practices used to appease the dead and to cleanse family members. Rituals are traditional rites of practice to give good luck or to protect community members from misfortune. Rituals function to maintain social order and are considered by many persons in indigenous communities to provide an appropriate balance between the natural and the spiritual world. Because rituals impact the lives of learners in their communities, the lesson helps students consider when cultural practices should be observed and when traditional practices should be questioned. A central issue raised in the lesson is whether a cultural community can force compliance to rituals when it goes against an individual member's will to participate.

In the lesson *Initiation from Childhood to Adulthood*, learners consider the qualifications for adulthood in their cultural communities. Issues such as social conformity and pressure are examined, as well as the advantages and disadvantages of male and female circumcision. The teacher shares a newspaper story of Lundi, a famous gospel singer from a rural Eastern Cape village, who argued against traditional circumcision, citing instances where young men have died due to complications and the lack of sterile conditions. Learners discuss how circumcision can be responsive to human rights and how individuals might deal with the negative implications from personal opposition to circumcision, such as being isolated from their cultural communities. Students consider the rationale indigenous communities provide for male and female circumcision, as well as how cultural practices could be responsive to pressures for social change.

Building Community

A democratic community is constructed as people recognize that their social contribution is necessary for creating and maintaining community.

In the lesson *Participation in the Community*, learners explore the importance of community participation and the personal qualities of citizenship, such as honesty and dedication, which enable productive work. They also consider instances where citizens who do not contribute to community building benefit from the efforts of others. To illustrate the need for community involvement by all of society's members, the story of the Hare is told.

> Once upon a time in the animal kingdom there lived different kinds of animals, Hare being one of them. The Hare was a very cunning animal and would always find excuses for not participating in communal activities like farming. However, when it came to sharing of the harvest, he was always ready. (Scenario constructed by curriculum team, as cited in Kubow & Fischer, 2004a)

Discussion of the story enables learners to consider issues such as playing tricks, being dishonest, and stealing from the community, which is juxtaposed with sincerity, social contribution, and active participation. The teacher summarizes the lesson by emphasizing that citizens have a moral duty to contribute in positive ways to their community, from which they reap social and economic benefits.

In the lesson *Empowerment*, students become familiar with the term, which is defined as the ability to assert influence on one's surroundings and circumstances. Because democracy is premised on citizens' competence to negotiate and dialogue with others, citizens must be confident and able to contribute to decision-making processes in their communities. A story is told of a community whose viewpoints had long been suppressed due to fear of retaliation from the ruling class.

> Once upon a time in a village community in a semi-arid area, the community there depended on government assistance and never thought they could be independent. A religious priest comes in and decides to try and trap rain water and build reservoirs. The villagers accept and take the advice. They tap water and use the same for irrigation. Then they start to harvest their own vegetables and become self-sufficient. (Scenario constructed by curriculum team, as cited in Kubow & Fischer, 2004a)

Learners discuss the different stages of the story, which moves from the people's state of hopelessness and dependence to the acceptance of an idea introduced to the community. Students are also given examples that illustrate the democratic and undemocratic acts of leaders, and they consider role models worth emulating. Democratic practices such as voting, standing up for those whose voices have been denied, and working with others regardless of different belief systems are addressed in the lesson.

The goal of the lesson is to help learners recognize that those who make informed decisions are proactive; they learn from past mistakes and are open to change.

The international project helped to clarify what some educators from Kenya and South Africa understand democracy to be, what is desirable and undesirable in their respective societies, and what kinds of issues should be addressed through culturally relevant classroom lessons. School curriculum and school practices can contribute to the development of a democratic culture and help sustain democracy as students become exposed to, and practiced in, the values and behaviors considered important to democratic life in their respective communities. Both communities and formal education can play important roles in fostering a citizen identity that simultaneously affirms human rights, individual autonomy, and diversity, while also providing a democratic foundation that helps hold a society together. To examine peoples' perceptions of democracy is to engage in the identity debate (i.e., who were are and where we are going as a community and nation), and to build communities that move society forward in socially desirable ways with the aim of realizing the kind of democracy its citizens envision.

CULTURE'S GENERAL FUNCTIONS AND THE DEVELOPMENT OF DEMOCRATIC CULTURE

According to one conception, "culture, in simple terms, is everything that human beings make or do" (Makgoba, Shope, & Mazwai, 1999, p. x). Mazrui (1990) developed a framework of roles that culture plays in a society. These roles, which orchestrate people's thoughts, values, and actions, can be termed *conceptual, behavioral, relational, evaluative, formative, communicative, purposeful, productive,* and *consumptive.* Mazrui's initial conceptualization, and my elaboration of this set of roles in democratic settings, was useful for thinking about the many dimensions along which democratic thought and action can be developed. Building upon Mazrui's (1990) cultural functions work, I have constructed a chart that identifies, describes, and elaborates on at least nine ways that culture shapes people's lives and then extend that analysis to consider the corollary of how democratic culture might be constructed (see Table 7.2). The chart is not meant to imply that these are the only ways in which culture functions or that there is only one kind of democratic culture to be developed. Rather, the chart serves as a tool for social educators involved in democratic work to consider cultural issues and differences that are part of lived experiences

Table 7.2. General Functions of Culture Applied to the Development of Democratic Culture

Cultural Functions	Democratic Application
conceptual—cognitive thought processes; acquiring knowledge through perception, intuition, and/or reasoning; memories and imaginations	*democratic awareness*—peoples' views of democracy are shaped by the cultural knowledge and different contexts to which they have been exposed; involves consciousness raising whereby people see the value of democracy for themselves
behavioral—responses by persons and/or groups to a particular set of conditions	*democratic action*—ability to act in democratic ways; democratic praxis directed toward non-racialism, equity, and liberation
relational—the structuring of social relations within a society often by status, age, gender, class	*democratic interaction*—the structuring of social relations in fair and equitable ways
evaluative—examining and judging the value and importance of something	*democratic assessment*—critical examination of social conditions and attention to the connection between knowledge and power
formative—influential in developing or shaping character and identity	*democratic identity*—personal, social, and national identity fashioned through freedom to define for oneself what is most important
communicative—language and modes of expression (e.g., music and art) as tools for expression and idea sharing	*democratic dialogue*—encounters where diverse opinions are sought and people are free to contribute their knowledge and positions with others
purposeful—satisfaction derived from needs and/or desires being met; one's purpose and meaning in life is identified and developed	*democratic attainment*—the realization of individual and group goals
productive—the ability to construct and exchange something of value (knowledge, materials, goods) to the community and to others	*democratic knowledge construction*—how democracy is systematically put together; producing conceptualizations of democracy to guide the building of society in socially just ways
consumptive—engaged in, causing, or encouraging the consumption of goods and materials	*democratic expenditure*—the kinds of investments that enable citizens to develop their ability and potential

and participants' nuanced understandings of democracy and citizenship within different democratic countries.

Conceptually, a person's cognition is shaped by knowledge, perception, intuition, reasoning, memory, and imagination. Applied to the development of democratic culture, people's democratic awareness is created by the different knowledge and contexts to which they have been exposed. *Behaviorally*, people respond to their geophysical and social conditions in particular ways that are influenced by their cultural norms or the challenges to those norms posed by social, economic, political, and geophysical factors. Democracy, therefore, is actualized through the democratic actions of citizens within their respective communities who choose to assert their human rights and to protect those rights for others. Democratic praxis is a kind of action that is directed toward non-racialism, equality, and liberation, and from which citizens are challenged to continually consider their knowledge and actions as they build their social environments. The construction of democratic spaces, then, requires attention to developing democratic knowledge, skills, and values/dispositions that are shaped by cultural norms and influences.

Relationally, culture often structures social relations by age, gender, class, and status. Thus, democratic interactions would be necessary to ensure that social relations do not limit individual autonomy and choice as a result of social hierarchies. In terms of culture's *evaluative* role, particular social and cultural norms lend themselves to certain examinations and judgments as to the value and importance rendered to people, places, and events. In a democratic society, citizens are called upon to critically examine the relationship between knowledge and power in their communities and in society at large, which requires the ability to engage in a continual democratic assessment of the practices in their respective environments. Culture also plays a *formative* role, for it is influential in shaping character and identity. Democratic identity—which functions at the personal and societal level—is shaped in relation to the degree of freedom that citizens have to define for themselves what is beneficial to them and their society.

In *communicative* terms, language and different modes of expression are tools for the sharing of knowledge, values, and ideas. Democratic dialogue, where diverse opinions are sought and people are free to contribute without fear, is a hallmark of a democratic society. As such, "a research process that encourages dialogic encounters" is central to developing "democratic imagination and human agency" and its facilitation in schools (Kubow, 2005, p. 24). Culture also provides *purpose* in life, as people derive satisfaction from their needs and desires being met. The corollary in a democratic society is the attainment of social and individual goals deemed favorable. There are also *productive* and *consumptive* functions of culture that serve to organize community life in particular ways, delineating to its members what is useful and of value to the community and guarding against or, in some cases, aiding the consumption of goods and sustaining practices that are harmful to the individual and the society. Citizens in democracies are encouraged to engage in active knowledge construction, to use their minds and goodwill to build communities in a socially just direction, and to encourage healthy consumptive habits. Moreover, the democratic expenditure required for social well being is dependent on the kinds of goods, materials, and practices that help develop citizens' abilities and potential to contribute to their society in positive ways.

In the lessons developed by the international curriculum team, the themes and issues the teachers want their learners to consider in the classroom attest to a complex intersection of culture and democracy. Formal education, as a social institution, plays an important role in shaping learners' views of themselves as citizens, their histories as members of South Africa or Kenya, and their conscious attempts to carry out their culture while fashioning democratic relations and structures. The lessons speak to culture's socializing force, with the power to sanction behavior that at times may be appropriate, and at other times may be a barrier to individual choice and autonomy. Learners are asked to consider whether there is room to question cultural traditions without penalty to their personal safety, security, and social belonging. The lessons also emphasize the importance given to positive social contribution, and to behaviors that will foster desirable social change exerted within and outside the community. Concerns about social conformity and pressure feature largely in the lessons, and the teachers want learners to explore the ways in which their own and other citizens' voices are enlarged or restricted by culture. Central to community building efforts is personal character (honesty, trust, respect, and hard work) and communication skills (discussion and negotiation). Character and communication help to guard against apathy and to effectively address social problems such as violence, discrimination, and inequality.

A TEMPORAL PERSPECTIVE TO GUIDE DEMOCRATIC WORK

Those engaged in democratic citizenship education efforts at home and abroad may benefit from an interpretive framework to assist in their explorations of democracy in diverse cultural settings. The classroom lessons developed by the South African and Kenyan teachers reflect a temporal consciousness or perspective; that is, the lessons have been constructed through their consideration of some of the historical conditions, contemporary realities, and envisioned trajectories (directions) of their communities and nations. In-depth examinations of democracy require attention to three temporal spheres: the past, the present, and the future (see Table 7.3). Within each sphere, sociocultural, political, and economic aspects should be considered for how they have fashioned democracy and peoples' responses within their communities in particular ways. Material and immaterial space simultaneously shapes these aspects and temporal spheres.[1]

A temporal perspective is useful in generating citizenship education curriculum because it draws upon knowledge that is reflective of the people and countries for which the curriculum is to be designed and implemented. An analysis of the lessons that emerged from the international project enabled me to develop these potentially useful frameworks on culture and democracy. Schoolteachers from South Africa and Kenya not only shared perspectives on the sociocultural, political, and economic issues impacting democracy and citizenship education, but the project provided a method for enabling the identification of key democratic themes, which then served as the conceptual content for the democratic lessons created. Using a method of open inquiry fostered learning about the African contexts in which these participants live and teach, and provided a way for the educators themselves to develop democratic lessons appropriate to and relevant for their students. When democracy is the focus of educational efforts, this is all the more reason for researchers to be concerned with the processes used with international participants. Attention must be given, therefore, to the development of democratic education content through democratic research approaches.

Table 7.3.   Culture and Democracy: Developing a Temporal Consciousness

	PAST (History)	PRESENT (Realities)	FUTURE (Direction)
	The Historical	The Contemporary	The Trajectory
Material Space: geophysical location, land, and resources *Immaterial Space:* values, knowledge, memory, rootedness, personal and collective identities, relationships, community	How sociocultural, political, and economic influences have shaped individuals, communities, and nations in the past; how historical conditions (internal and external) have changed cultures and nations; people's responses to their social challenges and the individual and collective influence exerted on their environments	How contemporary sociocultural, political, and economic influences shape present realities and pose challenges to the person, community, country, and world	How the future might be fashioned; developing citizens' social capacity to imagine democratic environments to guide community building in a desirable direction; fostering a sense of human agency to construct a socially just society and world

CONCLUSION

This chapter explored the intersection of culture and democracy in an international research project led by American project directors with teacher participants from two African countries. Because culture influences people's constructions of democracy, the notion of a one-size-fits all or homogenous brand of American democracy exported abroad is challenged by the life-worlds of individuals and communities in different locales who also exercise their right to question, to reflect, and to act in ways they consider beneficial for themselves and others. There is no need to crusade for democracy; rather, the practice of democracy, which involves seeking the knowledge and views of others in an environment where people can contribute their viewpoints, can cultivate a desire for, and efforts toward, democratic practice in homes, schools, communities, and countries. For U.S. comparative educators, our most valuable contribution will be the actual practice of democracy in the research studies and projects we conduct with international participants. The field of comparative and international education, which draws upon multiple disciplines in its appraisals of educational phenomena, offers the opportunity to explore the complexities associated with educating for citizenship in democracies around the globe. Comparative educators, whose training makes them necessarily sensitive to culture, have a prominent role to play in shaping the direction of cross-national democratic education efforts.

ACKNOWLEDGEMENTS

I want to thank all of the teachers from South Africa and Kenya who participated in the focus groups. Particular gratitude is extended to the curriculum team whose work is showcased in this chapter. The South African team members include: Henry Bheki, Pretty Pinky Mabasa, Sydney Msbenzi Mbuyazi, Zamangwane Ruth Bhengu-Mpungose, and Sibusiso Simamane. The Kenyan team members include: Daniel Odhiambo Maganda, Dr. Wycliffe Humphrey Odiwuor, Moses Teddy Ayomo Oketch, Florence Achieng Omondi, Hellen Onyango, and Grace Akeyo Were.

NOTE

1.   Nóvoa and Yariv-Mashal (2003) suggest that democracy entails both a material and immaterial space. Material space refers to people's lived experiences within particular physical locales. Immaterial space is associ-

ated with the imaginations and memories formed through associated living with people similar or dissimilar to us.

REFERENCES

Astiz, M. F., Wiseman, A. W., & Baker, D. P. (2002). Slouching toward decentralization: Consequences for curricular control in national education systems. *Comparative Education Review, 46*(1), 66–88.

Collinson, V., & Ono, Y. (2001). The professional development of teachers in the United States and Japan. *European Journal of Teacher Education, 24*(2), 223–248.

Crwys-Williams, J. (Ed.). (1997). *In the words of Nelson Mandela*. London: Penquin Books.

Fiske, E. B., & Ladd, H. F. (2004). *Equity: Education reform in post-apartheid South Africa*. Washington, DC: Brookings Institution Press.

Gutek, G. L. (1993). *American education in a global society: Internationalizing teacher education*. White Plains, NY: Longman.

Habermas, J. (1996). An alternative way out of the philosophy of the subject: Communicative versus subject-centered reason. In L. D. Cahoone (Ed.), *From modernism to postmodernism: An anthology*. Cambridge, MA: Blackwell.

Hahn, C. (1998). *Becoming political: Comparative perspectives on citizenship education*. Albany, NY: SUNY Press.

Karsten, S., Kubow, P., Matrai, Z., & Pitiyanuwat, S. (2000). Challenges facing the 21st century citizen: Views of policy makers. In J. Cogan & R. Derricott (Eds.), *Citizenship for the 21st century: An international perspective on education* (pp. 109–130). London: Kogan Page.

Kubow, P. K. (2005). African wisdom and democratic classrooms: South Africa and Kenya. *Education and Society, 23*(3), 21–33.

Kubow, P. K., & Fischer, J. M. (Eds.). (2004a). *Education for democracy: A democratic curriculum framework and lessons*. Lima, OH: CSS.

Kubow, P. K., & Fischer, J. M. (2004b). The Education for Democracy Project: Using democratic pedagogies to create indigenous curriculum. *INQUIRY: Critical Thinking Across the Disciplines, 23*(2), 7–12.

Kubow, P. K., & Fischer, J. M. (2006). Democratic concept development: A dialogic process for developing education curriculum. *Pedagogies: An International Journal, 1*(3), 197–219.

Kubow, P. K., & Fossum, P. R. (2007). *Comparative education: Exploring issues in international context* (2nd ed.). Upper Saddle River, NJ: Merrill Prentice Hall, Pearson Education.

Makgoba, M. W., Shope, T., & Mazwai, T. (1999). Introduction. In M. W. Makgoba (Ed.), *African renaissance: The new struggle* (pp. i–xii). Cape Town, South Africa: Mafube and Tafelberg.

Manganyi, N. C. (2004). Transitions. In N. C. Manganyi (Ed.), *On becoming a democracy: Transition and transformation in South African society* (pp. 3–10). Pretoria: University of South Africa Press.

Mazrui, A. A. (1990). *Cultural forces in world politics*. London: James Currey.

Mbeki, T. (1999). Prologue. In M. W. Makgoba (Ed.), *African renaissance: The new struggle* (pp. xii–xxi). Cape Town, South Africa: Mafube and Tafelberg.

McGovern, S. (1999). *Education, modern development, and indigenous knowledge: An analysis of academic knowledge production.* New York: Garland.

McLaren, P. (2003). Critical pedagogy: A look at the major concepts. In A. Darder, M. Baltodano, & R. D. Torres (Eds.), *The critical pedagogy reader* (pp. 69–96). New York: RoutledgeFalmer.

Nóvoa, A., & Yariv-Mashal, T. (2003). Comparative research in education: A mode of governance or a historical journey? *Comparative Education, 39*(4), 423–438.

Robins, S. L. (Ed.). (2005). *Limits to liberation after apartheid: Citizenship, governance, and culture.* Cape Town, South Africa: David Philip.

Schutz, A. (1995). *The life-world.* Dartford, England: Greenwich University Press.

von Lieres, B. (2005). Marginalisation and citizenship in post-apartheid South Africa. In S. L. Robins (Ed.), *Limits to liberation after apartheid: Citizenship, governance, and culture* (pp. 22–32). Cape Town, South Africa: David Philip.

CHAPTER 8

PUTTING EQUITY INTO ACTION

A Case Study of Educators' Professional Development in Twenty-First Century Kazakhstan

David Landis and Sapargul Mirseitova

INTRODUCTION AND OVERVIEW

In this chapter, we describe how an ethic of participatory citizenship is developing across a professional association of educators in Kazakhstan. Our discussion explores how members of this association, the Kazakhstan Reading Association (KazRA), created a nongovernmental organization governed by the entire membership of the association. Today, this group aims to provide opportunities for all members to vote in the election of representatives and to participate in setting goals and developing activities of the association.

The efforts that led to the creation of KazRA began in 1997 with the introduction of the Reading and Writing for Critical Thinking Project (RWCT). RWCT was a joint offering of the International Reading Association (IRA) and the Soros Open Society Institute of New York (OSI-NY)

Advancing Democracy Through Education? U.S. Influence Abroad and Domestic Practices, pp. 179–206
Copyright © 2008 by Information Age Publishing

and was built upon the concepts and methods of the highly successful Orava Project in Slovakia, which was funded by the United States Agency for International Development (USAID) (Meredith & Steele, 2000). Since 1992, the Orava Association for Democratic Education has introduced instructional practices that support students' active involvement in schools and communities. As a result of the efforts of educators in Slovakia, the RWCT has introduced a philosophy of education and methods of instruction that promote participatory citizenship through educational reform to a much larger group of educators and students around the world. Since 1997, RWCT has involved at least 50,000 educators in Eastern Europe, Central and Southeast Asia, and Central and South America (RWCT International Consortium, 2005).

Today, the KazRA and its regional entities sponsor RWCT in more than 420 schools and universities across the country of Kazakhstan. RWCT serves as the primary resource for assisting Kazakhstani elementary, secondary, and university educators, as well as their students with interactive, thought-provoking practices for participating in school reading and writing. KazRA trainers demonstrate and discuss more than 100 learning strategies that: (a) promote analysis of the strengths and weaknesses of arguments and positions that arise during discussions and problem solving; (b) provide experiences for building and expressing personal opinions and views; (c) encourage interest and participation in school reading and writing; and (d) raise questions and discussions to elaborate ideas and concepts across all school subjects. KazRA activities and publications are in great demand across a variety of schools, working groups, and academic levels. Each year, this association conducts in-service workshops for several groups of teachers and school administrators (about 200 participants, each receiving about 120 hours of training), while about 50 similar groups (about 1,500 participants in all) around the country pay their own fees to take part. Participation in the underwritten workshops is determined by a competition. In some of the fee-based workshops teachers pay the fees and in some cases their schools pay. While KazRA has trained more than 14,000 teachers so far, this figure represents only 2% of elementary and secondary teachers nationwide. In addition, KazRA also provides support in various related areas that include: publishing of professional journals and books, helping university faculty in writing course syllabi, and facilitating workshops for members of the National Academy of Education about current education needs.

Our discussion, which takes the form of a dialogue, is based upon 6 years of participant observation of classroom lessons across elementary, secondary, and university settings, workshops, national/regional/international conferences presentations, grant proposal writing sessions, meetings with government representatives, media interviews, student research of local communities, and other events. To construct this chapter, we reviewed our notes and official records related to these events and we conducted a focus-group discussion with a group of long-term project participants in order to check our developing interpretations. Our comments focus upon the following broad research questions:

- How have educators affiliated with KazRA appropriated the RWCT materials in light of linguistic, ideological, and societal differences that are part of cross-cultural cooperation?
- Given that the RWCT conceptual framework includes ideas about how people should relate to each other, how do educators negotiate between these ideas and the relational practices of their region and culture? And in what ways do the relations with international donors come into play?"

These broad questions are approached through a series of more specific questions:

- How have RWCT participants conceived of participatory citizenship?
- What are the social and institutional dynamics that influence the use of RWCT for promoting participatory citizenship, and what structures constrain or facilitate their successful implementation?
- How do customary educational practices and programs accommodate, challenge, or modify the kind of civic learning envisioned by the RWCT materials?

In order to discuss these sets of questions, our chapter is organized as a cross-cultural dialogue. During our conversation, we strive to communicate across cultural and linguistic differences in order to build understanding about education reform as a means for encouraging participatory citizenship. We discuss key historical events that led to the introduction of the RWCT project in Kazakhstan and early RWCT activities (during the years 1997–2000). Next, we explore the creation of the KazRA and the influence of USAID support, which began in 2000 and continued until 2006. To conclude, we discuss how the organization is currently functioning and make some predictions for the future.

RESEARCH METHODS

Our study utilized an observational method as a means of representing emerging ideas about citizenship and education reform that have been nurtured by the RWCT project and the KazRA during the past 8 years. As a research method, observations have long been used for studying educational issues and processes. In particular, we examined diaries, journal records, and other documents supplemented by retrospective narratives of key events as a means of recording and analyzing our observational data (e.g., Evertson & Green, 1986). This approach was selected in order to describe processes and ways of interacting that have developed during the formation of KazRA and its regional entities. Our goal was to construct a broad overview of the project as a backdrop for highlighting specific, descriptive information about key events. Categories and meanings for organizing our data were identified as our study proceeded.[1]

HISTORICAL BACKGROUND—
INTRODUCING RWCT IN KAZAKHSTAN

Schools have traditionally functioned as important sites for promoting national identity and allegiance to political, economic, and social systems. Teachers and students in Kazakhstan, for example, were expected to focus time and effort towards realizing Soviet scientific, ideological, and industrial policies during most of the twentieth century. Educators were to raise awareness of socialist ideology in order to supply the technical specialists required by the Soviet system (Kaiser, 1984; Olcott, 1987). Education planners introduced a variety of pedagogical methods including cooperative student groups in order to achieve these goals. Such methods tended to be dominated by questions, problems, and perspectives posed by the official school curriculum. Many classrooms, as a result, were places where teachers directed endless streams of information at students. Since the restructuring of the official Soviet bureaucracy in the late 1980s and Kazakhstan's declaration of independence on December 16, 1991, educators in Kazakhstan have more openly debated what scholarly and cultural traditions to honor and reestablish after 70 years of Soviet education directives as well as how to prepare their students to participate in an increasingly global culture in the twenty-first century.

By 1997, the OSI-NY and its national affiliates had committed to introducing RWCT to interested educators across the former Soviet-bloc countries. A "train-the-trainer" model was developed in which local educators first learned about the philosophical approach and methods through workshop demonstrations facilitated by IRA volunteers and began applying the practices in their own classrooms. By the second year the first generation participants began to train other teachers about RWCT. In this way, the RWCT approach was introduced in each local region by trainers who continue to serve as skilled teachers of the methods and who understand its theoretical and philosophical bases. RWCT was designed to encourage teachers to change from traditional information-focused models of instruction that emphasize memory and oral recitation, to a focus upon critical thinking, reading, and writing. Overall, RWCT aimed to increase students' capacities to take responsibility for learning, form independent opinions, show respect for the opinions of others, participate in critical review of the strengths and weaknesses of various arguments or solutions to problems, and engage in collaborative problem solving and discussion of possible courses of action and accompanying consequences. These activities were portrayed as fundamental to the formation of open, participatory societies.

Goals for teachers included: arranging educational activities and spaces that support student inquiry, making use of a method of lesson planning for promoting critical thinking and inquiry, incorporating strategies or techniques for comprehending, interpreting and discussing various texts, developing observational skills for learning more about teaching and encouraging professional development, and serving as a resource for other interested teachers. Goals for students involved in the project included: raising questions and carefully and systematically considering possible alternative answers, considering various perspectives of other people and examining their assumptions, developing responsibility for one's learning and use of resources, learning to cooperate with others by listening to them respectfully and working together, and developing habits supporting life-long learning and curiosity (Meredith, Steele, Temple, & Walter, 1997).

In order to accomplish these goals, RWCT and the IRA recruited more than 80 volunteer educators from around the world. Four volunteers were assigned to each participating country and were given responsibility for facilitating a set of eight in-service workshops, which were primarily offered during school vacations and summer breaks. The workshops incorporated a series of introductions, demonstrations, explanations, and guided practice/planning sessions so that teachers could apply the workshop ideas and practices in their classrooms. In between workshops, participating teachers were involved in monthly meetings to discuss their uses of the workshop content and they observed one another in their classrooms. In Kazakhstan, for example, the IRA volunteers typically visited for two or three week periods—facilitating workshops for 3–5 days; traveling to classrooms of the project participants to observe lessons and provide on-site consultations; and meeting with local and regional education officials to promote the project. Today, UNESCO (United Nations Educational, Scientific and Cultural Organization) recognizes RWCT, among 25 other educational projects, as an exemplary model for promoting crisis prevention and peace building (http://www.ibe.unesco.org).

Since 1997, a transnational network of supporters has influenced the formulation of KazRA and its presentation of the RWCT project. This support has included substantial financial contributions from USAID, the OSI-NY, Soros Foundation Kazakhstan, the Chevron and Shell oil companies, as well as other types of support from the KazRA, the Ministry of Education for the Republic of Kazakhstan, city departments of education in local communities across the country, the Hobart and William Smith Colleges, and the University of Northern Iowa, International Reading Association. The development and working out of these activities reflects the interrelations between these groups, their representatives, and local school directors, educators, parents, and children in participating schools. In the next part of the chapter, we utilize a dialogue format to consider various points of view about the influence of RWCT and the network of supporters mentioned previously in Kazakhstan educational settings beginning in 1997 and continuing to the present. To conclude, we review our key questions and offer summary comments.

DEVELOPING PARTICIPATORY CITIZENSHIP
THROUGH EDUCATION REFORM

In this section we discuss how the RWCT project was introduced in 1997 as well as the expectations that early groups of teachers and school directors held from 1998 to 2000.

Dialogue One

Sapargul: While you started with RWCT in 1997, I came to the project in 1999, and then, six months later I left Kazakhstan for eight months of Fulbright study in the U.S. Anyway, from my little experience during that time, I can say that one of our biggest challenges was the language issue—how to use the Kazakh, Russian, and English languages to work cooperatively and effectively—an issue that relates to other concerns about cultural aspects and pedagogical trends. Challenges posed by different languages still remain for our organization and we will return to discussing our challenges in more detail.

So, David, don't you think the language issue was to some extent over simplified during the workshop meetings and school observations? On the surface, it appeared that the IRA volunteers would say something, then interpreters would rephrase it in Kazakh or Russian, and then the national participants were expected to understand the idea. It reminded me of a behavioral approach to illustrating human communication. How did communication across languages work in reality?

David: I remember the very first workshop that I participated in, March 1998. My American colleague, Peter, and I were explaining the procedures for a cooperative learning activity known as "jigsaw." In this activity, the Russian-speaking participants joined small groups—each group studying a particular section of an article Then we asked each group to teach the information in their section to their colleagues. The participants were confused by the word "teach." Did we want them to prepare a lesson plan? Were we asking them to explain the article? In English, the verb "teach" can refer to several actions including: showing or demonstrating how to do something, giving information about a subject, encouraging another person to accept an idea, causing another person to understand an idea, or persuading/making someone to behave in a certain way. In Russian, however, these actions are indicated by different words such as: <обьяснить> to explain or illustrate, <учить> to give instruction, <принять> to accept an idea. The national participants certainly wondered what we meant by the word "teach," and we had not expected such different contexts and cultural meanings around this verb "teach." So all of us ended up with a real "puzzle!"

Peter and I decided to try again. So after a lunch break we demonstrated the "jigsaw" activity a second time, and drew attention to understanding the ideas presented in the article. Larissa, a teacher from the northern part of the country, explained during a retrospective discussion that she was not used to this kind of persistence. She had not expected that we would be tolerant in this kind of situation since her prior experience in school settings had been that any problems in teacher practice were usually blamed upon the teachers rather than those who were leading in-service presentations. She said that even today, when she has these kinds of situations in her classrooms, that she remembers how we tried again and did not give up when things were difficult.

Sapargul: Reconsidering how RWCT could have been introduced in
            Kazakhstan can raise further insight into relations of lan-
            guage, culture, and pedagogy. First, we could have done
            some preliminary activities to introduce the IRA volunteers
            and the local participants. To my mind, the IRA visitors had
            some ideas about the Soviet regime and education in the
            territory of the USSR, but they had little information about
            Kazakh history, traditions and culture. As for the Kazakh
            participants, they knew little about western education, his-
            tory, or culture. Do you remember how many problems, for
            example, were related to understanding just one word
            «оценка» since "evaluation" was interpreted so differ-
            ently? In the RWCT materials, "evaluation" meant observ-
            ing and appreciating students' processes of inquiry,
            reading, and writing in addition to reviewing final products.
            However, in Russian pedagogy, 'evaluation' means grad-
            ing—mostly focusing on giving points or marks.

David: Yes, I remember a story that Tamara[3] retold for us about
            "evaluation" as a form of critical thinking. She said, "*We
            were accepting critical thinking as though it was 'criticizing.' We
            told our colleagues that we would return from the workshop as
            great critics. In schools, this phrase was typically used in the context
            of saying what is wrong and what is bad and then giving a grade
            as result. Then I came and participated in the workshops and
            began to ask, 'What do the volunteers mean when they say 'critical
            thinking?' It's not what I expected.' Today I know that my first
            understanding is very far from what it means in reality. For me, I
            see that it means asking questions and considering other points of
            view.*" For me, her story tied together issues related to teach-
            ing and evaluation with the phrase "critical thinking."

Sapargul: At the same time differing expectations about what it means
            to be critical and to evaluate reflect more than just differ-
            ences in interpretation. The local teachers, those who are
            not in the project, still consider grading as the final action
            of each class, course and year, and evaluation of students'
            achievements is very formal. Even today, newcomers to the
            project think of "critical thinking" as "criticizing" and as
            they participate in workshops they remark, "*Oh, OK, it
            doesn't mean to criticize, so you should change 'critical thinking' to
            'creative thinking.'*"

I remember after class observations, for example, how many principals tried to avoid "critical" discussions by taking the IRA visitors away from the teacher being observed because they thought it was more important to demonstrate their hospitality than to make time for teacher reflection or "critical thinking" about the lesson. What do you think, why?

David: For the principals, showing hospitality was absolutely required and for us as North American educators it was important to show appreciation for all that had been done to help us feel welcomed. All of us were trying to cross differences in cultural expectations and pedagogical practices and so we worked hard to build relationships. Many expressions of thanks and appreciation were offered during lesson observations, meetings, meals, and coffee breaks. Through these social events, the foundations for future cooperation were established.

Sapargul: Besides, I think, the principals were not used to teacher reflection as important. Traditionally, classroom visitors could say very formal things and mostly they criticized what they saw and heard. The observed teacher was supposed just to listen and accept every comment. For the principals, the North American educator was not just an ordinary guest and even not from their own country, so they did their best to express national hospitality by taking away any kind of "business" relationship.

David: Several times during the early classroom observations, opportunities for teachers to interact with the visitors were strictly limited. As an North American educator, I expected that teachers would be allowed to discuss their lessons in detail with me as an observer. However, the reality was that I was guided to a "press conference" type of situation where my discussion with the teacher would be carefully guided through a series of general questions and comments such as: *Did you like the class? Did you like our kids? Do you like our school? Tell us something about your country. We would like to present this gift to you on behalf of our school community. Thank you for coming.*

Sapargul: At this period of time, it was an unbelievable situation when foreigners, moreover, North Americans, could come and visit just any school in Kazakhstan, even those in cities that had been formerly closed during the Soviet times because of military or industrial activities. It was for the principal very important and also all the faculty and children wanted to use this situation to learn more about countries such as the USA and Canada and therefore they didn't expect that you came for different purposes. They wanted to know how North Americans lived, not what details you noticed about teacher lessons.

Another huge difference that had to be taken into account was related to the national cultural view of respecting the age, experience and education of particular people such as elders, teachers, and administrators. Don't you think it was most difficult for a teacher to accept the RWCT point of view that a child can have his own opinion and it should be respected anyway? It was totally a new idea that the child comes to school already with her own knowledge and the teacher should eventually, and respectfully, develop it further and build on it. Do you remember how teachers were resisting subconsciously sharing their power in the classroom with children?

I remember a story told by another participant, Galina. She has been teaching Russian literature in a secondary school for several years and she was part of the original group of RWCT participants in Kazakhstan. She remembers when RWCT project directors came to observe her teaching. She did all the talking during the lesson and felt so proud of her guidance of students' answers to her questions and her use of her materials—a lesson that went according to all of the principles she had been taught during her pedagogical training. After the lesson, she asked one of the visitors, *"What do you say about my class?"*

He replied, *"How did you like your lesson?"*

She answered, *"It was good."*

He said, *"Ok. Congratulations."* He shook her hand. And he left her puzzled because she was expecting some criticism and advice about how to teach. She expected that he would criticize her lesson in detail and explain exactly how to use the materials in the proper way. Now today, she notices that his attitude toward her lesson opened up the possibility for her to think about her class. His reply meant that it is her job to think about it and take responsibility for improving it. She says this experience was a great lesson for her. All of these examples demonstrate the respect that in-country participants had for their international visitors. Anyway, what was the most remarkable thing during this period for you?

David: During this time, my observations of other teachers' lessons in Kazakhstan schools and my reading of documents related to RWCT reminded me that I ought to "critically" reconsider my teaching practices. One early piece of writing composed by staff at Soros Foundation Kazakhstan (1998), for example, proposed introducing RWCT to instructors of universities. This document, *Development of Critical Thinking* explained:

> Democratic pedagogical techniques are successfully used in any subject context. The key item in them is a priority common to all mankind and civil values: value and dignity of a human life, it's openness and readiness to cooperate, equal opportunities to begin, respect of diversity and dif-ferences among people, traditions, and cultures; not only tolerance as a democratic principle, but the demonstration of an interest towards what others are thinking about, even if their thoughts are opposite to our own.

Documents like this implied a set of basic civil values underlying an ethic of participatory citizenship and they drew my attention to critically reevaluating my own teach-ing practices. I started asking how my pedagogical activi-ties extended or denied basic freedoms of my students in my classes in the U.S. and how my students' situations compared with what I read and observed in classrooms in Kazakhstan.

Sapargul: For me it was a belief that we can do it—we can bring some changes into our education. I also think that period was sig-nificant for our organization because it brought together very motivated, dedicated-to-their-profession people. Though, at the same time that period was very challenging and some people could not meet the expectations and chal-lenges of our work, so they left.

Dialogue Two

In this section, we discuss the influence of USAID support beginning in 2000 and the rapid growth of the RWCT movement in Kazakhstan educational networks. We also consider the dynamic relations that were established during this time period between the Ministry of Education, the KazRA staff, teachers, and administrators at USAID, and the influence of those relations upon the implementation of democratic principles of citizenship and education reform in local schools. Finally, we discuss current developments in secondary and higher education in Kazakhstan.

Sapargul: By the year 2000, it became obvious that we should continue our work. Three years of Soros Foundation/OSI-NY support had concluded and we realized this period of time was not enough for us because we only raised the desire for change but we were still far from our goal of transformation. Teachers were eager to participate at RWCT workshops, to try strategies in their classrooms afterwards, but it did not become their part of educational philosophy. Three years are not enough for total transformation if one wants to change from just accepting information into weighing it, comparing it with actual situations and other resources, and then making the final decision about which of it to select or follow. Don't you think it was a critical moment in our work and our organization? It was a time when we were supposed to take some decisive steps. Otherwise, all our previous efforts would have resulted in a very formal attitude—that "critical thinking" means the use of strategies and using the strategies for the sake of strategies.

David: Yes, there was a risk that reading and writing for critical thinking could have been viewed as just a formula—a set of strategies and nothing more; but I remember steps that were taken to avoid that possibility. By the year 2002, for example, two national quarterly journals were being published for RWCT participants and their students. One publication became known as *Voice and Vision*, (2,700 copies printed and distributed each issue) a professional journal that continues to provide a place for elementary and secondary teachers to share their ideas and experiences related to RWCT philosophy and methods, with one issue each year devoted to higher education faculty interests. A second journal was also launched—*Baby Camel*—featuring writing and art from students (about 2,000 copies are printed and distributed each issue). Today, these journals are unique in Kazakhstan because they represent one of the few, if not the only, nation-wide forums where teachers and students can share and receive ideas about their issues and concerns in classroom teaching. By encouraging teachers and students to write and read, to speak about their views and insights, these publications have become an important way of promoting and deepening ideas about participation in classrooms and schools, and across the wider educational community in Kazakhstan. By making a place where teachers and students could express their viewpoints, people could see that our efforts were more than just strategies for classroom use; there was a more expansive vision in mind for participation.

Sapargul: In 2000, the first national conference took place. I believed that it should become an essential activity in transformation. So the point was if you are a thoughtful teacher and willing to bring some changes into your classroom you should be a good observer of your students in the situation in your classroom and willing to take immediate action and responsibility for it. It can be effective to take notes and after class to consider your thoughts about the situation and reflect upon why it happened and how I can support my students in their learning not only about what is in the textbook but also about life. If a teacher does these kinds of things, a second step may be, *"Oh, I should look around and consider other teachers and share my experiences."*

But in our traditional conferences we were used to situations where one person reports about very general common issues and gives theoretical support, and these kinds of reports were very far from teachers' concerns and students' learning and particular situations that happen every day in classrooms. When I was thinking about a new approach towards the conference, I came to some big challenges, like so many walls before me. It was like, *"These teachers have never seen other ways of presenting papers at conferences and expressing personal viewpoints, so how I should do this work?"*

So I decided to begin with the trainers of the project. There were 40 trainers at that time. I visited different regions and cities to work with those who expressed interest and helped them to consider themes for their presentations, titles, and how to fit them with our conference themes. During the past 6 years we proposed the following themes for our annual national conference: Opening Teachers' Floor for Speaking; The Power of Language and Learning About Language; Writing: From Sources to Present; Professional Development: Teachers' Viewpoints; School and University: Challenges, Inquiry, Findings; Citizenship Development: Patriotism and Moral and Education Mission.

These conference themes can be compared with traditional conference themes proposed by our Ministry of Education such as Quality of Pedagogical Education: Problems and Perspectives for Development. Themes like this are addressed to academicians, not to teachers. They are too abstract to help teachers with the realities of classroom situations, where teachers deal with differences around issues of language, power, cultural perspectives, and pedagogical practices.

We did not have e-mail at that time. The trainers sent their papers by regular postal mail and I responded in writing to each proposal and returned them. I worked with them as a reviewer—responding to multiple drafts from each trainer. Galina remembered how she worked with me to write her conference paper. After the first conference she felt so proud. Over time, she realized how she moved from just reporting about her topic to using the writing and preparation to think more deeply about her topic and gain new insights into it. Now the trainers bring this approach to conference preparation to newcomers and help them to write their conference presentations today.

After the third conference it was obvious that this kind of forum raised other issues. It was not just bringing personal experience to share with others. It was clear that conference writing and speaking was helping teachers to develop a process for professional development. I learned that teachers experience so many challenges when writing. Teachers were not used to viewing writing as a tool for professional development. They expected that only university faculty would write papers and present them at conferences. However, I realized how important writing was for their work and for encouraging their participation as members of the KazRA. So we began a book series called "Professional Development School." It was not just an impulse, but also a con-

scious effort across the project to encourage teachers to
write about education.

Sapargul: Encouraging teachers' professional growth through writing
about their teaching has led to some profound results. By
the year 2000, there were about 2,000 teachers certified as
RWCT participants and RWCT schoolchildren demonstrated their ability to argue respectfully, to admit that there
may be another viewpoint, which is different from theirs.
Both teachers and students were successful in learning
cooperative work.

Another interesting aspect of our teachers' professional
growth occurred through the influence of USAID priorities
and conceptions. How we organized our activities was influenced by USAID expectations for education and we revised
our goals to go further into civic education in line with our
business plan. As we were supporting teachers' professional
development with USAID money, we knew we ought to
think about how more people could benefit from it so when
the support came to an end we would not feel sorry that we
did not use it for many important things. We tried to carefully spend it and we saved money through in-kind contributions from local groups, adding these savings to further
activities. Our relationship with USAID helped us to analyze and reflect upon what we were doing. USAID was asking about the end results and what is the impact or
implications. Their requests helped us make our work an
ongoing process. USAID presented a good model about
how to organize business work, and our teachers learned
how to report, how to build business relationships, ways to
focus on time and format, and ways to include one's ideas in
business plan writing. There was a lot to learn from USAID.

But, anyway, we did not feel like we could say, "Now we
can stop looking for finances" even though we received
funding totaling 1.17 million dollars between 2000 and
2005. Always we were looking for money. It seemed like we
could never stop filing reports, requesting grants, and
thinking about the next proposals to write. Yet, as a result of
the continuing USAID support, we were able to maintain a
consistent focus for our activities and avoid becoming too
distracted by the goals and interests of multiple grantors.
So, RWCT became recognized across many levels of education in Kazakhstan. All important documents issued by the

Ministry of Education, for example, included critical thinking development as one of the skills to work on in schools. Besides being recognized by education administrators regionally and nationally, RWCT also became very popular among teachers across the country, and there continues to be a queue of those who want to take our workshops.

Earlier, we mentioned that teachers were interested in learning strategies in order to try them in their classrooms and it seems that another reason for the popularity of RWCT has been the use of the strategies. Somehow, using graphic organizers such as Venn diagram, engaging in cooperative learning interactions such as jigsaw or think/ pair/ share, and making time for written reflections and debates, attracted teachers' and students' interests in forming questions or opinions and putting more personal effort into lesson planning and in-class activities. While group work and related dialogical approaches such as role-playing had been part of the Soviet educational system, the strategies utilized by RWCT helped establish a type of critical thinking that moved beyond expected curricular questions and answers towards discussions that consider varying perspectives and circumstances, alternative sources of information, and ways to solve problems that were new and significant for teachers and students.

David: Another reason for the popularity of RWCT surely reflects the increasing opportunities for teachers to lead activities within their local regions. The national and regional conferences offer them a place to contribute their ideas for bringing change to their schools. Local committees provide a place for them to become involved with education reform in their area. So, national education reform is becoming realized through grass-roots teacher initiative within local areas. Today, RWCT teachers are recognized locally and nationally, they are invited by officials to present at regional conferences and demonstrate their teaching to others. During the past year, for example, more than 70 RWCT teachers advanced their qualifications and were promoted to higher professional categories.

Sapargul and David: In order to illustrate opportunities for teacher involvement, we take a closer look at a recent national conference that occurred in August of 2005. As we reconsidered the events of this conference, we noticed that the presenters made a conscious effort to adapt their presentations to the situations of those who attended their sessions. Many presenters, even those who were attending for the first time, revised their papers once they arrived at the conference location in order to encourage active involvement of their listeners with the topics of the sessions. It was as though they imagined themselves in place of those in the audience and made an effort to include them in the discussion. They were learning from each other about how to change their presentations to be more interactive. Coming from different regions they worked as a team. If one person from a region was presenting, other colleagues from the same area attended the session to support and help and to show concern and empathy for the presenter. In these ways they imagined themselves in the place of the presenter to encourage him or her to have a successful session.

In addition, it seems to us that the conference demonstrated a particular point described in early RWCT materials—that active participation by people influences later social behaviors. In particular, active involvement fosters habits of civility that bring together individual interests and agendas with concern for others and their interests and agendas. We believe that educational experiences involving inquiry, cooperative learning, and respectful discussions fostered by RWCT in the classrooms also encourage educators to put ideas about civil behaviors and equity into action at the conference.

During the national conference, for example, a number of committees met to guide the work of the KazRA. The charter and documents committee discussed ways to update KazRA legal documents. A publications committee explored ideas for involving more members in writing articles for the national journal and for encouraging them to view it more and more as their journal. This committee also discussed how to raise the confidence of members who don't believe they can write. Meanwhile, the conference chairperson committee—composed of the chairs of past, current, and the upcoming conference discussed particular changes in conference programs and how to encourage more people to submit proposals. For 2005, 197 papers were submitted and 156 were selected. An awards committee discussed criteria for nominations of "RWCT Teacher" and "RWCT School of the Year" among other awards. Across the committees, members were thinking about how to improve and bring to a higher level those new members that recently affiliated. So, experienced members helped newcomers to see themselves as people of importance and value within the KazRA social community. They talked about ways to include retired people as well as how to encourage students to begin to feel they are part of a big professional group.

After the conference, attendees gathered in special interest groups to discuss their future plans for particular conference sessions. In addition, conference attendees met in regional groups to discuss what they learned from the conference and what activities they will support in their regions and how to reach out to new teachers and students who are interested in participating. Through the work of these groups, conference attendees participated in the work of creating a social organization adapted to the tasks that committee members determined were important (cf. Moscovici, 1972).

Our observations of the various social events such as the annual auction for supporting education in orphanages and local schools reminded us that conference participants seemed to be developing a sense of how their personal goals and actions influenced the wider context of the KazRA community and its history. During this conference, for example, we observed that teacher participants took initiative to plan their conference presentations, guide the work of their committees, and organize other events. We believe that KazRA members have built a sense of history about the conference as an event during the past 7 years and have developed a sense of ownership for it.

Taken together, these observations implicitly demonstrate a sense of "democratic civility" that was in evidence during the 2005 conference. Conference attendees demonstrated through their support for one another that they were eager to cooperate so that everyone had an opportunity to participate and be recognized for their contributions. Rather than "civic duty" or obligation, participants showed habits of communicating and behaving that promoted responsibility toward the group, respect for others' views, and a willingness to share power and authority for making decisions (cf. Temple, 2001). In sum, the activities of this recent conference provide examples of KazRA members cooperating together to continuously form an association that encourages them to move beyond personal goals and interests toward shared activities that support engaged participation for the benefit of the group.

David: What have been some challenges for KazRA teachers?

Sapargul: One challenge was that students were accepting the changes easily while teachers were not able to change immediately. Teachers were accepting RWCT in their minds; but making a conscious effort to do things differently during lessons and activities was much more difficult. So, they needed time, more time than just 3 years. Besides, since new teachers come into the project each year, there always has been the possibility that RWCT may be viewed by them as a technique or just an instrument, so it would leave behind the whole philosophy of it—to listen to and hear others, and build your relationships with others the way you would like them to do it with you. RWCT meant respecting the views of other teachers and students by drawing together one's interests and agendas with concern for others and their interests. Also, there was always a related possibility that the RWCT activities and workshops may be only the starting point for change.

So, I continually looked for other opportunities to meet these challenges by building other relationships that could add to and extend what was already happening. In May of 2000, I returned from my study in the U.S. full of new ideas. From Ken Goodman I learned new insights about reading and writing. I observed how he addresses teachers by encouraging them to respect and support their students as readers and writers—letting students introduce personally important reading and writing.

In addition, I thought about Western interpretations of Vygotsky's ideas that teachers should consider students' zones of proximal development (ZPD) since students come to school with academic and community knowledge in their zones of development. His writing discusses the ZPD as the meeting of knowledge or experiences from social, cultural worlds with conscious awareness of oneself as an individual and the self-regulating processes of a psychological world— a meeting made possible through language as a social, cultural tool (cf. Berk & Winsler, 1995). I thought about his division of academic knowledge and community knowledge and how Westerners brought the two kinds of knowledge together to help and support the whole student, while in our country we view the zone of development as composed of these knowledge bases separately and we see only the academic knowledge as the point we should focus on when doing professional development. Even our student testing is oriented toward academic knowledge with little consideration for other knowledge that students can draw from. As a result of this comparison of viewpoints about Vygotsky, I decided that we should emphasize teacher research about students' funds of knowledge (Moll, Amanti, Neff, & González, 1992; Moll & González, 1997) and ethnographic student research about community life in our professional development efforts (Egan-Robertson & Bloome, 1998).

My visit also introduced me to new ideas about whole language and I changed my attitudes towards working with teachers. I should act more respectfully towards them and give them a chance to show what they want and where they want support. I learned that in the classroom the power belongs to the teacher. He or she is responsible for everything there.

Our teachers, again because of the big difference in viewpoints between Central Asia and North America, did not accept these ideas at once. If in your part of the world, teacher response is the most significant part of the professional development, here teacher views are discussed as a very scholarly, theoretical issue that has little relation with classroom teaching. Therefore, at that period of time I was quite sure that teachers should learn observational methods and do action research. As a result they would become confident about their teaching, planning their lessons and sharing their thoughts with each other they would go deeper into teaching philosophy and learn from it.

Time has passed, but classroom-based research remains a challenging issue. Today just a few teachers do serious action research because most school administrators do not support teacher research work. Few administrators are interested in teacher-initiated research or writing. It is not convenient for school administration if a teacher is busy doing something else, not directly assigned by the administration. Also, teachers do not have substitutes when they attend conferences or have professional meetings. School administrators may also argue that teachers should be busy at schools instead of doing work, which seems unconnected with their direct duties. It is always a problem to build communication between teachers across several schools; especially in rural places where teachers do not have access to electronic communication. In this section we discuss next steps of KazRA into future activities.

Dialogue Three

Sapargul: Today we think about our nearest future. To become more or less an independent organization, to become sustainable we need to continue professional development activities like publishing books and journals based on teaching and schooling; doing action research, and paying more attention to how children read and write. In other words our organization should become a place of professional development for teachers. It is important that teachers recognize that they need to grow. As a professional association, KazRA activities should be updated and offered on time. Also we should keep our cooperation with international professional organizations like IRA. At the same time we should continue to study teachers' needs in the country. In order to reach these goals, I hope that we will focus particularly on identifying university, elementary, and secondary faculty who wish to work with us. I believe that our schools should be centers of community outreach that support reading and writing. One way that outreach can occur is through involving students and teachers in community-based research that leads to beneficial social action projects and promotes equity for social participation. A particular emphasis at this time is introducing teachers and students to ethnographic inquiry as an approach to understanding schools in communities.

David: Beginning in 2002, four national teachers and I introduced about 70 students in Grades 1, 5, 8, and 11 to ethnographic research in order to learn about community knowledge and how such knowledge could serve as a beneficial education resource in classrooms. Comparisons were made with past and present approaches to ethnography and students gained experience with composing photographs, interviewing, map-making, field-note writing and cross-situational data analysis.

One example was a study by a small group of first grade students who were interested in a local department store. They began by drawing pictures of the store and discussing what store employees and shoppers would be talking about and what they would be doing in the store. Then the students went with their teacher to the store and began to talk with store clerks about their work and the products that were sold there. The students conducted interviews and composed photos of products and activities in the store such as paying for a purchase. Across these research activities, students wanted to find answers to the question, "What is a department store?" First, the students tried answering the question. It seemed simple to ask, but the answers were quite complicated. Students had difficulty answering it and even adults they interviewed could not agree with one another. Some people said it was a big store, others said it was a store where people can find anything because it has departments inside it. Students made lists of key terms and phrases they heard in the store such as salesperson, signs, cash box, purchase, counters, shop windows, and bills; they sketched possible relations between the terms using graphic organizers such as cluster webs to analyze what they heard. Some words such as "brand" suggested still further research since students became interested to find out where different products came from and how they were transported to Kazakhstan (see Landis, Kalieva, Abitova, Izmukhanbetova, & Musaeva, 2005). As a result of these and other activities, students drew upon academic content of their school subjects such as geography, spelling, handwriting, mathematics, social studies, and reading in order to discuss what they were learning about the activities of people in a local community setting outside the classroom.

Sapargul: In addition to student community research, I think our research about teaching and learning should go into more depth. That is, we should look closer at classroom practice and how students learn. We need to learn how to do group studies, try to avoid formal and inconsistent studies. One goal that should guide us in our work will be—doing what will support students' learning. Also it's equally important for us to learn to be involved in our community activities. I did not know before how it is important to train leadership skills also for our teachers. Teachers have a vocation to be a model of a good citizen—they, by profession, model ongoing reading and learning, so they are supposed to model ongoing active involved citizenship too.

In addition to teacher research, we will pursue closer contact with other educational institutions in the country. These connections should move beyond written agreements to include more informal cooperation through long-term working relationships: (a) we need to do some studies with the Ministry of Education; and (b) we could focus more on higher education by supporting cooperation between all pedagogical universities in the country.

In addition, it seems to me that a series of recent events will also influence our future activities. These events include the publication of the following government generated documents that will influence education at all levels in our country: (a) Conception of Education Development in Kazakhstan, 2004; (b) Conception of Development of Higher Pedagogical Education in Kazakhstan, 2004; (c) State Program of Education Development in Kazakhstan, 2004; and (d) Third National Congress on Education, November 2004.

According to these documents and discussions in our national legislature, educators are responsible for transforming the whole education system to reflect a humanistic, more equitable basis. Two particular changes indicated by these documents are implementing a credit-hours system and an all-national test for undergraduates in higher education and mandating more testing in secondary education. These two changes raised numerous other issues to the surface, among them: poor quality textbooks and the related all-national test that is based upon the textbooks, difficulties with writing course outlines and syllabi, and lack of experience working with students as individuals. Teachers complain that they do not know how to fill students' independent work time. Meanwhile the Ministry of Education continues to send prescriptions and deadlines for implementing the changes. No advisory assistance or materials are available for review since they are all mostly in English. The Ministry of Education pushes this process forward because Kazakhstan plans to enter WTO [Word Trade

Organization] and then EU. To achieve this goal, educators and students should participate in an international test—PISA [Program for International Student Assessment]. National education administrators, and school principals among them, began to study attentively Russian experiences with PISA. A Russian Federation summary concludes that Russian students struggled with analyzing the different points of view in texts (not only in reading but also in science) and in expressing one's opinions. Many students have low interest and engagement in reading and more students view learning as memorizing rather than understanding ideas and concepts. Our experiences with RWCT will help us challenge students and their teachers to move beyond memorization toward active participation in reading and writing, in and out of school.

DISCUSSION OF OUR GUIDING QUESTIONS

In this part of the chapter, we review our dialogue and reflect upon it in terms of the specific questions that were raised in the chapter introduction about RWCT participants' conceptions about citizenship and democracy, the social and institutional dynamics that influence the use of RWCT for promoting citizenship and what structures constrain or facilitate their successful implementation, and how customary educational practices and programs accomodate, challenge, or modify the kind of civic learning envisioned by the RWCT materials.

In dialogue one, we considered David's role as an North American educator and how differences in language, cultural expectations, and pedagogical practices influenced the application of RWCT in meetings between the IRA volunteers, the teachers and school principals. When time was limited, customary practices for showing hospitality took precedence over discussions about teacher supervision and debriefings of lesson observations. However, the priority given to showing hospitality and respect set the RWCT materials in a social, cultural context that valued meeting people from a different part of the world and communicated an interest in entering into cooperative relations with them. In this context, a democratic ethic was defined less as individual autonomy according to a liberal democratic tradition (e.g., Perlstein, 2002) and more as the construction of a community of mutual interests.

In dialogue two, we discussed a set of dynamic influences upon the ways RWCT was put into practice. This set includes goals of the KazRA organization for transforming education, the introduction of publications and the national conference as forums for encouraging writing and participation in more public places, the influence of USAID upon introducing teachers to business plan writing and transparent reporting, teacher-led activities at the national and regional conferences, writing and speaking as key influences for professional development, and theoretical ideas about teachers, student knowledge, and classroom-based research. While these influences support a focus on teachers as active participants in KazRA activities, yet the primary result did not develop "self-actualizing" adults who created their own individual environments (e.g., Perlstein, 2002). Rather, teachers developed ways of creating particular environments such as their regional and local committees, and conferences that are conducive to their collective professional and personal development, and they treated these environments as resources for their common good. At first, the RWCT materials provided an impetus for change, then KazRA and its members moved beyond a focus on the materials by creating a set of collective institutions and organizations such as the national conference and regional centers, along with supporting materials such as the publications, in order to function as a group. As a consequence, they created a social organization adapted to accomplish the tasks (e.g., Moscovici, 1972) considered as necessary and beneficial so that more people could participate. The current structure and functioning of the KazRA reflects the results of its members' creative activities and collective agency in developing an ethic of democracy suited to their cultural and pedagogical contexts.

In dialogue three, we considered Sapargul's role as executive director of KazRA and the importance of having a network of leaders who can set appropriate goals for future activities. The social changes being introduced by KazRA into the educational system in Kazakhstan do not just depend upon the constraints of the environment or the techniques advocated by the RWCT materials. In addition, KazRA national staff and its network of trainers continue to initiate changes that are always interacting with the goals and agency of other people in the Ministry of Education and elsewhere. Resistance or struggle with change is a necessary and beneficial part of the picture as well. From this perspective, it is important to consider who wants the changes and whose interests are served by the changes. Working out goals for future work will require continued discussions at KazRA conferences and committee meetings about topics such as arrangements of work and responsibilities, definitions of important concepts and ideas, and what power or influence is appropriate for various members (e.g., Mosovici, 1972).

Across the dialogues, we see increasing opportunities for members' participation in an educational organization where power is being exercised more and more through the activities of local entities as well as through a network of representatives who guide the work of conference planning, goal setting, and publication of journals and books. This association has brought people together to seek what is mutually beneficial to them as educators, students, and parents. The association has provided new and varied opportunities; it has promoted an ethic of caring for others; and it has raised members' willingness to take responsibility and initiative for its continued success. This description of an 'ethic of democracy' can be compared with other discussions about the evolution of different conceptions of democracy including: radical redistributions of capital and control, the influence of consumer choice and private enterprise, and questions about the capability of the market place to bring about equitable social relations (e.g. Wells, Slayton, & Scott, 2002).

Our analysis of the data for this study presents a different view of democracy—a view that focuses less upon the activities of autonomous individuals and their self-determined obligations (e.g., Perlstein, 2002), and focuses more upon the decisions of people to come together to form an association that encourages its members to move beyond their personal interests in order to bring about constructive social change within a set of civic values marked by social responsibility, respect, and compassion for one another.

NOTES

1.   Sources of data for our research included archival records of the projects well as focus group interviews at the 2005 KazRA national conference, and our in-person and e-mail dialogues as coauthors. In particular, we paid attention to historical events that seemed interesting to us or to our research participants, and we examined documents that indicated particular trends or directions of the KazRA.

   Our research procedures evolved in phases: the first phase generated ideas and recollections via e-mail about key events, a second phase produced a rough draft of possible dialogues distributed by e-mail, and a third phase included focus group interviews and discussions to generate additional perspectives about key events and to check our developing interpretations as we wrote the dialogues. Our decisions about which events to sample involved a back and forth process of consulting our research questions, exploring archival records, and making decisions about what additional information was needed (e.g, Spradley, 1980) based upon our dual role as researchers and participants in KazRA activities as we proceeded through the study.

   We invited five people to take part in a focus group discussion of key events on the basis of their status as first-generation participants of RWCT in Kazakhstan. They were eager to discuss their memories and recollections of key events and they retold several stories about a variety of national and regional project events and talked with us for about two hours. Our analysis procedures involved both inductive and deductive processes. We inductively examined our descriptive notes and archival records in order to construct units stated in the form of key ideas or principles for explaining principles and processes developed over time to guide the activities of the KazRA.

2. Workshop topics included: a theoretical and methodological framework, promoting critical thinking, encouraging reading, writing, and discussions during lessons, ideas for reading critically, and ideas for developing writing.

3. Participants gave permission for their real names to be used in this chapter.

REFERENCES

Berk, L. E., & Winsler, A. (1995). *Scaffolding children's learning: Vygotsky and early childhood education.* Washington, DC: National Association for the Education of Young Children.

Egan-Robertson, A., & Bloome, D. (Eds.). (1998). *Students as researchers of culture and language in their own communities.* Cresskill, NJ: Hampton Press.

Evertson, C. M., & Green, J. L. (1986). Observation as inquiry and method. In M. C. Wittrock (Ed.), *Handbook of Research on Teaching* (3rd. ed., pp. 162–213). New York: Macmillan.

Kaiser, R. G. (1984). *Russia: The people and the power.* New York: Washington Square Press.

Landis, D., Kalieva, R., Abitova, S., Izmukhanbetova, S., & Musaeva, Zh. (2005). Thinking through ethnographic reading and writing. *Thinking Classroom/Peremena, 6*(1), 5–13.

Meredith, K. S., & Steele, J. L. (2000). Education in transition: Trends in Central and Eastern Europe. In M. L. Kamil, P. D. Pearson, & R. Barr (Eds.), *Handbook of reading research* (Vol. 3, pp. 29–40). Mahwah, NJ: Erlbaum.

Meredith, K., Steele, J., Temple, C., & Walter, S. (1997). *The Reading and Writing for Critical Thinking Project.* Consortium for Democratic Pedagogy, International Reading Association, Hobart & William Smith Colleges, University of Northern Iowa.

Moll, L. C., Amanti, C., Neff, D., & González, N. (1992). Funds of knowledge for teaching: Using a qualitative approach to connect homes and classrooms. *Theory into Practice, 31*(2), 132–141.

Moll, L. C., & Gonzalez, N. (1997). Teachers as social scientists: Learning about culture from household research. In P. M. Hall (Ed.), *Race, ethnicity, and multiculturalism* (Vol. 1, pp. 89–114). New York: Garland.

Moscovici, S. (1972). Society and theory in social psychology. In J. Israel & H. Tajfel (Eds.), *The context of social psychology: A critical assessment* (pp. 17–68). London: Academic Press.

Olcott, M. B. (1987). *The Kazakhs.* Stanford, CA: Hoover Institution—Stanford University.

Perlstein, D. (2002). Minds stayed on freedom: Politics and pedagogy in the African-American freedom struggle. *American Educational Research Journal, 39*(2), 249–277.

RWCT International Consortium. (2005). *Reading and writing for critical thinking.* Retrieved February 9, 2007, from http://ct-net.net/ct_about

Soros Foundation-Kazakhstan (1998). *Development of critical thinking through reading and writing.* Almaty, Kazakhstan: Soros Foundation-Kazakhstan.

Temple, C. (2001). Interactive literacy education, engaged citizenship, and open societies. In D. Klooster, J. L. Steele, & P. L. Bloem (Eds.), *Ideas without boundaries: International education reform through reading and writing for critical thinking* (pp. 38–47). Newark, DE: International Reading Association.

Wells, A. S., Slayton, J., & Scott, J. (2002). Defining democracy in the Neoliberal Age: Charter school reform and educational consumption. *American Educational Research Journal, 39*(2), 337–361.

CHAPTER 9

FROM MONSOONS TO KATRINA

The Civic Implications of Cosmopolitanism

Payal P. Shah

[Teaching in Rajasthan, India] was just so amazing, and incredibly difficult, and the connections that I made and struggles that I went through were just so crazy. It has changed my life, now I know that this is what I want to do. There are so many places trying to do this, and I love doing this, so this is something that I want to do. Kids are kids, even in a place where they have a completely different life than yours, in a different place, they are just kids. It was just so great.

Kara

When I describe my summer I describe it as extremes. Many of the issues are different in India, but some are the same—just to a different extreme. Extreme tastes, extreme smells, extreme poverty, just extreme. There are problems everywhere; just different problems.

Rachel

Advancing Democracy Through Education? U.S. Influence Abroad and Domestic Practices, pp. 207–227
Copyright © 2008 by Information Age Publishing
207

INTRODUCTION

In an era of increased globalization, we are undoubtedly becoming more interconnected culturally, politically, and economically. Flows of people, ideas, and commodities have simultaneously intensified relationships between people, and increased diversity within individual countries. The blurring of national boundaries challenges traditional notions of citizenship, and thus the traditional educational aim of citizenship building. These changes obligate us as educators to reconsider our civic mission, and reexamine what we believe the role and function of civic education should be.

It has been widely acknowledged that our future generations must be equipped with the skills, knowledge, and perspectives to function in this diversifying society. International and global education (IGE) is a social movement that has answered the call to attempt to "globalize American education" (Anderson, 1990, p. 13). At its core, "global education promotes not only knowledge and awareness of other places and people, but also the ability to view events from a variety of perspectives other than one's own" (Sutton & Hutton, 2001, p. 2). This conception resonates with Martha Nussbaum's assertion that the development of empathy is an essential component of both a liberal education and the cultivation of humanity. Nussbaum (1997) writes in *Cultivating Humanity* that "as a world citizen our primary loyalty is to human beings the world over, having the ability to see themselves as human beings bound to all other human beings by ties of recognition and concern" (p. 9). What is the role of education in promoting such sentiment? How can we foster the dispositions, values, and conceptions of citizenship necessary to flourish in a global world?

While IGE often takes place in the classroom, many organizations attempt to equip students with global perspectives by placing them in challenging, interactive foreign settings. This chapter addresses the questions above through the experiences of 11 high school students who participated in a community-service global education program in Rajasthan, India. In July of 2005, I had the opportunity to develop and lead a group of 16 high school students, ranging in age from 15–18, on a 1-month community service program at an English language school in rural Rajasthan, India. The program was part of Global Exploration (a pseudonym) an organization based in the New England region of the United States which provides a variety of programs for American high school students. The goals of these programs are to give students the opportunity to engage in an educational summer experience that promotes individual growth and mutual respect through participation in communities around the world. This particular immersion-based education organization, one of at least a dozen that I am aware of, has been operating for over 50 years, and has impacted over 25,000 children. I conducted semistructured interviews with the students upon their return to the United States, supplementing data recorded as program leader and participant-observer, to explore the relationship of their experience in rural, undeveloped Western India to personal and civic identity, global and empathetic understanding, and perceptions of others, the United States, and themselves.

This chapter describes the latest stage of an ongoing reflective dialogue between myself and the students. I chose to take part in such a program with the explicit intention of pushing the students beyond the standard boundaries of global education programs to think deeply and broadly about issues of democracy and social justice. I also wanted to engage them to think about the specific role they, as privileged Americans, play in perpetuating inequality and poverty, not only in India, but also at home. As a researcher-practitioner, my perspective on global education and citizenship has been greatly influenced by the notion of cosmopolitanism. In this program, I sought to discover whether the goals of cosmopolitanism could be encouraged and supported in practice. It is with this intention that I structured the month long program. Intensive and reflective discussions throughout the program were followed up with more dialogue and reflection back in the United States.

This chapter first discusses the concepts of cosmopolitanism and world citizenship, with particular attention to their civic implications, and their relation to IGE. In my analysis of whether the students developed a sense of citizenship and responsibility towards the human community as a result of this IGE program, I found that this program did change the way the students perceive themselves and their world around them. However, I did not find that the students were able to make critical, transnational connections between issues that they saw in India (i.e., poverty and inequality), and their similar manifestations within the United States. I explore various theoretical perspectives—cognitive development, critical race, and White privilege theories—to explain why these students failed to progress to the most critical and reflective stages of global consciousness development. The chapter concludes with thoughts on the role IGE programs can play, in conjunction with formal education, towards a reconceptualization of civic education in the United States.

THE GOAL: WORLD CITIZENSHIP

Many academics, theorists, and practitioners advocate for the development of global citizenship, world citizenship, worldmindedness, and related stances, as part of their democratic citizenship (Alger & Harf, 1986; Anderson, 1990; Gutmann, 1993; Hanvey, 1976; Merryfield, 1995, 1998, 2000; Nussbaum, 1994, 1997). They apply diverse theoretical perspectives to reconceptualize the term "citizenship" and make it relevant to a world in which national boundaries are changing and blurring. As educators, we are charged with the dual purpose of developing citizens with national identity, allegiance, and loyalty, and of instilling in our citizens a respect for human rights and an ability to live in a global age (Alger & Harf, 1986; Hanvey, 1976; Kniep, 1986; Merryfield, 1995). However, these goals are not necessarily compatible. Nussbaum's (1994, 1997) conception of global citizenship—cosmopolitanism—reveals why we need to expand our notions of citizenship, and reformulate our conception of IGE. Nussbaum's particular conceptualization of global citizenship applies well in educational settings because it was originally conceived as part of a project to reformulate the notion of a "liberal education." Further, cosmopolitanism provides a conceptual basis for reconciling the sometimes conflicting nature of two purposes of education: the fostering of both national allegiance and universal care for all humans.

According to Nussbaum (1997), cosmopolitanism's core belief is that an ideal citizen is a "world citizen" whose primary loyalty is to human beings across the world; other associative ties—national, local, religious, group—are secondary. It accepts multiple dimensions of citizenship, with world citizenship being one such type to which we can all subscribe. While a variety of views about how to order diverse loyalties are possible, Nussbaum emphasizes that "we should still be sure that we recognize the worth of human life wherever it occurs and see ourselves as bound by common human abilities and problems to people who lie at a great distance from us" (p. 9). World citizenship or "cultivation of humanity" (p. 8) involves three central capabilities: the capacity for critical self-examination; the ability to see oneself as a human being bound to all other human beings; and the possession of a narrative imagination.

The capacity for critical self-examination is, in Socratic terms, "living the examined life." Living an examined life entails the ability to reason logically and to challenge all beliefs and traditions, including one's own. This capability fosters independent and critical thinking so that people need not defer to authority or tradition. This skill is essential in creating democratic citizens who demand and actualize a reflective and socially just society.

Cultivating humanity in this reflective and reasonable manner also requires citizens to understand how common needs and goals can be realized differently in different circumstances. Viewing citizenship in human terms—emphasizing the needs and capacities that link us to people beyond our close proximity—can help build the respect and tolerance necessary to live among people who conceive of living the good life in different ways. Respect for diversity and difference in thought and practice—to recognize someone with a diverse background as a fellow citizen—is essential in creating a supportive democratic society. Thus, extending traditional conceptions of citizenship beyond political boundaries is a core element of democracy and cosmopolitan philosophy.

Nussbaum's (1997) third capacity—the narrative imagination—features prominently in this case study because it exemplifies the ultimate goal of global consciousness. The development of this capacity goes beyond learning from facts, textbooks, or lectures, and extends understanding to empathizing. Central to the narrative imagination is connecting on an interpersonal level with people in circumstances and situations different from one's own. Developing this empathetic understanding allows citizens to acknowledge, and to begin to understand, the emotions and desires of people living very different lives. Nussbaum recognizes that the cultivation of this capacity is an ideal. Nonetheless, even in its most rudimentary form, it can be powerful in pushing people to think beyond what life is like in their own shoes, to what life is like in someone else's. Empathetic understanding is the key to transcending national loyalty with human concern—the greater and universal dimension of a reconceived global citizenship.

Efforts to create a more equitable, inclusive, and just society require that we problematize the world in which we live, recognizing that systems of inequality and oppression, like those producing environmental problems, transcend national borders. The concept of cosmopolitanism and world citizenship become especially relevant as we recognize that our society is becoming increasingly global and less national/local. Being a citizen in any country presently requires the empathetic understanding of different racial and ethnic groups, religions, cultures and beliefs. The cultivation of world citizenship, and the capacities inherent in developing it, are essential components in our ability to participate effectively in a world characterized by human diversity, cross-cultural interaction, dynamic change, and global interdependence (Merryfield, 1995).

INTERNATIONAL AND GLOBAL EDUCATION— A SUFFICIENT APPROACH?

IGE, the social movement dedicated to making American education more international or global (Anderson, 1990; Arum, 1987), is also "a dynamic concept that involves a journey or movement of people, minds, or ideas, across political and cultural frontiers" (Hansen, 2002, p. 5). IGE develops "the knowledge, skills, and attitudes that are the basis for decision making and participation in a world characterized by cultural pluralism, interconnectedness, and international economic competition" (Merryfield, 1995, p. 1). IGE is focused on helping students see things from a different perspective, and on enabling students to learn about their country's relationship to, and place in the larger world system. Thus, its civic implications—in helping people come to terms with their identity embedded in social and cultural plurality—are significant.

Specifically, international education includes all education that involves the study of other countries, cultures, and societies (Hansen, 2002; Merryfield, 1995; Sutton & Hutton, 2001; Tye, 1990; Ukpokodu, 1999). It encompasses the use of in-depth study and work to help build the knowledge and skills to function in a global world. In contrast, global education takes a more conceptual approach; it moves beyond the acquisition of knowledge about other nations and cultures, to a more holistic, and systems-oriented conception of shared human issues and situations (Hanvey, 1976; Sutton & Hutton, 2001; Ukpokodu, 1999). "The affective and action goals of global education call for a transformation in the awareness and interests of learnings, one that derives more readily from social situations than from 'book learning' " (Sutton & Hutton, 2001, p. 1).

It is evident that the goals of global citizenship and the goals of IGE, specifically global education, are closely aligned. Both conceptions call for a significant change in the way we see our role in, and think of, the world around us. Working together, they call for critical reflection upon humanity and upon one's place in the world. The rest of the chapter will analyze the degree to which the cross-cultural experience from one global education program was successful in engaging its participants to develop an expanded international, critical, and cosmopolitan world-view.

PROJECT AND METHODOLOGY

Global Exploration offers thematic programs, including language learning, global exploration, and global awareness, as well as partnerships with liberal arts colleges in New England that introduce high school students to college-level academic work. The program I led was centered upon community service, its only type of offering in India at the time.

The English medium school in which we worked in rural western India had been established more than a decade ago by an Indian textile and clothing company in order to give the children of its rural weavers and dyers the opportunity to obtain an English language education. Global Exploration was invited to create a program based at this school as a result of personal connections between the director of Global Exploration, and the head of the Indian textile and clothing company. In 2005, we participated in the third annual summer program based at this school. The American students spent three weeks at the school engaging in a variety of projects: English teaching to students in Grades 1–8; painting and designing newly constructed classrooms; leading reciprocal discussion groups twice a week with students on any topic about U.S.-India culture and society; and helping to build an access road to the school.

My main responsibilities as coordinator were to set up and to facilitate the projects and to support and engage the students in a critical manner that fostered their personal, emotional, and intellectual growth. The support and engagement aspects of the program were what most appealed to me about the position. Having the opportunity to lead focused group discussions for at least three hours daily was, according to the students, invaluable in reflecting upon and processing the challenging experiences they were having. These discussions were held in the evenings and were centered on pushing the students not only to recount and comment on activities, feelings, and thoughts of the day, but to contextualize their experiences in the larger global sociocultural context within which they were living. Issues of privilege, power, and potential for social change explicitly and implicitly wove their way into the conversations. I made a special effort to broaden the context of the discussions beyond the particular to the universal, in order to make this experience relevant to their lives back home. In addition to our discussions and time in the village working with the school, I arranged multiple site visits with various nongovernmental organizations in Delhi in order to provide the students with a more comprehensive view of Indian educational issues and Indian society.

Our discussions were illuminating for me as well. The depth to which students were willing and eager to discuss various social issues was surprising to me. Politically, most of the students characterized themselves as liberal. They were also aware of the problems resulting from comparing Indian issues to the "better" situation in America, and thus consciously attempted to refrain from comparisons of that sort. Additionally, the connections that they made while in India to their lives back home, and in particular to life in large cosmopolitan cities in the United States, were striking. A few of the students from California were deeply affected by the drought conditions in Rajasthan, and immediately drew parallels to the fact that the water situation in the United States may soon be as it is in India. Other issues, such as the purpose and goals of charity, the power of the English language, gender stereotypes, and the nature and goal of education, were discussed frequently. Working with children, and successfully communicating with people without knowing the language, appeared to affirm that as humans, there are powerful commonalities that bind us together. Often I would hear the students say that "kids are kids, no matter where you are they are the same." Similarly, one student, who developed a particularly close relationship with the young girls with whom we built a road, was touched by how much the girls she worked with meant to her. She was surprised that despite the fact that they never exchanged a word, and could barely begin to understand the everyday life experiences of the other, a relationship developed between them. Our discussions reminded me of the power that humanity potentially has over all of us—and this was a power of which the students seemed to be cognizant.

Once back in the United States, I maintained contact with the students. Many were struggling to make sense of their experiences in India even well after their return. In order to understand how the students were thinking about their experience once they had left India, and in what way this experience affected their perception of their community, country, the world, and more importantly, themselves, I conducted semistructured interviews with the participants. In November and December of 2005, 11 of the 16 participants engaged in interviews with me over the phone. Five students decided not to participate, because they perceived that they did not have the time for the in-depth conversations, which ranged from 3 to 5 hours in duration. These interviews covered issues from global awareness, international and domestic current event knowledge, feelings upon returning, current experiences in school, to whether they were able to discuss their experiences in India with friends, family, and teachers. They were aimed at allowing the students to relate and reflect on their activities now, in light of having recently returned from India. The interviews were semistructured, with a number of open ended questions that were prompted according to the particular direction of the responses. The dialogues or discussions were reciprocal in nature, allowing the participants to have a hand in structuring and leading the conversation.

The conversational nature of the interviews echoed the dialogical format we had used in India. I was equally a participant in the interview, and an interviewer. The close and trusting relationships that were already established with the participants contributed to the openness of the responses, and hence offered deeper insights than they might have otherwise had. I was their friend, confidante, main form of support, and instructor, and we had eaten together and shared lodging for 1 month. Because of our deeply shared experience, I wanted to "create conditions in which the object of research enters into the process as an active subject" (Acker, Barry, & Esseveld, 1983, p. 136).

Fifteen of the students who participated in my summer program attended high schools across the United States, while one student was from France. As the costs of participating in this program were quite high (around $7,000 for the month), and scholarships are limited, it is safe to conclude that most of the students come from middle to upper-middle class families. This was confirmed as I got to know the students and could ascertain their socioeconomic backgrounds. Of the 16 students on the trip, 5 were males, and 11 were females. Fifteen of the students were racially White in the U.S. context, while 1 student was Indian-American. All but one of the students attending public schools attended suburban high schools, while one student attended a school for gifted and talented students in a large metropolitan city. Others attended private college preparatory schools in large metropolitan cities. All of the students came from the East or West Coast, with the exception of one student who from Chicago. In general, these students came from very diverse areas across the United States.

FINDINGS

The results of my interviews strongly support the idea that cross cultural experiences, such as the Global Exploration program, change the way participants view the world around them. It was common for my students to state that they recognized the importance of being aware of international issues. In response to my question about why they felt that international awareness was important, the general response was that, as Americans, it is our duty to know what is going on around us. For example, Fiona stated:

> If we are supposed to be the leaders of the world, we should know what's going on in the world. And I'm not saying that we should be the leaders of the world, but if that's the position that we think that we are in, then we should know what we are getting into.

> Payal: And do you really think that we don't know much?

> Fiona: No. Not at all.

Stephanie added:

> Americans right now really feel that they are superior because we're one of the world's largest powers, and we don't learn other languages, we don't anything. Like in New York City, everyone is really assimilated together, but we don't really learn so much about everyone else's cultures, at least not as much as I think we used to. So that's what I mean, we really need to learn about other cultures.

Thus, the students themselves perceive that we, as Americans, are not sufficiently exposed to and aware of other cultures and international events. Common reasons cited for our ignorance point towards main-stream media being mainly focused on U.S. issues and events. To counter this, students, such as Allison, have begun exploring other media sources:

> I've started reading the BBC world news because I think it sort of gives a better view; England is not so centered on them specifically. So it's easier to find out about what is going on in the world.

Another common benefit of global education, expressed here by Catherine, is that of an increased awareness of global and social issues such as poverty and inequality:

> I have traveled a lot with my parents, and I've seen slums in South Africa and seen slums in Cairo, I had already done all of that. But with India I was really doing it on my own and my parents were not trying to show me any-thing—how the majority of people live—and I kind of felt it for myself, and I realized how important a problem it is—how poverty is a scary thing but at the same time there are some amazing things that come from it, like how that guy in the slums in Delhi said that he still has hope.
>
> I meet people at my school who have no hope in their lives, and they have three cars, and it just made me think about the world in a different way, and I think I had a good perspective on the world, I knew how everything was not easy, but when I experienced it first hand, there was some connection there. Also, seeing how some people were happy despite being in what we would call poverty. Like Jivaram [one of the men at the school who worked out in the forest with us], he had like two outfits, but he was fine, that was his life, and all the people in the village had been living like that for centuries, and why did they have to change?
>
> They're perfectly happy. And I really never thought of it that way, I had always thought of what our standards were. And seeing that was kind of, it made me interested in the whole idea of poverty, and what really is poverty. When we think about it, is it to our standards, or is it to people that are actually living in "poverty's" standards? So it just put a whole new spin on everything for me.

Catherine's excerpt demonstrates how the exposure gained from a cross-cultural experience enabled her not just to become aware of other places and people, but to also begin "to view events from a variety of perspectives other than one's own" (Sutton & Hutton, 2001, p. 6). Catherine also mentioned that doing an educationally oriented program, such as this one, provided her a very different experience than she could get traveling with her parents. It was the combination of being on her own, and being immersed in a situation where she made strong connections with others, that enabled this experience to have a transformative effect for her. Similarly, Kara states:

> One of the reasons [I wanted to do a Global Exploration program was that] I just wanted something different and out of the ordinary and a chance to see a different part of the world, because I knew that if I went with my father I would see it, but it would not be the same at all. It kind of put things in perspective, and it was quite shocking.

While this excerpt indicates that her, as well as many of the other students', initial desire to participate in this program was because of India's exoticism and "otherness," there is still a broadening of perspective. Experiences like these give participants the ability to learn about different events and gain insights from these events in an entirely different manner —a way that draws upon personal experiences, emotional reactions, and reflection in a manner that is very difficult to replicate in a classroom or from a text book. For example, Stephanie replied:

> I think I probably learned more in India then I did in three years of high school. In school everything is really safe and learning is mediated through teachers, and what you learn is from a text book, and you don't really get to practice it—I mean, it's not really practical. But when you're in a place, you're learning about the place, you really understand what you're learning the next second after you learn it because you're interacting with people and a culture and stuff; and it's really much better I think.

Fiona added:

> I think you could be taking classes on India and the problems and riches of India; you could learn about it for the rest of your life but you won't actually understand it until you go there. I think that you can learn about extreme poverty and extreme wealth and you can describe the smell, the sights, and the different people and the starving kids, but you're not going to actually know what it's like until a kid with such extreme parasites on his skin that they grow into lesions comes up to you and asks you for a bite of food. You just can't understand that.

Building on viewing global events from different perspectives, this experience offered the students an opportunity to see America from the outside, looking in. Global education proponents claim that cross-cultural experiences enable the students to make some observations about their home country that they might not had made had they not left the country (Anderson, 1990; Hansen, 2002; Merryfield, 1998, 2000). In their statements, many students confirmed this claim, and upon their return from

India became very critical of American society. For example, Allison stated:

> I had never really thought about it before but I was like, "Oh my gosh, we are the most selfish country!" I have never really thought of it that way, but once [I realized this], it was really an eye opener to the fact that it's a big deal when something really small happens to us, even though it happens a million times to other countries, and we don't really do anything for other countries, except maybe it runs on the news for a few days, but it wasn't like all the news for weeks like when it happens to us.

And Deena believes that

> Some people have lost [a general appreciation for life] because people are so wrapped up in the materialistic things, and looking into the future more. I feel like in India and in other countries there are stronger family ties. I know that that does not really affect people on a larger scale as a whole, but in India the family and extended families are really common as opposed to in America where there are really high divorce rates and stuff like that.

While the students were able to recognize that there are aspects of the United States that are problematic and warrant change, much of their insight and learning was focused on developing perspectives that enable them to understand and relate to the world outside of the United States and themselves. Most of the dialogue regarding what they learned and what they remember was quite particularistic: India has huge population issues; women in India occupy such and such a position in society; and so forth. The link between what is happening in India to what is happening on a global level—the interconnectedness of nations and issues—was not fully recognized or discussed.

A better understanding of transnational and global issues, such as the environment and poverty, was supported and cultivated through this program. However, global education aims to do more than provide students with an awareness of the world around them. In the words of Hanvey (1976), an attainable global perspective is one that also enables students to recognize and understand "problems that transcend the national, regional, or coalitional; human problems" (p. 166). While students recognize that environmental concerns—such as water and pollution—are concerns that affect all of us regardless of our geographic location, issues of poverty, inequality, and race were still regarded as being problems "there,"—and such a connection "here" was not readily made. An example that highlights this assertion can be found in responses to questions about how the students felt about the way U.S. society responded to the fallout from hurricane Katrina, which took place the same summer that students visited India. One student, Fiona stated:

> I thought [hurricane Katrina] was incredibly devastating, and it is our country, so people should be as concerned and as wanting to help as they are, but I think that that bubble [referring to an isolationist perspective that Americans tend to have], like do they realize that this happens every year to Indians during monsoon? And people are donating so much money, and these things are happening in other places that need our help just as much.

Many other students reacted in a similar way; while not wanting to devalue the situation at home, they were quite critical of how differently events at home and abroad are treated. Only three of those interviewed made a connection between the issues of poverty and inequality in the two countries, or reflected on how their experience with poverty and inequality abroad shed light upon similar situations at home. For the majority, even the aftermath of Hurricane Katrina did not invite comparisons of India's racial and economic inequality with that in the United States. Students responded not with surprise at the fact that people in the U.S. also live with poverty; rather, they felt that the media focused too heavily on the U.S. when similar and even more extreme poverty exists elsewhere. The students were not able to defamiliarize the familiar and use their experience in India to reflect more critically upon circumstances at home.

Among the students who did make a meaningful connection, Kara observed:

> Another thing that bugs me about fundraising is that all this money is being sent off to the far corners of the world that nobody really cares about—I mean fifteen minutes away there are people living in poverty or below the poverty line, and some people deny that that is even the case. Some people just cannot accept that, and it's like, well take a fifteen minute drive and you'll see. It's not the sending money that I care about, but that people don't care and people are just sending money off rather than sending it here, because there is definitely a need for the resources here as well.

Michelle commented that the program really gave her an appreciation of what she has, as well as made her realize how little others have:

> I see people who don't have as much as me, I am much more aware of that now, and a friend and I started something where we found a homeless family and got Christmas presents for them—we found out the ages and sizes of the kids and bought them a whole Christmas.

Additionally, while the general idea of diversity was mentioned by about half of the students as a reason why individuals should embark upon cross-cultural experiences, the idea that one could experience racial diversity across the U.S. was not realized. Only one of the students interviewed brought up the issue of race, and how being abroad and being immersed in a society that is racially different from the U.S. enabled her to reflect upon her own identity in the U.S. as a White female.

In the next section I will propose three perspectives that might explain why students who went through the Global Exploration program were not able to critically reflect on issues of race, inequality, and poverty here in the United States. The first theory is a psychological, cognitive explanation, and the second, critical race and White privilege theory.

Potential Explanations

a. Cognitive Development Approach

In reference to Robert Hanvey's (1976) stages of global awareness, we can see that most of the students who went through the Global Exploration program were able to gain the majority of the dimensions of a global perspective that he delineates, including: (1) "perspective consciousness"; (2) "State of the Planet" awareness; and (3) "cross-cultural awareness" (Hanvey, 1976, p. 162). The fourth and fifth dimensions, "knowledge of global dynamics,"—and "awareness of human choices" (Hanvey, 1976, pp. 165–166), are those that have yet to be realized. Embedded in these two dimensions of global awareness is the recognition that there are issues that cut across national borders—problems that are human problems, not geography-specific problems. Additionally, there is the recognition that there are thoughts, beliefs, and ways of acting that we assumed had benefits, but which now need to be questioned. In Hanvey's opinion, it is this "cognitive revolution" that constitutes the shift from a pre-global to global cognitions. Not surprisingly, this cognition is the hardest to attain, and according to Hanvey, society at large has yet to achieve it.

One possible explanation for why students who have had a cross-cultural experience are not always able to critically reflect on the issues of race, inequality, and poverty back in the United States, might have to do with age and the level of cognitive development achieved by the individual. Critical self reflection is a skill, or level of cognitive development, that is usually one of the last phases of development. Perhaps the participants of this program—high school adolescents—have not yet developed in this way. Psychologists, such as Piaget, Kohlberg, and Gilligan, have been interested in explaining how we learn, and have identified various stages that people generally go through in the process of learning. Piaget's theory of cognitive development identifies four main stages of development, with corresponding age groups where this cognition usually occurs.

Piaget's fourth stage, the "formal operational stage," is the stage where "logical use of symbols [is] related to abstract concepts" (Huitt & Hummell, 2003). Piaget believed that persons who reach the formal operation stage are able to think logically and abstractly. They can also reason theoretically. Piaget considered this the ultimate stage of development, and it might be seen as the type of thought process that people must have in order to critically reflect and go from a pre-global to global cognition.

However, Piaget's cognitive development theory assumes that development continues during adolescence (Crain, 1985). Under this presumption, Piaget's studies revealed that only approximately 35% of high school graduates in Western, developed countries obtain formal operations, and that many people do not think formally even during adulthood. Lawrence Kohlberg took Piaget's work further and developed additional stages that go beyond early adolescence into adulthood. Kohlberg's final stages, 5 and 6 are more theoretical and are concerned with society in general. Both stages require the individual to step back and think about what society is, and what makes a good society. In stage 5, people begin considering the values and rights within society, and "they then evaluate existing societies in terms of these prior considerations. They are said to take a—'prior-to society'—perspective" (Colby & Kohlberg, 1983, p. 22 as cited in Crain, 1985). Stage 6 takes this realization and conceptualization further by emphasizing justice. This conception of justice is universal, and in this stage individuals are guided by principles of justice which are oriented towards decision making that is based on equality. Finally, when people are in this stage of cognition, their commitment to justice supports a well functioning society that is fair and just; therefore individuals are more apt to engage in civil disobedience and question democratic practices and laws that are unjust (Crain, 1985). Kohlberg believes that acting in stage 6 is possible when people can see and evaluate decisions through the eyes of others, regardless of their particular position; they develop the ability to empathetically understand.

Regarding the development process itself, both Piaget and Kohlberg believe that progress along the stages is not a natural product of maturation. Biologically, we all do not automatically progress from one stage to another, nor is socialization (parents and teachers teaching their children to think in different ways) the main determinant of transition between stages. Kohlberg, in particular, stressed that moral development occurs when individuals are forced to think about certain issues and situations— and social experiences are key in stimulating mental processes that lead to new types of thinking (Crain, 1985). Thus, while development continues to occur throughout adolescence and into adulthood, initial social experiences in any form prove never to be too early, or ineffective. Furthermore, it appears that an experience during high school might provide an excellent "social experience" from which progression into stage 5 and 6 could be furthered.

b. Feminist Perspective of Cognitive Development

The Piaget/Kohlberg model of development just explored has limitations to it, not in terms of the process through which people go through in their moral development, but rather in terms of the actual stages of development and outcomes that it values and legitimizes. The Piaget/Kohlberg conceptualization of development has been criticized by Gilligan, among others, as privileging a male perspective and male process of development over a female one. As the majority of the participants in this study, and generally the majority of participants in global education programs, are female, it is prudent to pursue the implications of a feminist approach to cognitive development, and consequently cosmopolitanism.

Gilligan (1982) challenges Kohlberg's stages of development by stating that women develop differently; for females, morality centers not on rights and rules but rather interpersonal relationships and an ethics of compassion and care. This hypothesis by Gilligan calls into question the fifth and sixth stages of Kohlberg's model, and its focus on justice, and justice guided decision making. Gilligan instead proposes the idea that perhaps the ideal outcome of moral development might not be impersonal justice, but rather the development of a more affiliative way of living (Gilligan, 1982). Additionally, she concludes that women's morality is more contextualized and—contrasting to the methodology of Kohlberg— is tied to real ongoing relationships rather than to abstract solutions to hypothetical dilemmas.

Similarly, Noddings' (1984, 1992) discussion of the ethics of care, and her three fundamentals to caring—engrossment, receptivity, and reciprocity—focus on interpersonal connection and subjectivity, context, and relationships as determining individual action (Parsons, 2005). Gilligan's and Noddings' efforts to emphasize care and emotion as a desirable outcome of moral development and cosmopolitanism are useful in exploring why the Global Exploration participants have not yet achieved the later stages of Kohlberg's and Hanvey's models. There is a need for research in this area to be further developed; Gilligan (1982) vaguely hypothesizes that the integration of a more Kolhbergian line of moral development with her subjective approach occurs in adult years, but how such integration can be fostered has yet to be sufficiently explored or explained.

However, this perspective elucidates an important point regarding the broader conceptualization of global citizenship: there is a need to reevaluate whether the concept of global citizenship assumes that cosmopolitanism solely equates to justice. Conversely, it would be simplistic to say that in the case of females, cosmopolitanism should be equated with care. Rather, the two perspectives need to be seen in concert; they are neither dichotomous nor can they be separated from one another. In my view, inherent in caring is a sense of justice, and in justice there is caring. If we were to abstract the two, it would be difficult to conceptualize an inclusive, equitable, and just society. Further, I believe that Nussbaum's third capability—the narrative imagination—leaves considerable room for a feminist approach to morality, while perhaps the initial two capacities intertwine the concepts of justice and care. In any case, for the goal of conceptualizing citizenship, and for evaluating levels of achievement of moral and global perspective, multiple and comprehensive outcomes and orientations must be considered.

c. Critical Race Theory/White Privilege

Alternatively, the experiences people have as a result of their race and position in society may reduce their ability to progress to the most critical and reflective global cognitive stage of development, despite being positioned in many ways to be profoundly affected by a cross-cultural experience, such as that provided by Global Exploration. In her study of teacher educators, Merryfield (2000) concludes that the racial background of the United States. K–12 teachers studied played a significant role in how they came to realize and recognize issues of social stratification. According to Merryfield, people of color "acquired an understanding of discrimination and outsider status by the nature of growing up in a society characterized by White privilege and racism" (p. 4). White teacher educators, on the other hand, were only able to gain a sense of otherness and realization of systemic oppression by having experiences outside of the country—only in this way were they able to develop, in the words of W. E. B. DuBois (1989), a double consciousness.

The results of my study show that the experience of becoming a racial minority nevertheless did not proved them the experience of losing their privileged status—as White foreigners, they did not experience exclusion or oppression. As a result, being a racial minority in and of itself, was not enough to push the participants to examine their own society for systemic oppression, White hegemony, and class imposition. Only one of the students came to a realization regarding her Whiteness:

Actually today [in school] we were talking about stereotypes and minorities and we were talking about how it's fair to say that most African-Americans wake up every morning knowing that they are black, whereas when you are white you don't necessarily identify yourself. Or at least in my town I don't feel like that because there is not, well there's a small population of minorities, and in India it was the first time I was ever put in a minority, because we were the minority most of the time, when we did not see any other white people for weeks at a time. And that is when I first realized that I was white.

I mean of course I have always known that I was white, but I've never really realized that I was Caucasian, you know? I just remember that feeling.

This quote reveals that her experience in India was integral to her recognition of her Whiteness. However, external support, in this case in school, was also necessary to help her make this realization. The students in this study might not be able to critically reflect on their own lives and society due to being deeply embedded in their Whiteness. I believe that global education programs, like the Global Exploration Program, can play a large role in helping their participants examine their privilege. After all, issues of power, Western hegemony, race, and class were brought up in daily discussions in India. However, to continue the realization process once the students return home, and to turn the examination upon oneself and ones' society (capacities one and two of Nussbaum's conceptualization), requires further support. Critical race theory and White privilege theory raise race as an important issue for educators to address and consider; however, the procedures for deconstructing this privilege are not well elaborated. How do we as educators, and as concerned citizens, promote this type of deconstruction? How can we push these programs to go further, and directly address the issues of class and race privilege?

CONCLUSION

This study—11 students' experiences in and reflections on a 1-month immersion-based cross cultural experience—addresses some of the questions posed in the introduction, but raises equally as important questions as well. The chapter highlights the importance and significant effects of global education programs in the movement towards developing a world citizenship that emphasizes a cosmopolitan sensibility. After spending time in India, the participants of this study exhibited an awareness and concern for people living far away from them. They also began to recognize the transnational nature of many global issues such as pollution, lack of natural resources, and poverty. Yet it is the more abstract and theoretical components of cosmopolitanism—components that call individuals to reexamine their own contributions to global systems of inequality—that are still to be attained.

The study poses the question as to why these students in privileged race and class positions are not making the necessary connections to reach the ultimate dimension of world citizenship consciousness, despite the tremendous opportunity to engage in a global education program such as Cultural Exploration. Are they too young to fully realize the potential of such a program? Perhaps the values embedded within cosmopolitanism need to be reexamined and reconceptualized so that they are more inclusive of a larger variety of experiences. Perhaps the elite educational institutions that these children attend do not develop the essential capabilities of cosmopolitanism sufficiently in their classes. Further, is there ample opportunity for the students to engage with their experiences in the classroom? Most of the students I talked to were able to reflect upon their experiences in an environmental science class, or write about their experiences in English creative writing classes. Additionally, all the seniors in the program focused their college essays on their experience in India. There was discussion about individuals changing attitudes towards people living outside the United States, and discussion regarding their sense of who they were being called into question from this experience. However, none of the students felt as though they were pushed to extend their experiences to analyze whether similar situations (of inequality and power) exist here in the United States. This line of questioning on my part was mostly met with silence, and the acknowledgement that they should probably consider these things, but that they currently do not.

I believe that there is an urgent need for this type of supported critical reflection to be conducted with these students, because many of them will most likely assume positions of power in the future. Deeper levels of real-ization about power and race might enable them to use the privilege they are afforded to work towards social justice in global society. Global educa-tion programs provide their participants with one significant step on the path towards developing critically reflective and globally sensitive citizens. However, they are just one step. A school system that takes on the values embedded in cosmopolitanism is also necessary to support and push stu-dents to assume the challenges of adopting such a perspective.

Interestingly, a few months after the Katrina devastation occurred, Global Exploration launched a new domestic Gulf Coast Relief program as one of their "Global Awareness in Action" programs. The program is specifically intended to address firsthand the social and economic inequalities that exist in the United States, as revealed by the catastrophe. The catalogue describing the program states:

> In fascinating and disturbing ways, Hurricane Katrina has highlighted the fact that many of the dilemmas faced by developing countries are unre-solved here at home. By including a U.S. based project among our Global Awareness in Action programs, we hope to provide a context for under-standing our own difficulties. This program attempts to not only help pro-vide relief and aid, but to try to understand the root causes of the current social conditions in the US. Placing a domestic program at the center of a global education organization is an essential step in institutionalizing criti-cal self reflection amongst its participants. As awareness of the situation at

home increases, the "otherness" of situations around the globe may begin to recede, and the ideal of world citizenship may be easier to realize.

REFERENCES

Acker, B., & Esseveld, J. (1983). Objectivity and truth: Problems in doing feminist research. *Women's Studies International Forum, 6*(4), 423–435.

Alger, C. F., & Harf, J. E. (1986). Global education: Why? For whom? About what? In R. E. Freeman (Ed.), *Promising practices in global education: A handbook with case studies.* New York: National Council on Foreign Language and International Studies.

Anderson. L. F. (1990). A rationale for global education. In T. Kye (Ed.), *Global education: From thought to action.* Alexandria, VA: ASCSD.

Arum, S. (1987). *International Education: What is it?* A Taxonomy of International Education of U.S. Universities Council On International Education Exchange. Occasioanl Paper # 23.

Crain, W. C. (1985). *Theories of development.* Upper Saddle River, NJ: Prentice Hall.

DuBois, W. E. B. (1989). *The souls of Black folks.* New York: Bantom Books.

Gilligan, C. (1982). *In a different voice: Psychological theory and women's development.* Cambridge, MA: Harvard University Press.

Gutmann (1993). The challenge of multiculturalism in political ethics. *Philosophy & Public Affairs, 22*(3), 171–206.

Hansen, H. M. (2002). Defining international education. *New Directions for Higher Education, 117,* 5–12.

Hanvey, R (1976). *An attainable global perspective.* New York: American Forum for Global Education.

Huitt, W., & Hummel, J. (2003). Piaget's theory of cognitive development. *Educational Psychology Interactive.* Valdosta, GA: Valdosta State University. Retrieved November 28, 2005, from http://chiron.valdosta.edu/whuitt/col/cogsys/piaget.html

Kniep, W. M. (1986). Defining a global education by its content. *Social Education, 50*(6), 437–466.

Merryfield, M. (1995). *Teacher education in global and international education.* Washington, DC: ERIC Clearninghouse on Teaching and Teacher Education. (ERIC Document Reproduction Service No. ED 384 601)

Merryfield, M. (1998). Pedagogy for global perspectives in education: studies of teachers' thinking and practice. *Theory and Research in Social Education, 26*(3), 342–379.

Merryfield, M. (2000). Why aren't teachers being prepared to teach for diversity, equity, and global interconnectedness? A study of lived experiences in the making of multicultural and global educators. *Teaching and Teacher Education, 16*(4), 429-443

Merryfield, M. (2002). The difference a global educator can make. *Educational Leadership, 60*(2), 18–21.

Noddings, N. (1984). *Caring: A feminist approach to ethics and moral education.* Berkeley CA: University of California Press.

Noddings, N. (1992). *The challenge to care in schools: An alternative approach to education*. New York: Teachers College Press.

Nussbaum, M. (1994). Patriotism and cosmopolitanism. *The Boston Review 19*(5), 3–4.

Nussbaum, M. (1997). *Cultivating humanity*. Cambridge, MA: Harvard University Press.

Parsons, E. C. (2005). From caring as a relation to culturally relevant caring: A white teacher's bridge to black students. *Equity and Excellence in Education, 38*, 25–34.

Sutton, M., & Hutton, D. (2001). *Concepts and trends in global education*. Bloomington, IN: Clearinghouse for Social Studies/Social Science Education. (ERIC Document Reproduction Service No. ED 460 930)

Ukpokodu, N. (1999). Multiculturalism vs. globalism. *Social Education, 63*(5), 298–300.

CHAPTER 10

BUILDING TOWARDS DEMOCRACY IN APARTHEID SOUTH AFRICA

A Pioneering Partnership for Training Black School Leaders, 1989-95

Ronald R. Atkinson and Judy L. Wyatt

INTRODUCTION

By 1989, South Africa—and South African education—was in a state of crisis. Both international and internal opposition to the apartheid regime had reached unprecedented levels. International sanctions and boycotts were exerting pressure on both the South African economy and White South Africa's collective psyche. Internal resistance had led the government to declare yet another state of emergency, the third time it had implemented this repressive policy. Disruption and violence rocked many of South Africa's urban Black townships, including Black schools, as Black students by the tens of thousands joined the front lines of the

Advancing Democracy Through Education? U.S. Influence Abroad and Domestic Practices, pp. 229–255
Copyright © 2008 by Information Age Publishing
229

antiapartheid struggle. Groups ranging from the banned African National Congress (ANC) inside South Africa to USAID abroad recognized that reform of the educational sector was critical to any effort to undermine apartheid and to create a truly democratic South Africa, not just because schools and universities germinated the seeds of the grassroots resistance, but because the vast majority of the country had been systematically denied access to learning.

This chapter presents a case study of a genuine partnership between an African educational initiative and U.S. assistance and expertise that was both creative and effective, without distorting or preempting the goals of the aid's beneficiary. The main partners were Teacher Opportunity Programmes (or TOPS), the largest educational nongovernmental organization (NGO) in South Africa at the time, the University of South Carolina (USC), and two historically-Black universities in South Africa, the University of the Western Cape (UWC) and the University of Durban-Westville (UDW). Beginning in 1989 with a needs assessment involving more than 150 Black teachers and principals across the country (Wyatt, 1989),[1] the partnership developed and implemented a highly integrated two-track program in school management and leadership for Black educational leaders in South Africa. One track consisted of a year-long, locally-based in-service course; the other was an international program leading to a master's degree.[2]

The initial needs assessment research, the scholarship then current on effective school leadership, and the impetus of the broader political struggle then underway in South Africa converged to promote a single overarching goal for the program. That goal was to facilitate the movement of school leaders away from the authoritarian, top-down style of managing and leading schools that had been the norm under apartheid to a more open, participatory, democratic philosophy and practice.

The in-service track of the program ran for 6 years, from 1990–95 (2 years as a pilot program, 4 thereafter). During this period, approximately 2,000 principals and other Black school leaders from all across South Africa completed and passed the year-long course. An evaluation conducted towards the end of the program in 1994 by researchers at the University of Cape Town found that many of the participants surveyed had actually become more participatory and democratic in the way that they managed and led their schools after taking the course (Gilmour & Soudein, 1994).

The second track established the first master's level program in South Africa devoted explicitly and exclusively to educational management and leadership. Forty-eight students, representing every region of South Africa, enrolled in this 2-year MEd program from 1992–95. The program produced two unprecedented achievements in Black postsecondary (and postgraduate) education in South Africa: nearly half of these students were women, and the pass rate exceeded 90%. Students spent one semester of full-time study at USC, and then returned to their schools in South Africa. They completed the remainder of their course work at the UDW during school holidays, and then conducted field research for their MEd. theses. The program was funded by more than seventy companies and foundations in South Africa and the United States, with a major grant of $1.7 million from the U.S. Agency for International Development.

The Sociohistorical Context

Geographically, South Africa is about the size of the Southeastern United States, with a 2004 population of approximately 43.4 million people. Based upon the old apartheid racial classification system, which created official categories that determined where one could live, which schools one could attend, and what life chances one would have, Africans are—and have been—the vast majority, totaling over 32.5 million people, or just over 75%. Apartheid not only divided Africans from other racial groups, but from each other, according to various ethnic and linguistic categories. But Africans in general were most disadvantaged under apartheid.

Whites, both Afrikaans-speaking Whites, or Afrikaners, and English-speaking Whites, constituted the dominant minority, numbering about 5.8 million (13.6%). Afrikaners are Whites of mainly Dutch descent, who arrived in South Africa in 1652, when the Dutch East India Company established a fort at the southwestern tip of Africa, which then expanded to become Cape Colony. Afrikaners have always been the leading White group by population (and usually in terms of political power as well). English-speaking Whites first came to South Africa when Britain took over Cape Colony in the early nineteenth century, but only established a numerically significant presence after the discovery of diamonds and gold in the late nineteenth century.

"Coloured" is a South African term—and an official apartheid category —referring to people of mixed race. The term was originally applied to descendants of Cape Colony slaves (imported into the colony from shortly after its founding in the mid-seventeenth century, and freed in 1833), and remnants of a pastoral group called Khoi that disintegrated following Cape Colony expansion onto their land. Some Coloureds speak Afrikaans as their home language, others English; they number 3.7 million, 8.6% of the population.

Finally, Indians (or Asians) are the smallest and most recently arrived major population group in South Africa. Totaling just over a million people, they are concentrated along the northeast Indian Ocean coast, where original immigrants were brought in by the British to work on British-owned sugar plantations in the second half of the nineteenth century. Mahatma Gandhi first developed his nonviolent approach to opposing British colonial rule in South Africa.

Established in 1948, apartheid was constructed upon earlier colonial policies of segregation and discrimination that had their origins in the second half of the seventeenth century, but whose impact became pronounced upon South Africa's African majority only towards the end of the nineteenth (Callinicos, 1981; Davenport & Saunders, 2000; Keegan, 1996; Thompson, 2001; Worden, 2007). It was then that the discovery of rich diamond, and then even richer gold, fields provided both the reason and the means for Whites in South Africa to extend much greater control and dominance over Blacks than had previously existed. While fiercely competitive in many ways, British colonial and commercial interests, on the one hand, and Afrikaners on the other, worked together (or at least in parallel) in this regard. Using a variety of tactics, including force or the threat of force, Whites were able to establish political control, take over 90% of the land, and impose taxes on a vast Black majority. Doing so forced ever increasing numbers of Africans onto the labor market, most importantly in the mines (which needed and used their labor to become the world's largest suppliers of gold and diamonds), but also on White farms and in other unskilled jobs in South Africa's growing towns and cities. With the loss of political autonomy and most of their land, Africans had few options other than working for Whites to earn cash to pay taxes or for other needs in an economy that was increasingly based on money.

The election in 1948 of an Afrikaner-dominated National Party government resulted in a system of even harsher and more pervasive segregation, discrimination, and White social control over Blacks known as apartheid—literally "separateness." The implementation of apartheid ideology and structures focused considerable attention on education (Hartshorne, 1992; Hyslop, 1990a; Kallaway, 1984; Nkomo, 1990).

The architects of apartheid knew that in order to shape society along the lines that they envisioned, it was necessary to plan and control schooling, especially for Afrikaners and Africans: Afrikaners were educated under the rubric of "Christian-National Education," in order to inculcate Afrikaner nationalism, strict segregation, and White supremacy; the Africans, under a "Bantu Education" policy designed (under Afrikaner "guardianship") for Africans to learn to serve the dominant White minority and to "know" and "accept" their place. An Institute of Christian-National Education policy document states:

We believe that the calling and task of White South Africa with respect to the native is to Christianize him and to assist him culturally, and that this calling and task has already found its clearly defined expression in the principles of guardianship, no levelling, and segregation. Thus we believe that any system of [African] education should be based on these principles.... [W]e believe ... that it is the right and duty of the State in co-operation with Christian Protestant churches to provide for and control native education ... with the proviso that the financing of native education does not take place at the cost of European education. (Rose & Tunmer, 1975, p. 127)

"Bantu education" can only be understood within the context of "separate development," a key component of apartheid ideology that is based on a firm commitment to White supremacy hidden behind Orwellian double-speak. Separate development extended earlier colonial notions of segregation and divide-and-rule, furthering the fragmentation of South Africa's Black majority. Indians and Coloureds were divided even more sharply than before from both Whites and Africans, and ethnic distinctions and differences among Africans were further hardened and heightened. A plethora of laws, including the Bantu Self-Governing Act (1959) and Bantu Citizenship Act (1970), created the mechanisms for establishing the ultimate expression of separate development, the fictively "independent" or "self-governing" entities originally called "Reserves," then "Bantustans" (and finally, "homelands").

The eventual idea was that Africans would not be citizens of South Africa, even if they were born, lived, and worked there their entire lives. Instead they would have citizenship in one of the homelands, leaving South Africa as a "White" country. Over time, 10 of these homelands were created. They were scattered—often in small, isolated pieces—in crazy-quilt fashion across, but mostly at the margins of, "White" South Africa. None were economically viable. All were crowded well beyond reasonable carrying capacity by people forced by law to live there. There were few jobs and few other ways to make a living (Lelyveld, 1985; Sparks, 1990).

The ideals of separate development permeated apartheid legislation on education, beginning with the Bantu Education Act of 1953 that established, in law, separate and highly unequal education for Africans. Eventually, 18 different Departments of Education were created—5 White, one Coloured, one Indian, and 11 African (one for each of the 10 homelands; one for Africans in "White" South Africa proper). All of these were tightly administered through top-down, authoritarian, apartheid-based, and ultimately White-controlled bureaucracies.

At the same time that apartheid ideology and government strategy based educational policy for Africans on separate development and the homelands, a two-fold social crisis within "White" South Africa created a different dynamic. First, rapid urbanization beginning in World War II placed enormous strains on urban structures, resulting in squatter camps, bus boycotts, trade unionism, and general unrest among urban Blacks, including young people. Second, expanding industry during the 1950s and '60s required Black semiskilled and even skilled labor, and business and industry leaders began to push for more education and training for Blacks. Thus, from the early to mid-1950s, state policies towards Blacks, particularly Africans, were compelled to include efforts to stabilize the urban work force, train semiskilled laborers, and control unrest and delinquency. As a result, education was expanded for both urban Blacks and Africans in the homelands (Christie & Collins, 1984; Chisolm, 1984; Hartshorne, 1992; Hyslop, 1988; Levy, 1991).

Indeed, the period from 1950 to 1970 saw the number of Blacks, especially Africans, in schools and other educational settings rise dramatically, from just over 1 million in 1950 (about three-fourths of them Africans) to 3.4 million in 1970 (more than 2.7 million of which were Africans). Throughout this period the vast majority of these students were in primary school (and among Africans, in lower primary), though secondary schooling also grew.

This dramatic expansion in numbers was not matched by comparable increases in funding. However much expenditures rose, they did not keep pace with growing enrolments, and remained extremely low in terms of the amount spent per student. Limited funding meant that Black school facilities were typically poor and overcrowded. Qualified Black teachers, moreover, were in short supply, and were paid far less than their White counterparts. But perhaps the best indication of the financial state of Black education was per capita funding in relationship to spending for Whites. In 1949, just before the establishment of Bantu education, the per capita spending for African pupils was approximately one seventh that for Whites; for Coloureds and Indians the figure was about two fifths. By 1970, gaps had widened greatly, so that the per capita funding (including capital expenditures) for African students was one twentieth that for Whites, while for Coloured students it was one fifth; and for Indians, just over one quarter (Hartshorne, 1992; South African Institute of Race Relations, 1951–52, 1961, 1970, 1989–90, 1992; Unterhalter, 1991).

From the beginning, Bantu education was recognized by Africans for what it was—a system of education that was not only separate, but intentionally unequal and inferior, designed to train Africans to perform at "the level of certain forms of labor" and no more. It is no surprise, then, that efforts to contest this system began even as it was being imposed (Davis, 1972; Hartshorne, 1992; Hyslop, 1987a, 1987b, 1989, 1990a, 1990b; Lodge, 1984). Such challenges, along with those by Coloureds and Indians against their apartheid schooling, recurred with lesser or greater strength and effectiveness over the next 45 years, both shaping and being shaped by broader political dynamics in the society at large.

The vibrant oppositional politics of the 1950s, including active opposition to apartheid education, did not survive into the next decade. Instead, the 1960s were marked by a heavy-handed repression that quashed and outlawed most oppositional political activity and many organizations, including the main (and mainstream) ANC (Gerhart, 1978; Lodge, 1983).

Still, by the late 1960s challenges to apartheid began to emerge. Black universities and urban secondary schools were a primary site of such challenges, spearheaded by the Black Consciousness movement, led by Steven Biko. The followers of Black Consciousness rejected the categories of apartheid and imposition of inferior status on all Black groups, demanded control of their own institutions and destinies, and affirmed pride and strength in their Blackness. The movement helped promote an ideological unity within the disadvantaged majority. For the first time many who were designated Africans, Coloureds, and Indians began to identify themselves collectively as "Black." More broadly, the emergence of Black Consciousness epitomized important new developments in opposition to apartheid, situated firmly within Black education. Indeed, given the decimation of extraparliamentary opposition and the pervasiveness of state terror, Black education provided one of the only places, at that time, where such opposition could develop (Cross & Chisolm, 1990; Gerhart, 1978; Marx, 1992).

In June 1976, Black education was catapulted to the front lines of the larger political struggle against apartheid. The flash point was Soweto, the sprawling African township near Johannesburg (with a population then in the neighborhood of 2 million). Mass demonstrations by students erupted there, sparked by the government decision to impose Afrikaans—"the language of the oppressor"—as a medium of instruction for certain subjects in African schools. Similar student protests quickly spread to other townships, and just as quickly took on broader antiapartheid, antiracist, and anti-Bantu education overtones. From June 1976 to the end of 1977, more than 1,000 students were shot by state security forces, and many others beaten, detained, maimed, and tortured (Brooks & Brickhill, 1980; Hirson, 1979; Kane-Berman, 1978).

Following the Soweto uprisings, school boycotts became a common mobilizing strategy for students. This was especially true after 1983, when the government introduced a new tri-cameral parliament. The government touted this as a move away from apartheid, even though it came about as a result of a Whites-only referendum, excluded Africans altogether, and made the Indian and Coloured chambers distinctly junior. Students were a crucial constituency of the broad-based antiapartheid movement that developed as a response, exceeding the level of popular resistance and mobilization of the 1950s and 1976–77. Frequently throughout the 1980s and early 1990s, more than a million students at a time were engaged in boycotts of classes in protests against both apartheid education and the apartheid system more generally.

Even more than before, the state responded to student and other oppositional politics with repression and violence. Three states of emergency followed in quick succession, each more deadly than its predecessor. Tens of thousands were imprisoned (and often tortured); thousands were killed. Probably two thirds or more of these were in their teens or early 20s, many of them secondary school or university students. Thus schools, students, and sometimes teachers were often on the front lines of the virtually uninterrupted, large-scale struggles against apartheid that engulfed South Africa from 1983 into the 1990s (South African Research Service, 1983, 1984, 1986, 1987, 1989, 1992; Lelyveld, 1985; Lodge & Nasson, 1991; Marx, 1992; Sparks, 1990; Worden, 2007).

This was a remarkable time in South Africa's history. As in a number of other parts of the world (especially the former Soviet Union and elsewhere in East-Central Europe), the end of the 1980s and beginning of the 1990s brought political shifts on a scale and at a pace virtually unthinkable just a few years before. In South Africa, 1989 was the year of what would be the country's last apartheid elections, conducted in the face of massive popular opposition. By the next year, Nelson Mandela and many other political prisoners were released from jail and the bans upon the ANC and many other antiapartheid organizations were lifted. Amidst the ongoing violence and strife of the next 4 years, negotiations toward the first truly democratic elections in the country's history were brokered.

In April 1994, the majority of South Africans voted for the first time, ending (at least in a formal sense) more than 40 years of apartheid. A government of national unity with a strong ANC majority was installed, headed by President Nelson Mandela. In the following year, South Africa was reintegrated into the international community. Mandela's moral authority provided a leadership that soothed White fears—as much as, or more, than could have been imagined—while also symbolizing the ascendancy of Blacks to political power. Political violence declined dramatically, although violent crime almost immediately began a climb that has continued into the new century.

Clearly, the enormous backlog of social and economic problems created or exacerbated by apartheid remains a formidable obstacle to a better life —and life opportunities—for most of South Africa's disadvantaged majority. But the 1994 and subsequent elections, and the new governments elected, have meant that these problems, including those in education, can at least begin to be addressed, with far less turmoil and bloodshed, and far more accommodation and goodwill than anyone could have conceived in the decade (or even 5 or 6 years) before the watershed year of 1994 (Sparks, 1995, 2003; Worden, 2007).

The Genesis of the School Management and Leadership Program

Apartheid education caused incalculable damage to Black children and youth, and to the disadvantaged majority population in general. As noted above, Bantu education did supply schooling for much larger numbers of students, especially at the primary level. But postprimary education increased as well. The number of students completing secondary school courses and sitting final exams grew from around 2,000 in 1960 to over 250,000 by 1990. But the results of the system were its own indictment: (1) more than 50% of those taking the school-leaving exams each year failed (and by the later 1980s the failure rate hovered at or even above 60%); (2) pass rates in mathematics and the sciences were even worse, ranging between 10% and 20%; (3) less than 1% of the pupils starting school matriculated 12 years later; and (4) for those who did finish and did well enough on their exams to make it to university, the failure rate of first-year students at historically Black institutions of higher education was 80%, the direct result of poor school preparation (South African Institute of Race Relations, 1992).

The grossly inadequate and inequitable apartheid system of education was symptomatic of the South African government's fundamental failure to address the needs and aspirations of its disadvantaged Black majority. One response to this failure was the emergence, especially over the 1980s, of one of the most dynamic and flourishing NGO sectors in the world. Literally thousands of NGOs were established, operating in almost all areas of Black community life. Given the nature of the apartheid system and its widely-accepted illegitimacy, many of these NGOs functioned as "third-generation NGOs"—NGOs that work for policy changes on regional and national levels in order to promote systemic change (Korten, 1987). In apartheid South Africa, this almost always included the promotion of greater participatory and democratic management, leadership, and (ultimately) governance. Not surprisingly, one of the main areas of NGO focus, including third-generation NGOs, was education, where by 1990 more than 2,000 NGOs were active. As Alexander (1990) has argued, these NGOs were important both as responses to immediate needs and as transitional launching pads for more thorough processes of change. At their best, in the words of Es'kia Mphahlele (1990), they draw from the "souls of the people and shed light on what education can and ought to be ... and provide what the State system does not even want to contemplate" (pp. 37, 46; see also Bot, 1989; Chisholm, 1992; Etheridge, 1986; Honey, 1991; Lee, 1991; Millar, Raynham, & Schaffer, 1991; Swainson, 1991; Wyatt, 1993, pp. 123–52; Wyatt & Cress, 1992).

The largest of the educational NGOs by the late 1980s was TOPS. TOPS was founded in 1982 by a group of community, educational, and private sector leaders—Black and White, from all across South Africa—to begin addressing some of the major problems of Black education (Murphy, 1987). Over a series of meetings the group developed a core vision and set of principles:

> The group was adamant that TOPS must remain completely independent of the government in order to maintain credibility within the Black community; TOPS would be privately run and financed with no government involvement. The aim of TOPS would be to contribute to educational development in Black communities by addressing the expressed needs of teachers. TOPS would be local- and school-based, which would allow teachers to study within their local regions. And [at least in the beginning] TOPS would focus mainly on primary education. (Wyatt, 1993, pp. 132–33)

A major reason for the initial emphasis on primary education was the high percentage of Black (especially African) primary school teachers who had not graduated—or "matriculated"—from secondary school (Standard 10, or Grade 12). More than 70% of African primary school teachers in the early 1980s had only completed Standard 8 (Grade 10), plus 2 years of teacher training (DeLange Commission of Enquiry into the Provision of Education in South Africa, 1983). This was sufficient to teach in Black primary schools (and before the 1970s, Blacks could teach primary school after completing Standard 6 (Grade 8) plus 1 year of teacher training). But the same year that the *DeLange Report* highlighted the problem, the government suddenly enacted new standards. In order to be a qualified teacher, the new law required "matric" (to have successfully completed secondary school), plus 3 years of teacher training. With the stroke of a pen, some 80,000 Black teachers were pronounced un- or underqualified, which among other things meant that they would earn less than half the salary of "qualified" teachers. The government took no steps to develop programs for upgrading these teachers. This left Black communities on their own to deal with this overwhelming backlog of now-designated "untrained" and "under-trained" teachers, which became a burning issue for both these teachers and the communities in which they taught.

TOPS stepped into the breach. It developed an academic component that focused on providing tutors at an expanding roster of locations around the country to help teachers in the six subject areas required for the national school leaving examination. Many thousands of Black primary school teachers, the vast majority women, enrolled in the after school and vacation courses and gained their matric. TOPS was aware from the beginning that obtaining matric did not necessarily improve Black education in the classroom. But it greatly improved the earning power and opportunities for further study of the individuals involved. And even more importantly, it demonstrated the TOPS program's broader, long-term commitment to the Black community.

This initial emphasis was soon complemented by the development of TOPS' second major component, Methodology, introduced in 1986 and designed to help teachers improve their knowledge and teaching skills in the crucial subjects of English, mathematics, and science. The third and final major component of TOPS was in school management, to develop management and leadership training for principals, deputy principals, and heads of departments. This proved more difficult to develop, as management and leadership training for school leaders was a relatively new concept in South Africa and research on Black school leadership was almost totally lacking. Several attempts by TOPS to develop this component over the mid to late 1980s failed to get off the ground (Wyatt, 1993, pp. 126–35, 164–66).

In the midst of these false starts, the present authors met Professor Merlyn Mehl in 1986 while he was in the United States on sabbatical leave from the UWC. About to be named the new National Director of TOPS, Professor Mehl had been invited to the USC to make several presentations on South Africa and South African education. In an afternoon meeting near the end of his visit, Mehl,

> asked JLW if she might be interested in coming to South Africa to work with Teacher Opportunity Programmes (TOPS) in conducting a needs assessment to determine what teachers and principals saw as the major issues and problems affecting the management of their schools. This meeting … set off a series of developments that has, among many other things, moved large numbers of people across oceans and continents, linking South African and South Carolinian lives and careers in ways that could have been only dimly imagined that first afternoon. (Atkinson, Wyatt, & Senkhane 1992, 1993, p. i)

Following a preliminary visit to South Africa later in 1987 to work out details, Wyatt (then a PhD student in educational leadership and policies at USC) returned to South Africa in early 1989 to begin the needs assessment research. At this time, research in many parts of the developing world conducted by the World Bank (1988), as well as numerous studies in the United States (for example, Boyer, 1983; Brookover Beammer, & Elthin, 1982; National Commission on Excellence in Education, 1983), indicated that one of the single most important factors (perhaps even *the* most important factor) in improving education was the school principal.

Nowhere, of course, do principals and the schools that they lead operate in a vacuum. Principals and their schools are always embedded within communities and influenced by the political, economic, and other social forces that impinge upon and operate within those communities. In the South Africa of the late 1980s and 1990s, the particular nature of those broader social forces placed all Black school leaders in a particularly problematic and ambiguous position. Central to the problem was the fact that Black school leaders were employed by, and in a fundamental sense were thus representatives of, an official system that had *no* credibility with most Black school leaders or with the teachers, students, and parents in the communities in which they worked. Within this general context of structural and emotional paradox, Black school leaders faced innumerable problems, three of which will be highlighted here.

First, they almost invariably came to their leadership positions, including as principal, without the benefit of formal training, and rarely received any subsequently. Until 1992, when TOPS, USC, and UDW established the MEd program described briefly above, there had been no postgraduate degree programs in South Africa focused specifically on this field. In addition, there were no professional organizations for principals, no literature specializing in the problems faced by principals in Black South African schools, and few opportunities for contact among principals to discuss ideas, programs, or problems. Several years earlier the government had instituted a limited course in school management with which many Black school leaders were familiar, but which few had actually taken. Appropriately called "Top Down," the program foundered for two fundamental reasons: (1) the training course, purchased from an American corporation, was based on a corporate sector model that ignored the structure and unique mission of schools and the real problems of Black school administrators; and (2) as befitted its name (and the way in which apartheid education operated more generally), the program's content and implementation were orchestrated from above, with no consultation with, or input from, the people directly affected. This effort failed to gain acceptance among participating principals and their constituents, to deliver contextually relevant management and leadership training, or to develop the capacity to deliver such training in the long term.

Second, as Black educational leaders, Black school principals and their deputies were in an especially exposed and difficult position within the broader South African political dynamic during the 1980s and 1990s. They were employed by authoritarian and highly centralized bureaucratic departments that were crucial components of the apartheid system and that as a result had no credibility in Black communities. In times of crisis, which had been frequent since the protests of school children that swept across South Africa in 1976 (beginning in the country's largest Black township, Soweto) and almost continual since 1983, Black school leaders were frequently caught between the demands of their respective departments and those of their students, teachers, and communities. Especially for Black school leaders with a deep commitment to those students, teachers, and communities—and there were many—the conflictual conditions within which they had to operate demanded leadership and management skills of the highest order.

Third, management and leadership in Black schools was made exceedingly difficult by a school environment characterized by resource scarcity, rigid and rule-bound bureaucracies, and a broader political context in which the various education departments, students, parents, and teachers often had deeply conflicting views about what the principal should be or do. The communities where these schools were located, moreover, were marked by widespread (and growing) unemployment and poverty which impacted on schools in myriad ways.

The TOPS Needs Assessment

The TOPS needs assessment research involved meetings and interviews with more than 150 teachers and principals throughout South Africa (Wyatt, 1989). Such widespread, grassroots participation helped ensure that real problems were identified, and provided the means for grounding any subsequent training program in the expressed needs not only of practicing school leaders but also of the teachers that they led. This approach, moreover, demonstrated TOPS' commitment to developing a school management and leadership training program in which broad-based, participatory involvement played a central role.

The TOPS organization, with offices located throughout the country, provided crucial structure, support, and access into Black communities. At the time, world-wide sanctions were in place against South Africa, including an academic boycott. The researcher was from a country whose government policies under the Reagan administration provided support for a beleaguered South African regime. In order to conduct research in Black communities in such a contentious area as education, it was vital to be associated with a credible organization so that the researcher was not seen as violating international sanctions or supporting the apartheid system. By 1989 the exiled ANC had revised its earlier total academic boycott and supported the involvement of outside individuals deemed to be clearly working to benefit the disadvantaged majority and committed to the larger political struggle. Affiliated with both TOPS and the most active antiapartheid institution of higher education in the country, the UWC, the present authors had been vetted prior to their arrival in South Africa by a

UWC committee in unofficial contact with the ANC and in compliance with ANC guidelines on outside academics.

Working under the auspices of TOPS was also decisive at local levels. There were several reasons why teachers and principals might have been apprehensive and suspicious. In addition to being American, the researcher was also White and female. Asking people to give open and honest responses to sensitive questions within the context of the highly politicized and contentious environment of Black schools required credibility and trust. This was a tall order, especially given the broader political environment. In 1989, a state of emergency was in effect throughout South Africa, and individuals were being detained daily for political activities, or even criticizing the government. Any atypical behavior or activities—even attending meetings where a White foreigner asked questions and discussed problems related to school management and leadership—could be stressful or even risky for participants. Overcoming these obstacles was only possible because of the national presence of TOPS, its track record in improving Black education and the lives and skills of Black teachers, and the institutional credibility that this brought.

The results of the needs assessment revealed both similarities and striking differences among teachers and principals in terms of what these two groups saw as the main problems and issues affecting the management and leadership of their schools.

The problem areas that were consistently identified by both groups tended to be the broad, underlying difficulties affecting almost all Black South African schools. Some of the most important and consistently noted of these issues included:

- A pervasive scarcity of resources, including such areas as personnel, classroom space, books, and other equipment, teaching aids, electricity, water, and toilet facilities.
- Political and economic uncertainty and disruption.
- The authoritarian nature, rigid bureaucracy, and rule-bound hierarchy of the various Black education departments, which were often replicated in individual schools (at the time the program began, as noted above, eighteen separate departments of education in South Africa operated among different racial and ethnic groups, and in various geographical areas).
- The lack of management and teaching materials/training.
- The isolation of principals from colleagues.

In addition to these shared issues and problems, teachers and principals also generated separate—and quite distinct—lists of their own. The most common responses of teachers (including heads of departments) were broadly critical of principals and their current approaches to managing and leading schools. Principals (and school inspectors, to whom principals answered) were accused of typically lacking leadership and administrative skills; of being autocratic, bullying, threatening, and domineering; of being possessive concerning the school (saying such things as "This is *my* school; I'll do what I like"); and of showing favoritism and discrimination instead of treating all teachers fairly, equally, and with respect, regardless of age or gender.

Teachers also complained that there was a lack of communication and feedback, including no appropriate system for dealing with staff grievances. And teachers wanted the principal to welcome ideas and input from the teaching staff; wanted to be involved in planning, organizing, and discussing problems; and in general wanted more cooperation and democratic participation in running the school.

Principals and deputy principals, on the other hand, tended first to emphasize their need for training in various areas. Those areas most often identified included (1) budgeting and other financial aspects of school management; (2) crisis management and/dealing with conflict situations; (3) dealing with grievances from teachers and students; (4) staff development, motivation, and guidance; and (5) developing community/parent relations.

In addition, many principals and deputy principals expressed concerns about the lack of orientation for new principals; the need for more study leave for principals; bullying and domineering school inspectors; the need for more communication and consultation with their respective departments; and the lack of responsibility shown by many teachers.

The TOPS Pilot Program

At a TOPS national conference held at the University of Cape Town in December 1989, a group of TOPS principals from across South Africa decided that the needs assessment just described should provide the basis for developing a pilot in-service program for training principals and other school leaders. Conference members selected a committee, eventually called the TOPS National Facilitating Committee for Management, to begin producing materials for the program (Wyatt, 1990). Commencing work in early 1990, the resultant pilot program was field-tested during 1990–91 and 1991–92.

Feedback from this field testing was a crucial component in the ongoing development of the program. In addition, in September 1990 Chair of the facilitating committee, Professor R. I. M. Moletsane, and another management committee member, Mr. Zeph Senkhane, paid a month-long consultative visit to the College of Education at USC. Following this, five USC faculty and PhD student Judy Wyatt traveled throughout South Africa during May and June 1991, consulting with teachers, principals, and community leaders. This process of interaction and consultation contributed greatly to revising and upgrading materials for the full-fledged in-service program, titled "The Effective Principal."

The In-Service TOPS School Management and Leadership Program

Following the visit by the USC team to South Africa during May–June 1991, a seven-person team of TOPS personnel and USC faculty began the process of materials revision that resulted in the first edition of *The Effective Principal* (Atkinson, Wyatt, & Senkhane, 1992; with an Introduction by Atkinson & Wyatt, 1992a). These seven (the three editors and four main authors) were joined in January 1992 by the first group of six students in the TOPS, USC, and UDW MEd Program in Educational Management and Leadership. Over the next 5 months (January–May 1992), the expanded team drafted, discussed, reviewed, and revised the units of *The Effective Principal: Participant's Manual*. During June and July of 1992, further revisions, editing, and production of both the *Participant's Manual* and *Facilitator Guide* (which included additional material to assist in the effective facilitation of each unit) were completed at the TOPS Media Office in Cape Town, in time for the first Facilitator Training Program in July 1992.

Another round of revisions in 1993 resulted in a second edition of the course material, slightly re-titled (reflecting the broader political developments in the country) as *The Effective Principal: School Management and Leadership for a New South Africa* (Atkinson, Wyatt, & Senkhane, 1993), with a revised Introduction (Atkinson & Wyatt, 1993a, which provides the basis for substantial portions of the present chapter). Each of the original 18 units was reviewed and revised by a team of South African school leaders (the second group in the MEd program) and USC faculty, and a new Unit 19 was added on issues and problems facing women school leaders (Tonnson, Pigford, & Wyatt, 1992; Wyatt & Atkinson, 1992). As the list of contributors to this effort had shifted and expanded, it was decided not to designate specific authorship of individual units. Instead a complete list of contributors (which ran to 37 names) was included in the "Acknowledgements to the Second Edition."

This lengthy and elaborate process of materials development was intended to demonstrate the commitment of TOPS to the involvement of teachers and principals in the design, evaluation, and refinement of the program and the course materials on which it was based. It was a commitment not only to attempt to produce materials of the highest quality, but to do so within the participatory, cooperative, and democratic framework that the course and course readings emphasized. The process resulted in insights and inputs far beyond the capability of any individual or small group. Such broad-based consultation and collaboration between academics and practitioners (and South Africans and Americans), moreover, was crucial to the goal of developing materials that were relevant to South African schools, teachers, and school leaders, something particularly important at the critical juncture in South Africa's history during which this work was done.

Facilitator Training

One of the clearest results of feedback from the pilot program indicated the need to provide training for facilitators. In response, the first TOPS Facilitator Training in School Management and Leadership was held at two venues in and near Johannesburg from July 6–17, 1992. The training team consisted of five faculty members from the USC, three TOPS personnel, and the first six MEd students. The 40 participants came from across South Africa, 5 from each of the eight regions into which TOPS divided South Africa (corresponding roughly with official administrative divisions in the country). In 1993 and 1994, the number of participants in facilitator training each of those years (held during the July school holidays in the Orange Free State) was approximately 100, enabling many more people to become trained facilitators and far greater numbers of school leaders across the country to participate in the course.

Facilitator training was an intense experience. Each year's nearly 2-week program was organized to include six or more contact hours per day, with reading and preparation time occupying many additional hours. The sessions were highly interactive and required both preparation ahead of time and active participation during the sessions themselves. Throughout the training, participants worked in teams made up of both other participants and the trainers.

While the discussion of some units was facilitated by the trainers, each participant was responsible for cofacilitating two of the 19 units. The purpose of the sessions was not only to present and discuss content, but to develop skills in presenting the material in highly interactive ways. A particular focus was to lead groups in a way that both modeled and encouraged participants to engage in behaviors compatible with the open, democratic, and participatory nature of the course content, including the giving and receiving of positive and constructive feedback. This basic approach, developed for and during the first facilitator training program, continued to characterize the successor programs in 1993 and 1994 (see Atkinson & Wyatt, 1992b, 1993b, 1994). While the open nature of the process encouraged critical reflection and feedback, most suggestions for improving the program had to do with wanting more time to go through and process the material, wanting follow-up sessions, and some criticisms of the venues for the training. Otherwise, feedback from participants in these intense facilitator training sessions was almost universally positive. To provide just a few illustrative examples:

- "No other course has been as rich as this one."
- "The fact that we were treated as equals by our Facilitators made us to review the way we treat our teachers, students and parents."
- "The training has so developed me both personally and profession-ally, I don't have the words to describe the impact. I feel very confi-dent to go out there and share the experiences with my colleagues back home. The materials covered the areas of school management and the facilitators made it come alive."
- "I have attended many courses but feel that this two weeks was the most effective. The programme was heavy but the way it was pre-sented made the time fly by and one was unaware of the tremen-dous amount of work one was going through. It was a lovely learning experience presented by a very professional and dedicated group of presenters."
- "Thanks for the best two weeks of my life as a principal."
- "At times when I was faced with problems at my school I felt that I should quit and join another profession. I am happy to say that the experience I got here has made a great impact in that I am already looking forward to when my school reopens. I will be able to share [this training] with my staff and other principals. I believe that the culture of my school will change and the teachers will be more involved in decision making."

Finally, in Gilmour and Soudien's evaluation of the 1994 Facilitator Train-ing Program, they wrote:

Without exception each of the participants interviewed expressed their unconditional support and gratitude for the TOPS programme.... Several of the interviewees repeatedly spoke of how the course had helped them to reflect on their own practice. "If I want to change my school" said one "I will have to look at myself first and where I'll have to change" .... A participant from East London where the programme has only recently been introduced commented that his participation in the [facilitator training] programme "had been an experience of a life-time. The experience is enriching to see so many positive people, to see so many people with this outlook towards education." (pp. 24–25)

An Overview of Course Content

As noted above, the text of *The Effective Principal* (Atkinson, Wyatt, Senkhane, 1993) consisted of a revised introduction, 18 substantially revised units, and a new unit 19 on women school leaders. The *Participants' Manual* consisted of three volumes; the *Facilitator Guide* was augmented with a new fourth volume of additional readings. Each unit was organized so that it began with a brief statement of the purpose of the unit, followed by an overview of the unit, and then by a discussion of the basic concepts and principles addressed in the unit. In addition, each unit (except the first) included sets of required additional readings and workbook activities, and all included a brief self-test (the correct answers to which were included at the end of each volume).

Volume 1 focused on a range of topics that introduced broad, underlying information, approaches, techniques, and skills central to effective school leadership. In addition to the Introduction, the volume consisted of the following six units: (1) Facilitating Learning; (2) Understanding The Adult Learner: Teaching Teachers; (3) Dealing Effectively With Groups; (4) Communicating Effectively in Schools; (5) Improving Problem Solving; and (6) Schools as Organizations.

Volume 2 focused on school leadership, looking especially at ways that principals and other school leaders could work in open, critical yet supportive, and participatory ways with the teaching staff to make them better teachers. The units in Volume 2 were: (7) School Leadership; (8) The Instructional Process: Helping Teachers Teach Effectively; (9) The Supervisory Process: Working with Teachers; (10) Clinical Supervision: Working with Teachers to Improve Instruction; (11) Staff Development: Helping Teachers Become All They Can Be; and (12) Teacher Induction: Inducting Beginning Teachers into Teaching.

Volume 3 discussed a variety of issues and problems that concerned both Black schools and the broader environment in which they were situated and which affected school principals in their roles as both managers and leaders. These units emphasized democratic, participatory, and transparent management and leadership, and included: (13) Principals and School Effectiveness; (14) School and Community Relations; (15) Responding to Conflict; (16) Professional and Principled Behavior; (17) Managing the School Budget; (18) Organizational Change in Schools; and (19) Issues Facing Women School Leaders.

Although the overall TOPS management were aware of the oft-expressed desire for formal certification procedures for both participants and facilitators in the TOPS School Management and Leadership Program, the necessary details to establish such formal certification were never worked out. This ended up being one of the main shortcomings of the program, and certainly one of the major frustrations of program participants, including its codirectors (and present authors).

The MEd Program

In parallel with—and contributing in important ways to—the field-based, in-service training program was the first master's degree program in South Africa devoted explicitly and exclusively to educational management and leadership. Initiated by TOPS, this cooperative, capacity-building program was housed at the UDW, drawing upon the relevant programs and expertise already established at the USC.

The establishment of this postgraduate program for training Black school leaders was envisaged as a second component crucial to improving education and expanding opportunities for South Africa's disadvantaged majority. Such a program, especially one housed at a widely respected, historically Black university such as UDW, was seen as a new and powerful means to develop high-level Black educational and community leaders. These leaders, moreover, would be equipped with academic credentials that would position them to play key roles in shaping the overall direction of educational reform in a future, postapartheid South Africa that was being forged at the time.

As with the TOPS in-service program, the MEd program was grounded in fundamental ways in the results of the needs assessment discussed above. Of particular importance in this regard, it is worth noting again that the commitment to democratic and participatory processes characterizing both the needs assessment and the development and content of the in-service program. This provided a degree of relevance, legitimacy, and credibility that could not have been achieved otherwise. Such credibility, as well as a continuation of the same participatory ethos, was indispensable in establishing a new postgraduate degree program at UDW.

It is also significant that the MEd program was closely linked with TOPS' in-service training. Indeed, participation as a trainer and as a producer or refiner of materials in the in-service program were among the most crucial responsibilities and requirements of each MEd student. This approach had several important consequences.

First, the links between the MEd and in-service tracks of the school management and leadership program helped to ensure that those who had the opportunity to obtain the necessary educational background, and were selected to benefit from the opportunity to pursue a postgraduate degree, would plough some of the knowledge and skills acquired in their studies back into their communities and regions. Second, the MEd links with the in-service program provided for an important and appropriate integration of practical experience and ongoing community involvement with the research skills, theoretical understanding, and analytical work best learned in an academic setting. Third, by integrating the in-service and master's programs so that they reinforced one another, the professional development and empowerment of school leaders from disadvantaged communities was advanced to a far greater degree than if either component had proceeded without this linkage between academic work and field practice. And finally, the TOPS in-service program served as a primary vehicle for identifying, assessing, and recruiting principals for the MEd program.

Over the 4 years of student intake (from 1992–95), 48 students, as noted above, entered the MEd program, from across South Africa. Nearly half were women and more than 90% completed and passed the course. While some of these successful master's students have subsequently left education as opportunities in other fields opened to them as part of the transition to a new, postapartheid South Africa, many others have taken lead roles in the new, unified Ministry of Education.

A Brief Postscript

TOPS, along with most educational NGOs, did not survive the transition to a legitimate government and single education system that followed the historic 1994 elections. The rapid and dramatic shift in funding and attention away from the NGO sector to the new government brought an end to both tracks of the school management and leadership program described in this chapter. Even though this shift was in many ways understandable, even necessary, it did not occur without cost to South African education. The educational NGO sector, as indicated above, had produced a wide range and large number of exciting and innovative programs that had contributed greatly to Black education. Such creativity was not sustainable in the new government educational system, as it necessarily focused on the massive problems of consolidating and transforming 18 separate apartheid education departments into one postapartheid ministry.

But the ending of the TOPS school management and leadership program occurred only after a core of talented and committed Black school leaders received academic credentialing previously unavailable. This gave them access to opportunities and positions of leadership in the new Ministry of Education—and provided that Ministry with people who had acquired knowledge and skills that could help move it forward in the difficult period of transition from the multiple education departments and long-term damages of apartheid. And before the program ended, some 2,000 Black principals and other school leaders had taken the in-service course that spoke to their needs—and to the needs of their teachers, schools, and communities—to manage and lead schools more effectively. This meant, most basically, helping them to do so in more participatory and democratic ways, ways that fit into the much broader struggle that was trying to bring about a new, postapartheid South Africa. And while the postapartheid South Africa that has so far emerged from that struggle falls far short, in so many ways, from the hopes, aspirations, and ideals upon which the struggle was based, the University of Cape Town evaluation of the in-service program (Gilmour & Soudien, 1994) indicated significant changes made by those who had participated in the course. To whatever extent the 2,000 participants in the TOPS course utilized more effective, participatory, and democratic ways of managing and leading schools—and it seems as if this occurred to a far greater extent than we could have hoped—this could have positively affected tens of thousands of teachers, who could have in turn perhaps improved the learning and educational experience more generally of hundreds of thousands of students.

It was an exciting, even exhilarating, opportunity to have been a part of this endeavor, during an exciting, exhilarating period in the history of South Africa.

NOTES

1. The term "Black" is used throughout this chapter as a general term referring to anyone who was, or would have been, officially classified under apartheid as "African," "Coloured" (mixed race), or "Indian"/"Asian." All of these terms, along with "European" or "White," will be used for both the pre-apartheid and apartheid eras. Unfortunately, the continuing legacy of apartheid means that both educational and general life opportunities continue to be determined in large part by apartheid-based racial categories.
2. The most comprehensive discussion of TOPS and the school management and leadership program can be found in Wyatt (1993, pp. 123–98).

REFERENCES

Alexander, N. (1990). *Education and the struggle for national liberation in South Africa: Essays and speeches by Nevelle Alexander (1985–1989)*. Braamfontein, South Africa: Skotaville.

Atkinson, R., & Wyatt, J. L. (1992a). Introduction. In R. R. Atkinson, J. L. Wyatt, & Z. Senkhane (Eds.), *The effective principal* (pp. 1–12). Cape Town, South Africa: Teacher Opportunity Programmes.

Atkinson, R., & Wyatt, J. L. (1992b). *Report on Facilitator Training, TOPS School Management and Leadership Programme, 6–17 July 1992.* Cape Town, South Africa: Teacher Opportunity Programmes.

Atkinson, R., & Wyatt, J. L. (1993a). Introduction. In R. R. Atkinson, J. L. Wyatt, & Z. Senkhane (Eds.), *The effective principal: School management and leadership for a new South Africa* (pp. 1–9). Cape Town, South Africa: Teacher Opportunity Programmes.

Atkinson, R., & Wyatt, J. L. (1993b). *Report on Facilitator Training, TOPS School Management and Leadership Programme, 7–18 July 1993.* Cape Town, South Africa: Teacher Opportunity Programmes.

Atkinson, R., & Wyatt, J. L. (1994). *Report on Facilitator Training, TOPS School Management and Leadership Programme, 15–26 July 1994.* Cape Town, South Africa: Teacher Opportunity Programmes.

Atkinson, R. R., Wyatt, J. L., & Senkhane, Z. (Eds.). (1992). *The effective principal: Participants' Manual* (3 vols). *Facilitator Guide* (3 vols.). Cape Town, South Africa: Teacher Opportunity Programmes.

Atkinson, R. R., Wyatt, J. L., & Senkhane, Z. (Eds.). (1993). *The effective principal: School management and leadership for a new South Africa* (2nd ed.). *Participants' Manual* (3 vols.) *Facilitator Guide* (4 vols.) Cape Town, South Africa: Teacher Opportunity Programmes.

Bot, M. (1989, May). Black education and the role of the private sector. *South African Foundation Review*, 181–187. Johannesburg: South African Foundation.

Boyer, E. L. (1983). *High school: A report on secondary education in America.* New York: Harper & Row.

Brookover, W. B., Beammer, L., & Elthin, H. (1982). *Creating effective schools: An in-service program for enhancing school learning climate and achievement.* Holmes Beach, FL: Learning.

Brooks, A., & Brickhill, J. (1980). *Whirlwind before the storm: The origins and development of the uprising in Soweto and the rest of South Africa from June to December 1976.* London: International Defence and Aid Fund.

Callinicos, L. (1981). *Gold and workers 1886–1924: A people's history of South Africa.* Johannesburg, South Africa: Ravan Press.

Chisolm, L. (1984). Redefining skills: Black education in South Africa in the 1980s. In P. Kallaway (Ed.), *Apartheid and education: The education of Black South Africans.* Johannesburg, South Africa: Raven Press.

Chisolm, L. (1992). South African education in the era of negotiations. In South African Research Service, *South African Review 6: From "Red Friday" to Codesa* (pp. 279–293). Johannesburg, South Africa: Raven Press.

Christie, P., & Collins, C. (1984). Bantu education: Apartheid ideology and labour reproduction. In P. Kallaway (Ed.), *Apartheid and education: The education of Black South Africans.* Johannesburg, South Africa: Raven Press.

Cross, M., & Chisholm, L. (1990). The roots of segregated schooling in twentieth-century South Africa. In M. Nkomo (Ed.), *Pedagogy of domination: Toward a democratic education in South Africa* (pp. 43–74). Trenton, NJ: Africa World Press.

Davenport, T. R. H., & Saunders, C. (2000). *South Africa: A modern history* (5th ed.). New York: Palgrave Macmillan.

Davis, R. Hunt (1972). *Bantu education and the education of Africans in South Africa.* Athens: Ohio University Center for International Studies.

DeLange Commission of Enquiry into the Provision of Education in South Africa (1983). *The DeLange Report.* Pretoria, South Africa: Human Sciences Research Council.

Etheridge, D. (1986). The role of the private sector in education and training. In R. Smollen (Ed.), *Black advancement in the South African economy.* London: Macmillan Press.

Gerhart, G. (1978). *Black power in South Africa: The evolution of an ideology.* Berkeley: University of California Press.

Gilmour, J. D., & Soudien, C. A. (1994). *An evaluation of the management component of the TOPS programme, 1993–94.* Rondebosch, South Africa: School of Education, University of Cape Town.

Hartshorne, K. B. (1992). *Crisis and challenge: Black education 1910–1990.* New York: Oxford University Press.

Hirson, B. (1979). *Year of fire year of ash: The Soweto revolt: Roots of a revolution?* London: Zed Books.

Honey, M. (1991, October). *NGO and Private Sector Cooperation: When There's a Common Will, There's a Way.* Paper presented at the Conference on NGOs in Development, hosted by the Department of Development Administration, University of Stellenbosch, South Africa.

Hyslop, J. (1987a). Food, authority and politics: Student riots in South Africa, 1945–1976. *African Perspective* (new series), *1*(3–4), 3–41.

Hyslop, J. (1987b). The concepts of reproduction and resistance in the sociology of education: The case of the transition from "Missionary" to "Bantu" education, 1940–1955. *Perspectives in Education*, *9*(2), 3–25.

Hyslop, J. (1988). State education policy and the social reproduction of the urban African working class: The case of the Southern Transvaal 1955–1976. *Journal of Southern African Studies*, *14*(3), 446–76.

Hyslop, J. (1989). School boards school communities and educational politics: Aspects of the failure of Bantu education as a hegemonic strategy, 1955–1976. In P. Bonner, I. Hofmeyr, D. James, & T. Lodge (Eds.), *Holding their ground: Class, locality and culture in 19th and 20th century South Africa* (pp. 201–225). Johannesburg, South Africa: Ravan Press.

Hyslop, J. (1990a). *Social conflicts over African education in South Africa from the 1940s to 1976.* PhD thesis, University of Witwatersrand, Johannesburg.

Hyslop, J. (1990b). Teacher resistance in African education from the 1940s to the 1980s. In M. Nkomo (Ed.), *Pedagogy of domination: Toward a democratic education in South Africa* (pp. 93–119). Trenton, NJ: Africa World Press.

Kallaway, P. (Ed.). (1984). *Apartheid and education: The education of Black South Africans.* Johannesburg, South Africa: Ravan Press.

Kane-Berman, J. (1978). *Soweto: Black revolt, White reaction.* Johannesburg, South Africa: Ravan Press.

Keegan, T. (1996). *Colonial South Africa and the origins of the racial order.* Charlottesville: University Press of Virginia.

Korten, D. C. (1987). Third generation NGO strategies: A key to people-centered development. *World Development, 15*(Supplement 1), 145–159.

Lee, R. (1991, October). *No perfect path: Cooperation for development.* Paper presented at the Conference on NGOs in Development, hosted by the Department of Development Administration, University of Stellenbosch, South Africa.

Lelyveld, J. (1985). *Move your shadow: South Africa in Black and White.* New York: Times Books.

Levy, N. (1991). Matching education with employment: Targeting the Black labour force. In E. Unterhalter, H. Wolpe, T. Botha, S. Badat, T. Dlamini, & B. Khotseng (Eds.), *Apartheid education and popular struggles* (pp. 19–34). Johannesburg, South Africa: Ravan Press.

Lodge, T. (1983). *Black politics in South Africa since 1945.* Johannesburg, South Africa: Ravan Press.

Lodge, T. (1984). The parents' school boycott: Eastern Cape and East Rand townships, 1955. In P. Kalloway (Ed.), *Apartheid and education: The education of Black South Africans* (pp. 265–295). Johannesburg, South Africa: Ravan Press.

Lodge, T., & Nasson, B. (Eds.). (1991). *All, here, and now: Black politics in South Africa in the 1980s.* Cape Town, South Africa: Ford Foundation and David Philip.

Marx, A. W. (1992). *Lessons of struggle: South African internal opposition, 1960–1990.* New York: Oxford University Press.

Millar, C., Raynham, S.-A., & Schaffer, A. (Eds.). (1991). *Breaking the formal frame: Readings in South African education in the eighties.* Cape Town, South Africa: Oxford University Press.

Mphahlele, E. (1990). Alternative institutions of education for Africans in South Africa: An exploration of rationale, goals, and directions. *Harvard Educational Review, 60*(1), 36–47.

Murphy, J. G. (1987). *A model for in-service training of underqualified Black teachers in Southern Africa.* Johannesburg, South Africa: Fransman Scott Printing.

National Commission on Excellence in Education. (1983). *A nation at risk: The imperative for educational reform.* Washington, DC: U.S. Department of Education.

Nkomo, M. (Ed.). (1990). *Pedagogy of domination: Toward a democratic education in South Africa.* Trenton, NJ: Africa World Press.

Rose, B., & Tumner, R. (Eds.). (1975). *Documents in South African education.* Johannesburg, South Africa: A. D. Donker.

South African Institute of Race Relations. (1951–1952). *Race relations survey.* Johannesburg: South African Institute of Race Relations. (Originally *Survey of Race Relations in South Africa*)

South African Institute of Race Relations. (1961). *Race relations survey.* Johannesburg: South African Institute of Race Relations. (Originally *Survey of Race Relations in South Africa*)

South African Institute of Race Relations. (1962). *Race relations survey.* Johannesburg: South African Institute of Race Relations. (Originally *Survey of Race Relations in South Africa*)

South African Institute of Race Relations. (1970). *Race relations survey.* Johannesburg: South African Institute of Race Relations. (Originally *Survey of Race Relations in South Africa*)

South African Institute of Race Relations. (1989–1890). *Race relations survey.* Johannesburg: South African Institute of Race Relations. (Originally *Survey of Race Relations in South Africa*)

South African Institute of Race Relations (1992). *Race relations survey.* Johannesburg: South African Institute of Race Relations. (Originally *Survey of Race Relations in South Africa*)

South African Research Service. (1983). *South African Review 1: Same Foundations, New Facades?* Johannesburg, South Africa: Ravan Press.

South African Research Service. (1984*). South African Review 2.* Johannesburg: Ravan Press.

South African Research Service. (1986). *South African Review 3.* Johannesburg: Ravan Press.

South African Research Service. (1987). *South African Review 4.* Johannesburg: Ravan Press.

South African Research Service. (1989). *South African Review 5.* Johannesburg: Ravan Press.

South African Research Service. (1992). *South African Review 6: From "Red Friday" to Codesa.* Johannesburg: Ravan Press.

Sparks, A. (1990). *The mind of South Africa: The story of the rise and fall of apartheid.* London: Heinemann.

Sparks, A. (1995). *Tomorrow is another country: The inside story of South Africa's road to change.* New York: Hill and Wang.

Sparks, A. (2003). *Beyond the miracle: Inside the new South Africa.* Chicago: University of Chicago Press.

Swainson, N. (1991). Corporate Intervention in Education and Training, 1960–89. In E. Unterhalter, H. Wolpe, T. Botha, S. Badat, T. Dlamini, & B. Khotseng, B. (Eds.), *Apartheid education and popular struggles* (pp. 95–115). Johannesburg, South Africa: Ravan Press.

Thompson, L. (2001). *A history of South Africa* (3rd ed.). New Haven, CT: Yale University Press.

Tonnson, S., Pigford, A., & Wyatt, J. L. (1992). *The TOPS needs assessment for women educational leaders.* Cape Town, South Africa: Teacher Opportunity Prigrammes.

Unterhalter, E. (1991). Changing aspects of reformism in Bantu education: 1953–89. In E. Unterhalter, H. Wolpe, T. Botha, S. Badat, T. Dlamini, & B. Khotseng (Eds.), *Apartheid education and popular struggles* (pp. 35–72). Johannesburg, South Africa: Ravan Press.

Worden, N. (2007). *The making of modern South Africa: Conquest, apartheid, democracy* (4th ed.). Cambridge, MA: Blackwell.

World Bank. (1988). Education in Sub-Saharan Africa: Policies for adjustment, revitalization and expansion. Washington, DC: The World Bank.

Wyatt, J. L. (1989). *Report on TOPS needs assessment of school management: South Africa research conducted by Judy L. Wyatt, March–August 1989*. Cape Town, South Africa: Teacher Opportunity Programmes.

Wyatt, J. L. (Ed.) (1990). *The TOPS School Management Programme*. Cape Town, South Africa: Teacher Opportunity Programmes.

Wyatt, J. L. (1993). *The role of universities and non-governmental organizations in educational restructuring in South Africa: The case of training Black school leaders.* PhD dissertation, University of South Carolina.

Wyatt, J. L., & Atkinson, R. R. (1992). *Leadership training for Black Women principals and other school leaders. Report and proposal for funding.* Cape Town, South Africa: Teacher Opportunity Programmes.

Wyatt, J. L., & Cress, K. (1992, April). *The role of non-governmental education agencies in South Africa: The case of Teacher Opportunity Programmes (TOPS) preparing Black principals.* Paper presented at the annual meeting of the American Educational Research Association, San Francisco.

ABOUT THE AUTHORS

Ayman Alsayed holds a master's degree in international education and development. He has worked both overseas and in the United States as a counselor and educator, providing services to a range of clients including children, youth and families, refugees and new immigrants, and former prisoners. His primary areas of interest in research and practice are student and family counseling and advocacy and civic education for democratic development.

Ron Atkinson (ronald-atkinson@sc.edu) is an associate professor in the Department of History and Director of African Studies at the University of South Carolina. From 1990–96 he was the U.S. co-project director of the TOPS School Management and Leadership Training Programme, which developed both the first master's degree program in educational management and leadership in South Africa and a field-based, in-service program to train large numbers of Black school leaders in their home regions throughout South Africa. Both of these were joint endeavors involving USC, the University of Durban-Westville (an historically Black South African university), and Teacher Opportunity Programmes, then the largest educational nongovernmental organization in South Africa. There were 50 students in the master's track of this program and nearly 2,000 participants in the in-service component. Both before and after this, his work has focused mainly on the long-term history and current developments in northern Uganda, which has been the site of a brutal and devastating 21-year war.

Patricia Buck is an assistant professor of education at Bates College in Lewiston, Maine. Patricia's work focuses on issues related to forced migration, education, and gender. In her forthcoming book *Gender, Schooling, & Forced Migration: Somali Women's Multinational Refugee Journey* (due for publication by Information Age Press in 2008) Patricia traces Somali refugee women's journeys from Somalia through protracted stays in the Dadaab refugee camps in Northeastern Kenya, and, finally, to settlement in a small city in the United States. Her work focuses on the interstices of educational opportunity, gender identity negotiation, and refugee life as experienced by Somali women. Patricia has also published scholarly articles on interracial relations among U.S. middle school students and on urban teachers? positionality in regard to impoverished students and communities. In partnership with CARE Kenya, Patricia is currently conducting ethnographic research on the impacts of educational policy and practice on gender identity formation among girls and women living in the Dadaab refugee camps.

Benjamin Justice is an assistant professor of education and coordinator of the Social Studies Education Program at Rutgers University. During the initial stages of writing this essay, he received assistance from a 2005–2006 National Academy of Education/Spencer Post Doctoral Fellowship. He is the author of *The War That Wasn't: Religious Conflict and Controversy in the Common Schools of New York State, 1865–1900* (SUNY 2005), as well as various book chapters in edited volumes. His work has appeared in the *Journal of American Education, History of Education Quarterly, Teachers College Record, Social Education, Philosophy of Education*, and *New York History*. He is currently writing a history of American imperial education, from colonial times to the present.

Patricia K. Kubow (pkubow@bgsu.edu) is associate professor in educational foundations and inquiry at Bowling Green State University. Her research and scholarship are focused on democratic education, indigenous knowledge, and cross-cultural pedagogies applied to teacher education, curriculum development, and educational policy. She is founder and director of The Center for International Comparative Education (ICE) at Bowling Green State University and is currently involved in comparative studies of democracy, indigenous knowledge, and education in sub-Saharan Africa. Kubow's articles have appeared in such journals as *Comparative Education Review, Pedagogies: An International Journal, Asia-Pacific Journal of Teacher Education and Development, Higher Education in Europe*, and *Phi Delta Kappan*. She is also lead author of the textbook standard, *Comparative Education: Exploring Issues in International Context*, now in its second edition and published by Pearson Education/Merrill Prentice Hall.

David Landis is associate professor of language education and directs the MA in TESOL program at the Kazakhstan Institute of Management, Economics, and Strategic Research in Almaty, Kazakhstan. Prior to his move to Kazakhstan, he taught reading and writing methods courses at the University of Northern Iowa from 1995–2006. His research involves ethnographic and sociolinguistic perspectives and concepts to understand students' writing and reading in classrooms and home and community settings. He is interested in ways to link students' experiences outside of school with academic reading and writing. He and his colleagues have published research in journals such as *Language Arts, Journal of Adolescent and Adult Literacy, Reading & Writing Quarterly,* and *Thinking Classroom* as well as in books such as *RWCT Methods and Philosophy in Action* (2004) and *Ideas Without Boundaries: International Educational Reform Through Reading and Writing For Critical Thinking* (2001).

Bradley A. U. Levinson, an anthropologist, is associate professor of education at Indiana University. His research interests include student culture and identity formation, the ethnography of education policy, immigrant education, and citizenship education for democracy. His books include *We Are All Equal: Student Culture and Identity at a Mexican Secondary School* (Duke University Press), *Policy as Practice* (with Margaret Sutton, Greenwood) and *Schooling the Symbolic Animal: Social and Cultural Dimensions of Education* (Rowman & Littlefield.)

Sapargul Mirseitova for many years was lecturing and teaching English at the University of World Languages in Almaty, Kazakhstan. In 1991, she defended her dissertation on English Grammar in Moscow. In 1994, she completed her master's program at Grand Canyon University in Phoenix, Arizona. More recently, she did further research work in the field of education as IREX grantee at the University of Colorado and as a Fulbright Scholar at the University of Arizona. Since 1998, she has been involved in the international program "Reading and Writing for Critical Thinking." At present she is the president of the Kazakhstan Reading Association and the head of the Laboratory of Contemporary Educational Research at Kazakh State Pedagogical University for Young Ladies in Almaty, Kazakhstan. She regularly publishes her findings in the Kazakhstan Reading Association's journals and books. English readers can find her work written together with the United States and Canadian educators in Thinking Classroom and IRA online issues.

Payal P. Shah is a doctoral student in the Education Policy Studies Program at Indiana University, focusing in international and comparative education. Her research centers on issues of equity and justice in education in the United States and abroad, specifically in relation to gender, international development, and education. In addition to her interest in multicultural, global, and international education, Payal conducts research on girls' education policies and program in Western India.

Kathleen (Kathy) Staudt, PhD (University of Wisconsin 1976), is professor of political science and director of the Center for Civic Engagement—going into its 10th year—at the University of Texas at El Paso. Author of a dozen books, four of which focus on the U.S.-Mexico Border, her forthcoming *Violence and Activism at the Border: Gender, Fear, and Everyday Life in Ciudad Juárez* will be available from the University of Texas Press in 2008. Kathy teaches courses on public policy, women/gender, democracy, and borders, the last of which is required for students in UTEP's EdD program. Most of these courses utilize problem-solving, community-based teaching and learning approaches. Kathy is also active in the Paso del Norte Civil Rights Project, Border Interfaith, the Nonprofit Congress, and the Coalition Against Violence.

E. Doyle Stevick (stevick@gwm.sc.edu) is assistant professor of educational leadership and policies at the University of South Carolina, where he also founded and serves as director of the Office of International and Comparative Education (http://www.ed.sc.edu/ice/). He is an active member of the Comparative and International Education Society, where he founded the Special Interest Group in Citizenship and Democratic Education (CANDE), serving for 3 years as Chair. (The University of South Carolina will co-sponsor the CIES conference in 2009, in Charleston, South Carolina.) Previous publications include *Reimagining Civic Education: How Diverse Societies Form Democratic Citizens* (Rowman & Littlefield.) Currently, he is preparing a volume on Holocaust Education across Central and Eastern Europe.

Margaret Sutton is associate professor of educational leadership and policy studies. She teaches foundations courses in the teacher preparation programs as well as instructing graduate students in international and comparative education and in policy studies. Her research concerns cultural change both outside and inside the United States, with research and publications on educational policy formation in international assistance agencies; gender and education in the Third World; comparative multicultural policies; the sources and forms of global awareness among children and youth in the United States; and on citizenship and education around the world.

Judy L. Wyatt conducted the original research for, and was then (from 1990–96) the U.S. co-project director of, the TOPS School Management and Leadership Training Programme, which developed both the first masters' degree program in educational management and leadership in South Africa and a field-based, in-service program to train large numbers of Black school leaders in their home regions throughout South Africa. Both of these were joint endeavors involving USC, the University of Durban-Westville (an historically Black South African university), and Teacher Opportunity Programmes, then the largest educational nongovernmental organization in South Africa. There were 50 students in the master's track of this program and nearly 2,000 participants in the in-service component. After this, she spent 4 years as director of South Carolina Healthy Schools, one of 13 such state-wide initiatives funded by the Center for Disease Control and Prevention, then resigned to take care of (and eventually take in) an aging mother. She is currently self-employed.

INDEX